Library of Jewish Studies

LITERATURE OF THE SYNAGOGUE *Edited, with introductions and notes, by* JOSEPH HEINEMANN *with* JAKOB J. PETUCHOWSKI

BEHRMAN HOUSE, INC. | PUBLISHERS | NEW YORK

ACKNOWLEDGMENTS

The editors and publisher thank the following for permission to reprint:

Schocken Books, Inc., for "In the Middle of the Night," Jacob Sloan, tr., in Nahum N. Glatzer, ed., *The Passover Haggadah*, pp. 87–89, © 1953, 1969.

Jewish Publication Society of America for "The Royal Crown," Israel Zangwill, tr., in *Selected Religious Poems of Solomon ibn Gabirol*, pp. 83–84, 87–88, © 1924, 1952, 1974 (paperback); and for "O God, Thy Name," Nina Salaman, tr., in *Selected Poems of Jehudah Halevi*, pp. 127–29, © 1924, 1952, 1974 (paperback).

Library of Congress Cataloging in Publication Data
Main entry under title:
Literature of the synagogue.
   (Library of Jewish studies)
   Includes bibliographies and index.
   1. Jewish prayers. 2. Midrash—Translations into English. 3. Sermons, Hebrew—Translations into English. 4. Sermons, English—Translations from Hebrew. 5. Piyutim—Translations into English. I. Heinemann, Joseph. II. Petuchowski, Jakob Josef, 1925–
III. Jews. Liturgy and ritual. English. Selections. 1975.
BM665.R37   296.4   75–25536
ISBN 0–87441–217–X.   ISBN 0–87441–237–4 pbk.

© *Copyright 1975 by Joseph Heinemann*
© *Copyright 1975 by Jakob J. Petuchowski for "The Poetry of the Synagogue"*
Published by Behrman House, Inc., 1261 Broadway, New York, N. Y. 10001
Manufactured in the United States of America

CONTENTS

PART TWO / SERMONS

PART THREE / THE POETRY OF THE SYNAGOGUE

Glossary   287
Index   289

PREFACE

THE SELECTIONS offered in Parts One and Two of this volume reflect texts of prayers and sermons of the Talmudic period. Both prayers and sermons were part of the synagogue service in Talmudic times (especially on Sabbaths and festivals), together with scriptural readings from the Pentateuch and the Prophets. Later, when the regular prayers became fixed even in their wording, poems (known as *piyyutim*) were composed to vary and enliven the prayer service; examples of such synagogal poetry are offered in Part Three of this volume, prepared by Professor Jakob J. Petuchowski.

For the texts from the Babylonian Talmud and from Midrash Rabbah, I have based myself on the translations published by the Soncino Press, London; for the one from the Mekhilta, on the translation of J. Lauterbach, published by the Jewish Publication Society of America; in each case I have changed and adapted the English extensively. The texts from Sifre and from Midrash Tanhuma, as well as Saadia's "Paraphrase of the Weekday Amidah," were translated by Mrs. Batyah Rabin of Jerusalem. Rabbi Richard S. Sarason of Brown University, Providence, Rhode Island, translated the Palestinian version of the weekday Amidah. Rabbi William G. Braude very kindly put at my disposal the manuscript of his translation of Pesikta de Rav Kahana (now published by the Jewish Publication Society of America) and especially translated the homily from Deuteronomy Rabbah ("The Lord your God has multiplied you"). I benefited greatly from both these translations, which I used freely; Rabbi Braude cannot, of course, be held responsible for the more literal translations offered here.

References to prayers not quoted in the book are given according to page numbers in Philip Birnbaum, ed., *Daily Prayer Book* (New York: Hebrew Publishing Company, 1949).
The following abbreviations have been used throughout:

Bab.	Babylonian Talmud
Birnbaum	Philip Birnbaum, ed., *Daily Prayer Book*
Jerus.	Jerusalem Talmud
Tos.	Tosefta

Joseph Heinemann
Jerusalem

PART ONE

PRAYERS

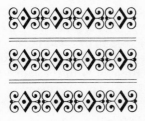

PRAYER is as old as man, answering, as it does, some of his deepest needs. Whenever and wherever man has been in distress, he has invoked the aid of higher powers, and in return for blessings and abundance, he has ever given thanks. The wealth of material collected by Fritz Heiler in *Prayer* [1] demonstrates the enormous variety in form and content that prayer has assumed in different ages and different societies; yet even more striking is the underlying oneness both of the concept of prayer itself and of many of its basic features—common, it would seem, to all human cultures.

Institutionalized prayer may not be quite as ancient as spontaneous prayer, but it, too, was known in the oldest civilizations, like those of Egypt and Babylonia, where prayer played a prominent part in the complex rituals accompanying temple ceremonies and sacrifices. Often prayer was invested with magical powers; its recital required expert knowledge. Only a properly trained priest knew the words in their exact order and could recite them with the intonation necessary to ensure their efficacy.

The ancient Jewish prayer found in the Bible is in one sense continuous with the kind of prayer that had been practiced in Egypt and Babylonia. But the ideas and motifs of biblical prayer differ qualitatively from the preceeding pagan models, not only because they express the monotheistic view but because they do not resort to crude bargaining with the Deity; because spiritual issues take precedence over requests for material benefits; and because the prayers are permeated by a sense of the intimate relation between the individual and his God, in whom he trusts and whose love and guidance he desires. All traces of magic have disappeared by the time we come to biblical prayer, which does not seek to impose man's will on heaven through devices and formulas designed to compel the Deity's consent to man's request. There are prayers in the Bible of both the individual and the cultic type, the latter represented especially by many of the Psalms—unsurpassed in poetic beauty and expressive power.

But if biblical prayer represents a departure from its pagan predecessors, an even more revolutionary development occurred in Judaism during the era of the Second Temple (fifth century B.C.E. to 70 C.E.), when there gradually came into being the entirely novel institution of regular community worship. So familiar to us has this institution become, not only in Judaism but in Christianity and Islam as well, that we tend to take it for granted; yet its conception and development was a tremendous innovation. Community prayer has a character utterly different both from spontaneous individual prayer and from the kind of Temple prayer exemplified (in Judaism) by the Levite songs and psalms. It is no longer simply an incidental or subordinate accompaniment to some other cult or ceremonial. In the new congregational concept, prayer itself becomes an act of worship sufficient unto itself. It does not require a sacred place for its performance, nor does it need a consecrated, chosen body of priests to carry it out. Similarly, community prayer, as it was conceived and practiced from Second Temple days on, is not just a means of expressing emotions of gratitude and of awe, or of pouring out man's needs. No longer does prayer depend on the mood of the worshiper or on his state of mind; no longer is it limited to occasions of joy or sorrow. It has become fixed, obligatory; it is recited regularly at set hours and in a certain, definite form and style. Prayer is now conceived as *avodah* (worship: literally, service)—a term that had previously been used to denote the sacrificial service in the Temple.[2]

A new mode of avodah—of service to God—thus comes into being, equivalent to the sacrificial cult in the Temple and possessing the same qualities: a regular, prescribed ritual by which Israel fulfills its duty of worship. But this new avodah has novel features. Sacrifices had been the exclusive prerogative of the Temple priests, while the people, on whose behalf the cult was performed, had been passive bystanders at best. The avodah of prayer is now carried out by the congregation itself, wherever it assembles. Once prayer is conceived as a valid form of avodah, it can become an integral part of the religious life of each community, and can acquire definite forms and patterns of its own.

Historically, prayer as a new type of avodah at first took its place alongside the sacrificial service, as an addition or complement to the Temple cult: "Prayers were instituted corresponding to the daily sacrifices" (Bab. Berakhot 26b). By means of such prayer any community was able to offer its own symbolic sacrifice, in addition to the regular sacrifices offered in the Temple on behalf of the community but not by it. Various sources from the Second Temple era testify that worshipers were conscious of this close correspondence between prayer and sacrifice; they looked upon their prayers as an act analogous to Temple worship, and hence they would pray at the very hours the daily sacrifices were being offered in the Temple: "and at the time of the sacrifices every man is obliged to pray . . . (Josephus, *Contra Apion*, 2:23); "and the whole multitude of the people were praying without at the time of the incense" (Luke 1:10); "and the incense of that evening was now being offered at Jerusalem in the house of God and Judith cried unto the Lord. . . ." (Judith 9:1). Only after the destruction of the Temple did prayer become a substitute for the now defunct sacrificial cult, acquiring a still more central and vital position in Jewish religious life as the only form of public worship available.

In the years immediately following the Destruction, the rabbis of Yavneh took it as one of their foremost tasks to fashion an order, and to establish precise, comprehensive rules for the regular recital of the prayers (Bab. Berakhot 28b et al.). But even then only the general outline and contents of the prayers were laid down. The actual wording remained fluid and was left to the individual worshiper or the reader. Official versions came into being only gradually; the first complete order of prayers known to us is that of Amram Gaon in the ninth century. We cannot determine accurately what the text of any given prayer may have been prior to this date, although it may be assumed with a fair degree of certainty that the texts of the main prayers, as they are preserved in all the rites extant today, reflect at least one of the versions current in early Rabbinic times.

The new style of worship was conceived from the outset primarily as community worship, since it, like the Temple avodah, was carried out on behalf of all Israel. In the new mode of service, however, any group of at least ten male, adult Jews (*minyan*) was considered to represent the entire nation and was entitled to speak in its name. The congregational character of set prayer finds its most striking outward expression in the exclusive use of the pronoun "we" by the speaker; there is no instance of such a prayer being formulated in the first person singular.[3] The weekday *amidah* (Eighteen Benedictions)— the set prayer par excellence—is often described in Talmudic sources as a petition "for the needs of the community," or "for the needs of Israel." To be sure, the rabbis never went so far as to deny someone who either would not or could not join a minyan the right to recite the obligatory prayers on his own; on the contrary, he was considered duty-bound to do so. But even in such cases, the individual used the same prayers as the community and recited them at the same time; he, too, prayed as "we" because he, too, considered himself a representative of the community. Still the individual's right and duty to recite the set prayers were to some extent limited and of doubtful standing. The rabbis who gave final shape and order to the fixed prayers disagreed among themselves as to whether an individual praying on his own was required to recite the entire Eighteen Benedictions every day or could substitute a shortened version (Mishnah Berakhot 4:3); they held that certain prayers, such as the additional prayer (*musaf*, recited on Sabbaths and Holy Days), could not be recited save in a "town congregation" (Mishnah Berakhot 4:7); and parts of the liturgy could not be recited at all without a minyan (Mishnah Megillah 4:3—nowadays the *Kedushah* and the *Kaddish* are included in this category). Hence, in some respects at least, the recital of the fixed prayers by an individual was thought to lack completeness and to be inferior in status to community worship.

This is not to say that the new mode of prayer implied a lessening of the weight of the individual in worship or a lowering of his status in general. The exact opposite is true: in the only type of avodah known previously, the Temple service, the individual—if present at all—was merely an onlooker, devoid of any function. The new style of congregational worship was, in comparison, carried out by the very individuals of whom the congregation was composed. No longer was the avodah performed by specially chosen priests; instead, the "avodah of the heart" was recited—was indeed required to be recited—by all those present. Nor was the function of the Temple priest in any sense transferred to the reader who spoke or chanted the prayers aloud; the latter, known in Talmudic sources as *sheliah tzibbur*, the "emissary of the congregation," was precisely that and no more. He held no office, he needed no qualifications (other than the elementary ability to recite the liturgy), and he certainly was not consecrated in any way; any member of the congregation was eligible to serve as emissary. Moreover, if many worshipers did not themselves speak the prayers but only listened to the reader, it was only because they were unable to do so (prayers were not written down and had to be either memorized or, to some extent, improvised during recital). Their roles were not passive; they were obliged not only to listen but also to chant frequent responses, by means of which even the ignorant became active participants in the service.[4]

Although the service and liturgy of the early (Eastern) Christian church were undoubtedly modeled on Jewish community prayer, they came gradually and increasingly to differ from the Jewish prototype in this essential feature: in the Church the role of the *leiturgos* ("leader of prayers") in time became a prominent one, and eventually he came to be looked upon not as an "emissary of the congregation," but largely as an intermediary between the community and God; his participation in the service thus became indispensable. A similar development, indeed, has taken place in modern times among Jewish congregations in the West, where the reader or cantor has been invested with special ritual functions, clothed in clerical garb, and elevated to the clergy. But all this is essentially foreign to the tradition which first created set community prayers as the main form of worship. In this form of avodah, all congregants are equal and none holds a special prerogative; nor does this style of worship presuppose or even tolerate the idea of mediation between the congregation and God.

Congregational prayer, then, allowed for—demanded—the active participation of the individual. It was never meant in the first instance to take the place of personal, spontaneous worship, which had its own rationale. Personal prayer serves as the immediate, direct expression of the religious feelings and needs of each person, in his own way, and at whatever time he feels the need. In Jewish tradition this kind of prayer has led a continuous existence; although it has played a part within the framework of congregational worship it has never been confined to that. There are dozens of personal prayers in Talmudic literature. They are mostly short, simple in style and diction, containing just a few brief petitions. Almost invariably they address God as "thou." They tend to have a standard opening formula, such as "May it be thy will, O Lord, my God" or just a direct address, such as "My God," "Master of the World," "Our Father," and the like.

The coexistence in Jewish liturgy of two different types of prayer serving different functions—spontaneous self-expression on the one hand and regulated, obligatory worship on the other—made it imperative to design ways of distinguishing between them. This was the more necessary because both types did intermingle, in fact to a large extent, as spontaneous or personal elements were interwoven with the set synagogue service. Moreover, since for a long time even the fixed prayers were not worded in a single obligatory way but were re-formulated and improvised in various styles, some method had to be found to distinguish between the two. For this purpose the *berakhah*-formula was developed. This formula serves either at the beginning, the end, or both, of each unit of the prescribed liturgy: if at the beginning, it consists of the words, "Blessed art thou, O Lord, our God, King of the Universe"; if at the end, "Blessed art thou" (followed by a few words summarizing the main content of the preceding passage). There are no obligatory prayers without the berakhah-formula (with the exception of the *Kaddish*, which originally was not part of the fixed synagogue-prayers); conversely, the use of this formula was prohibited in private, individual prayers. Originally—as can be seen in the Dead Sea Scrolls—many alternative formulas were used: "I thank thee" in place of "Blessed art thou," or other appellations for God instead of the Tetragrammaton. But by the third century C.E. the berakhah-formula had been singled out and became the standard form for fixed prayers as opposed to personal ones.[5]

It is interesting that the "Lord's Prayer" of the New Testament (Matt. 6:9ff.) clearly belongs to the type of private, personal prayer, as it was practiced among Jews in that period. It has most of the main characteristics of style and form, and several of its motifs and phrases have parallels in other private prayers of the period (though thematically its opening strikingly resembles that of the *Kaddish*). In addition, the instructions preceding the actual prayer clearly stress the virtue of private, individual worship: "And when you pray you shall not be as the hypocrites are: for they love to pray standing in the synagogues and in the corners of the streets . . . but you, when you pray, enter into your closet and when you have shut your door, pray to your Father which is in secret . . ." (ibid., 5–6). Evidently Jesus is here upholding the tradition of personal prayer as against the organized public worship of the Synagogue; prayer in one's own private room, shut off from others, instead of congregational prayer; brief, plainly styled petitions, instead of the series of comparatively long and elaborate benedictions; prayer in the Aramaic vernacular instead of in Hebrew (which by then was no longer commonly spoken); simple prayers which anyone could compose and speak himself instead of being dependent on the reader—all this seems to be implied in Jesus' advice and in the model prayer proposed by him. Of course the Church, in developing its community-style worship and liturgy, largely modeled on the example of the Synagogue, did not act on this advice.[6]

Later, Jewish congregational worship lost many of the elements of variety and spontaneous change that had been characteristic of it. Certainly one of the reasons for this development was the decision that prayer should be uttered in Hebrew (even though Jewish law permits prayer in other languages); in most countries of the Diaspora, Jews no longer had full command of that language. Nevertheless synagogue prayers always strove, as Shalom Spiegel wrote, "to retain and reconcile both the requirement of agreement and that of informality. . . . There continued for generations the deliberate tendency to keep the prayers fresh and fluid. . . . By asking with variety of circumstances also for variety of words, the Synagogue admitted or even invited into its midst the craftsmen of words, the poets. . . . The Middle Ages followed the Rabbinic age in the endeavor to preserve both obedience to tradition and individual assertion."[7]

THE BREATH OF EVERY LIVING BEING

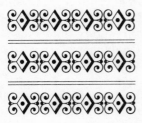

INTRODUCTION

ORIGINALLY, *in the days of the Tannaim, the official morning service in the synagogue began with the reading of the* Shema *and the benedictions preceding it. Among pious circles, a custom also existed of reciting a number of chapters from the Book of Psalms prior to the official opening of the service. Thus, "R. Jose said: Let my lot be among those who complete the praise every day" (Bab. Shabbat 118b) —i.e., among those who recite the concluding chapters of the Psalter every day (especially the last six, 145–150). Eventually this preliminary section, consisting of Psalms and other songs of praise collected from the Bible, was incorporated into the morning service; it is both preceded and followed by a benediction (Birnbaum, pp. 51–69), even though there is no explicit Talmudic source for the latter. On Sabbaths and festivals, more chapters from Psalms are added (Birnbaum, pp. 301ff.); and on those occasions the exalted hymn given below is recited before the concluding benediction. While this hymn in its present form may be a combination of several compositions, originally independent of one another and used alternatively, there can be no doubt that most of the text is ancient and that it is the outstanding example of early Rabbinic origin of an elaborate hymn of praise. One indication of its early date is the inclusion of a phrase from the first benediction of the Amidah in its Palestinian version, "O God,*

9

great, mighty, and awesome, most high God, Creator of heaven and earth" (see "The Weekday Amidah"). Current versions of the Amidah instead have: "who bestowest lovingkindness and art Master of all things" (Birnbaum, p. 82). Moreover, a third-century Amora identifies the "Benediction of the Song" (Mishnah Pesahim 10:7)—recited after the Hallel (Psalms 113–118) on Passover eve—as "The breath of every living being" (Bab. Pesahim 118a); hence the opening part, at least, of this hymn must have been known to him. However the composition was not originally intended for use after the Hallel, but as a conclusion to the recital of the last chapters of Psalms; for its opening verse "The breath of every living being shall bless thy name . . ." takes up, in paraphrase, the concluding verse of the Book of Psalms: "Let every thing that has breath praise the Lord" (Psalms 150:6). A part of the hymn is also quoted in the Talmud (Bab. Berakhot 59b) as part of a seasonal prayer of thanksgiving for rain.

While not employing strict meter or rhyme—an indication of very early origin—this hymn uses a great variety of stylistic devices and rhetorical forms, which make it especially impressive and greatly heighten its effect. A few such are: the series of hyperboles, "Though our mouths were full of song as the sea, and our tongues of exultation as the multitude of its waves"; the short rhythmic sentences, following one another: "From Egypt didst thou redeem us, and from the house of bondage didst thou release us"; the heaping up of synonyms of praise, such as "they shall all thank, bless, praise, glorify, extol . . . thy name" (and, similarly, again in the concluding benediction: "song and praise . . . hymn and psalm . . .").

Equally interesting and effective is the use of Bible quotations, interwoven into the composition, for example, ". . . and we will bless thy holy name, as it is said: 'Bless the Lord, O my soul' "; the quotation "The Lord slumbers not, nor sleeps" (Psalms 121:4) is immediately elaborated upon by a long series of other epithets some of them known to us also from the second benediction of the Amidah, (Birnbaum, p. 83); while the verse "All my bones shall say: 'Lord, who is like unto thee' " (Psalms 35:10) is preceded by a detailed description of the homage offered by each member of the body separately. However, in some instances the use of Scripture in this hymn embodies a feature unusual in liturgy: the Midrashic treatment of biblical verses. The quotation from Deuteronomy 10:17 (which as noted is also a quotation from the first benediction of the Amidah) —"God, great, mighty, and awesome"—is taken up again, and commented upon, word by word, in the manner of the Midrash: "God— in thy power and might; great—in thy glorious name; mighty—for ever; and awesome—by thy awesome acts. . . ." Another Midrash is embedded in the following passage: "For every mouth shall give thanks unto thee, and every tongue shall swear unto thee; every knee shall bow to thee, and every body shall prostrate itself before thee." Here each clause of Isaiah 45:23: "That unto me every knee shall bow, every tongue shall swear" is provided with a complementary phrase interpreting it.[1]

These and many other literary and stylistic devices the author(s) undoubtedly employed consciously and with purpose. On the other hand, several acrostics discovered in this composition by medieval commentators and, in part, indicated graphically in printed prayerbooks, would seem on closer examination to be entirely fortuitous.

THE BREATH OF EVERY LIVING BEING

The breath of every living being shall bless thy name, Lord our God, and the spirit of all flesh shall continually glorify and exalt thy fame, our King; from eternity to eternity thou art God. Besides thee we have no King who redeems and saves, sets free and delivers, who supports and has mercy in all times of trouble and distress; we have no King but thee.

He is God of the first and of the last, the God of all creatures, the Lord of all generations, who is extolled with many praises, and guides his world with kindness and his creatures with mercy. *The Lord slumbers not, nor sleeps;* he arouses the sleepers and awakens the slumberers; he makes the dumb to speak, looses the bound, supports the falling, and raises up the bowed.

To thee alone we give thanks. Though our mouths were full of songs as the sea, and our tongues of exultation as the multitude of its waves, and our lips of praise as the wide-extended firmament; though our eyes shone with light like the sun and the moon, and our hands were spread out like the eagles of heaven, and our feet were swift as deer, we should still be unable to thank thee and to bless thy name, Lord our God and God of our fathers, for one thousandth or one ten-thousandth part of the favors which thou hast conferred upon our fathers and upon us. Thou hast redeemed us from Egypt, Lord our God, and released us from the house of bondage; during famine thou hast fed us, and provided us with plenty; from the sword thou hast rescued us, from pestilence thou hast saved us, and from sore and lasting diseases thou hast delivered us. Until now thy mercy has helped us, and thy kindness has not left us: forsake us not, Lord our God, for ever. Therefore the limbs which thou hast spread forth upon us, and the spirit and breath which thou hast breathed into our nostrils, and the tongue which thou hast set in our mouths, shall all thank, bless, praise, glorify, extol, revere, hallow and assign kingship to thy name, O our King. For every mouth shall give thanks unto thee, and every tongue shall swear unto thee; every knee shall bow to thee, and every body shall prostrate itself before thee; all hearts shall fear thee, and all the inward parts and reins shall sing unto thy name, as it is written, *All my bones shall say, Lord, who is like unto thee? Thou deliverest the poor from him that is stronger than he, the poor and the needy from him that robs him* (Psalms 35:10). Who is like unto thee, who is equal to thee, who can be compared to thee, O God great, mighty, and awesome, most high God, Creator of heaven and earth? We will praise, laud, and glorify thee, and we will bless thy holy name, as it is said: *Bless the Lord, O my soul; and all that is within me, bless his holy name* (Psalms 103:1). Thou art God in thy power and might, great in thy glorious name, mighty for ever and awful by thy awesome acts, the King who sits upon a high and lofty throne.

He who inhabits eternity, exalted and holy is his name; and it is written, *Exult in the Lord, you righteous; praise is seemly for the upright* (Psalms 33:1).

By the mouth of the upright thou shalt be praised, by the words of the righteous thou shalt be blessed, by the tongue of the loving ones thou shalt be extolled, and in the midst of the holy thou shalt be hallowed.

In the assemblies of the tens of thousands of thy people, the house of Israel, thy name, our King, shall be glorified with joyous cries in every generation; for such is the duty of all creatures toward thee, Lord our God and God of our fathers, to thank, praise, laud, glorify, extol, honor, bless, exalt and adore thee, even beyond all the words of song and praise of David the son of Jesse, thy anointed servant.

Praised be thy name for ever, our King, the great and holy God and King, in heaven and on earth; for thee, Lord our God and God of our fathers, song and praise are becoming, hymn and psalm, strength and dominion, victory, greatness and might, renown and glory, holiness and sovereignty, blessings and thanksgivings, henceforth and for ever. Blessed art thou, O Lord, God and King, great in praises, God of thanksgivings, Lord of wonders, who makes choice of song and psalm, O King and God, the life of all worlds.

THE SHEMA AND ITS BENEDICTIONS

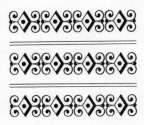

INTRODUCTION

BESIDES THE AMIDAH *prayer—referred to in Talmudic sources simply as "the Prayer"—the reading of the Shema constitutes the other major part of the obligatory daily community worship. Originally, these two were independent units of "orders of prayers"; for on the one hand the Shema is recited only in the morning and in the evening, but not in the afternoon service; while on the other hand it was not obligatory to recite the Amidah in the evening prayer according to the custom prevailing in Tannaitic times (and according to the halakhic ruling still in force). Moreover, the Mishnah (Berakhot I, 2 and IV, 1) sets different time limits for these two "services," clearly implying that they were not always recited jointly.*

However, in the early Amoraic period the ruling came to be generally accepted that "the benediction concerning redemption," i.e., the benediction following the Shema, should be joined to the "prayer," i.e., to the Amidah following it (Bab. Berakhot 9b); this held at first for the morning service and then eventually for the evening service as well (once the recital of the Amidah became customary also in the evening). The purpose of this ruling presumably was to ensure the recital of both the Shema and the Amidah in the synagogue—a practice that would involve great difficulties if each of them constituted a separate service; its effect, undoubtedly, was to create a more com-

prehensive service, consisting at a minimum of these two parts joined together.

The Shema in the morning and evening, preceding as it did the recital of the Amidah, marked the inception of worship. It was in turn preceded by the "invitation to worship" addressed by the reader to the congregation, "Bless the Lord who is to be blessed," followed by the response, "Blessed is the Lord, etc."

The reading of the Shema itself is made up of three separate Bible passages: Deuteronomy 6:4–10; 11:13–22; Numbers 15:37–41. The recital of the first two, mornings and evenings, is considered a precept because of Deuteronomy 6:7, ". . . and you shall speak of them [these words] . . . when you lie down and when you rise up" (and the similar formula in Deuteronomy 11:19). Numbers 15:37ff., is recited in order to carry out the precept, ". . . that you shall remember [i.e., mention] the day when you came forth out of the land of Egypt all the days of your life" (Deuteronomy 16:3 and Numbers 15:41; this specific passage was probably chosen because it mentions the commandment of the fringes, thus fitting in with the commandment of the phylacteries mentioned in the preceding two passages of the Shema). According to most sages, this precept was to apply only in the daytime, not at night; hence in the ancient Palestinian rite the passage from Numbers was recited only in the morning service (Mishnah Berakhot I, 5; Bab. Berakhot 14b). The order of the first two passages is dictated by the consideration that "one should accept upon oneself the yoke of the kingdom of Heaven [i.e., of God] first, and [only] afterward the yoke of the commandments" (Mishnah Berakhot II, 2); the recital of Deuteronomy 6:4ff., is taken to imply submission to God's sovereignty. To these Bible passages is added, immediately after Deuteronomy 6:4, one non-biblical sentence, "Blessed be the name of his glorious kingdom for ever and ever," which originated as a response voiced by the people in Temple services after the Tetragrammaton was pronounced by the priests (Mishnah Yoma IV, 2; Tos. Ta'anit I, 13). It is likely that in the Shema this sentence serves the same function, namely, a response to the pronouncing of the divine name in Deuteronomy 6:4. Originally, the Shema was recited antiphonally by reader and congregation (Tos. Sotah VI, 2–3). This *manner of recital was eventually discontinued. There was then no longer a need for the congregational response, yet the formula, "Blessed be the name, etc.," was retained, although it was said silently and not aloud.*

The three passages constituting the Shema originally were preceded by yet a fourth: the Decalogue (Mishnah Tamid V, 1). But at about the time of the destruction of the Temple this practice was discontinued, lest it lend support to the heretical view that only the ten commandments, but not the rest of the Torah, were of divine origin (Bab. Berakhot 12a; Jerus. ibid. I, 3c). This change is reflected also in the phylacteries of ancient Judea: those found at Kumran contain the Decalogue, while those of the Bar-Kokhba period no longer have it.[1]

The recital of the Shema in itself is not prayer in the strict sense. In prayer man addresses God; in these Bible passages God addresses Israel. And while the recital implies the worshiper's identification with the import of the passages ("acceptance of the yoke of the kingdom of Heaven," etc.), the Shema could not have become a prayer-service proper were it not for the benedictions preceding and following it, in which the worshiper gives praise and thanks to God and explicitly identifies himself with, and responds to, the Shema itself. This framework of benedictions, by means of which the Shema becomes a prayer-service, differs in the morning and evening (Mishnah Berakhot I, 4).

In the morning service, the first of the two benedictions preceding the Shema (called Yotzer after its opening phrase) is not related to the Shema itself, but gives praise to God for renewing sunlight in the morning and thereby, renewing creation itself; it is, in fact, a typical and appropriate morning prayer. It has been preserved in some ancient sources (among them Saadya's prayerbook) in an extremely short version:

> *Blessed art thou, etc., who formest light and createst darkness, who makest peace and createst all things; who in mercy gives light to the earth and to them that dwell thereon and whose goodness renews the*

creation every day continually. Blessed art thou, O Lord, Creator of the lights.

Against this, the current version (and even more so the one for the Sabbath, given below) has been expanded by a variety of poetic and semi-poetic additions, such as "God, the Lord over all works, blessed is he . . . ," which has an alphabetical acrostic at the beginning of each line (a similar, much shorter, piece is used on weekdays), and a variety of stylistic devices, among them a Midrashic-type exposition at the end of the first section (cf., below: "There is none to be compared unto thee and there is none besides thee, . . .").

Even though the Sabbath version is greatly embellished, only one of the additional sections—"To the God who rested from all his works, etc."—specifically refers to the Sabbath. (This section was almost certainly not composed as a continuation of the preceding one, as it appears today, but began "[the] God, who rested . . ." and was linked with the opening formula of the benediction "Blessed art thou. . . .") Here God is praised, not in general terms as the creator of the world, but for the specific "work" of the seventh day: namely, the creation of rest; the "Psalm of the Sabbath" is quoted, as if the Sabbath day, itself, were singing this song of praise to God. This—undoubtedly very early—semi-poetic elaboration of the benediction is, in our present versions of the Shema, unique to the Sabbath, although a composition for Thursdays, in exactly the same manner and style, was found in the Cairo Genizah; it refers to the acts of creation of the fifth day and incorporates the daily psalm for Thursdays:

> . . . fish and fowl, also sea monsters did the earth . . . bring forth and did give birth to cattle, creeping things and beasts. These are the works of the fifth day, on which were created the swarming creatures of the seas; and the fifth day [itself] offers praise and says: Sing aloud unto God our strength; shout for joy unto the God of Jacob (Psalms 81:2). Therefore let all his creatures bless the living God, let them render praise and greatness to God who is the creator of the swarming creatures of the seas and of the creeping creatures of the earth. Be thou blessed, our Savior, . . .

It seems logical to assume that such pieces were composed for each day of the week and that at some time it was the custom (probably in

Palestine) to vary the text day by day with a kind of midrash based on the section of Genesis relevant to that day and on the "Psalm of the Day" (Birnbaum, pp. 139ff.).

Most striking among the additions to this benediction is the Kedushah, i.e., the sanctification of God by the angelic choirs, based on the descriptions in Isaiah 6:1–3 and Ezekiel 1:4–3:13. The contradiction between the different formulas of praise ascribed to the angels in Isaiah and Ezekiel is solved in the Midrashic manner—through the assumption that there are two choirs, singing antiphonally. The Kedushah appears again, in a more elaborate form, in the Amidah (see "The Kedushah"). Undoubtedly, it was intended, in the first place, for recital in congregational prayer only, and the Gaonim insisted that even in the Yotzer benediction it is to be omitted in non-congregational prayer (hence the short version of Saadya, quoted earlier, which is intended for individual worship, does not contain it). The Kedushah has its place in this benediction through an association of ideas: God created the luminaries, who are but his servants, faithfully carrying out his will—as are the angels who give praise to their Master every morning.

The second benediction, unlike the first, is directly related to the Shema: it gives praise to God who showed his love for Israel by the gift of the Torah and the commandments. Its stress on God's love corresponds to the twice-repeated injunction in the Shema that Israel love God with all its heart; this now becomes a response to divine love, and the mutuality of the relationship is emphasized. The short petitions interwoven in the text of the benediction are probably later additions.

The benediction following the Shema is made up of two components: the first is an affirmation of faith—a formal and explicit acknowledgment by the worshipers that all that is stated in the biblical passages just recited is "true and certain, established and enduring." The latter part gives thanks for the redemption from Egypt, linking with the last verse of the Shema: "I am the Lord your God, who brought you

*out of the land of Egypt." On this note, the benediction concludes:
"Blessed art thou . . . who hast redeemed Israel."*

Apart from their specific content and function, the ideas expressed in
each of these three benedictions are interconnected. The first praises
God for creation (of light), the second for the giving of the Torah at
Sinai, the third for the redemption from Egypt. Creation, revelation,
and redemption are the three cornerstones of the traditional Jewish
view of history, designating its beginning, its great turning point,
and its goal. Their appearance together in the three benedictions of
the Shema (and elsewhere in traditional prayers) is certainly not
fortuitous, as was pointed out by medieval commentators and by
Franz Rosenzweig in Star of Redemption in modern times. This holds
true even though redemption in the third benediction specifically
refers to the redemption of Israel from Egypt rather than the messianic redemption of the future, for in Jewish tradition the one was
understood to be the prefiguration of the other. Characteristically, the
third benediction, though overtly concerned with giving thanks for
the past, concludes in most rites with a prayer for messianic redemption, as in the Ashkenazi rite: "O Rock of Israel, arise to the help
of Israel, . . ."—a simple, poetic composition, each line of which
concludes with the word "Israel."

The inner link among the three benedictions is reinforced ver-
bally. In the first, God is praised for having created light (or) in the
physical sense. The second is concerned with the Torah, the spiritual
light of the soul ("Enlighten our eyes in thy law"; see the whole of
Psalms 19 and especially 9; Prov. 6:23). And redemption, too, is called
"light" metaphorically (e.g., Isa. 9:1: "The people that walked in
darkness have seen a great light"); even though it is not thus alluded
to in the third benediction, interestingly enough the first benediction
ends: "Cause a new light to shine upon Zion and may we all be
worthy soon to enjoy its brightness." This last passage, though objected to by some of the Geonim as out of context, has nevertheless
been retained in the Ashkenazi rite.

In the evening, the second and third benedictions express the
same ideas, though formulated differently and more briefly. The first,
however, instead of stressing the renewal of light in the morning,
emphasizes that God brings night and darkness as well. (The Talmud
[Bab. Berakhot 11b] insists that reference be made in the evening

prayer to God as the creator of light, and in the morning prayer to God as the creator of darkness—undoubtedly, to repudiate dualistic religions, like Zoroastrianism, which assign light and darkness to two opposing divine forces [Isa. 45:7; and note the exchange of "evil" for "all things" at the beginning of the Yotzer benediction].) Since the motif of Creation is not emphasized in the first evening benediction, the evening series as a whole does not feature the association, mentioned above, of the ideas of creation, revelation, and redemption that characterize the morning service; hence it stands to reason that the morning series of benedictions is the original one, and was later adapted for use in the evening as well.

In the evening a further benediction is recited after the one concerning redemption—"Grant . . . that we lie down in peace . . ."—which, in contrast to the preceding three, is a petition for personal protection from night dangers, when a man is asleep and off guard. This prayer was added because the recital of the Amidah, with its manifold petitions, was originally not obligatory at night and the Shema and its benedictions constituted the entire evening service; this was felt to be insufficient—a prayer-service must, of necessity, contain petitions as well as praises—and thus an additional prayer was attached to the evening Shema service. Its conclusion, especially in the version used on Sabbaths and festivals rather incongruously strikes a national note, stressing protection and peace for the land of Israel and Jerusalem.

THE SHEMA AND ITS BENEDICTIONS

1. Blessed art thou, O Lord our God, King of the universe, who formest light and createst darkness, who makest peace and createst all things.

All shall thank thee, and all shall praise thee, and all shall say, there is none holy like the Lord. All shall extol thee for ever, Creator of all things, O God who openest every day the doors of the gates of the East, and cleavest the windows of the firmament, bringing forth the sun from its place, and the moon from its dwelling, giving light to the whole world and to its inhabitants whom thou hast created in thy mercy. In mercy thou givest light to the earth and to those who dwell on it, and in thy goodness renewest the creation every day continually; O King, who alone wast exalted from aforetime, praised, glorified, and extolled from days of old. Eternal God, in thine abundant mercies, have mercy upon us, Lord of our strength, Rock of our stronghold, Shield of our salvation, thou Stronghold of ours! There is none to be compared unto thee, and there is none besides thee; there is none but thee: who is like thee? There is none to be compared unto thee, Lord our God, in this world, and there is none besides thee, our King, in the life of the world to come; there is none but thee, our Redeemer, in the days of the Messiah; neither is there any like thee, our Deliverer, in the resurrection of the dead.

God, the Lord over all works, blessed is he, and ever to be blessed by the mouth of everything that has breath. His greatness and goodness fill the universe; knowledge and understanding surround him; he is exalted above the holy *Hayot* and is adorned in glory above the celestial chariot; purity and rectitude are before his throne, kindness and mercy before his glory. The luminaries are good which our God has created: he formed them with knowledge, understanding and discernment; he gave them might and power to rule in the midst of the world. They are full of luster, and they radiate brightness: beautiful is their luster throughout all the world. They rejoice in their going forth, and are glad in their returning; they perform with awe the will of their Master. Glory and honor they render his name, exultation and rejoicing at the remembrance of his sovereignty. He called unto the sun, and it shone forth in light: he looked, and ordained the figure of the moon. All the hosts on high render praise unto him, the Seraphim, the Ophanim, and the holy Hayot ascribing glory and greatness.

To the God who rested from all his works, and on the seventh day exalted himself and sat upon the throne of his glory; who robed himself in glory on the day of rest, and called the Sabbath day a delight. This is the praise of the Sabbath day, that God rested thereon from all his work, when the Sabbath day [itself] offers praise and says *A Psalm, a song of the Sabbath day, it is good to give thanks unto the Lord* [Psalms 92:1–2]. Therefore let all his creatures glorify and bless God; let them render praise, honor, and greatness to the God and King who is Creator of all things, and who, in his holiness, gives an inheritance of rest to his people Israel on the holy Sabbath day. Thy name, Lord our God, shall be hallowed, and thy remembrance, our King, shall be glorified in heaven above and on the earth below. Be thou blessed, our Savior, for the excellency of thy handiwork, and for the bright luminaries which thou hast made: they shall glorify thee for ever.

Be thou blessed, our Rock, our King and Redeemer, Creator of holy beings, praised be thy name for ever, our King; Creator of ministering spirits, all of whom stand in the heights of the universe, and proclaim with awe in unison aloud the words of the living God and everlasting King. All of them are beloved, pure and mighty, and all of them in dread and awe do the will of the Master; and all of them open their mouths in holiness and purity, with song and psalm, while they bless and praise, glorify and reverence, sanctify and ascribe sovereignty to the name of the Divine King, the great, mighty, and dreaded One, holy is he; and they all take upon themselves the yoke of the kingdom of Heaven one from the other, and give permission to one another to hallow their Creator: in tranquil joy of spirit, with pure speech and holy melody they all respond in unison, and exclaim with awe:

Holy, holy, holy is the Lord of hosts: the whole earth is full of his glory [Isa. 6:3].

And the Ophanim and the holy Hayot with a noise of great rushing, upraising themselves toward the Seraphim, over against them offer praise and say:

Blessed be the glory of the Lord from his place [Ezek. 3:12].

To the blessed God they offer melodies; to the King, the living and eternal God, they utter hymns and make their praises heard; for he alone performs mighty deeds, and makes new things; he is the Lord of battles; he sows righteousness, causes salvation to spring forth, creates remedies, and is revered in praises. He is the Lord of wonders, who in his goodness renews the creation every day continually, as it is said, *To Him that made great lights, for His mercy endures for ever* [Psalms 136:7]. O cause a new light to shine upon Zion, and may we all be worthy soon to enjoy its brightness. Blessed art thou, O Lord, Creator of the lights.

2. With abounding love hast thou loved us, Lord our God, great and exceeding mercy hast thou bestowed upon us. Our Father, our

King, for our fathers' sake, who trusted in thee, and whom thou didst teach laws of life, be gracious unto us and teach us. Our Father, merciful Father, ever compassionate, have mercy upon us and put it into our hearts to understand and to discern, to mark, learn, and teach, to heed, to do, and to fulfill in love all the words of instruction in thy Torah. Enlighten our eyes in thy Torah and let our hearts cleave to thy commandments, and unite our hearts to love and fear thy name, so that we be never put to shame. Because we have trusted in thy holy, great, and revered name, we shall rejoice and be glad in thy salvation. O bring us in peace from the four corners of the earth, and make us go upright to our land; for thou art a God who works salvation. Thou hast chosen us from all peoples and tongues, and hast brought us near unto thy great name for ever in faithfulness, that we might in love give thanks unto thee and proclaim thy unity. Blessed art thou, O Lord, who hast chosen thy people Israel in love.

Hear, O Israel, The Lord our God, the Lord is One.
Blessed be the name of his glorious kingdom for ever and ever.

You shall love the Lord your God with all your heart, and with all your soul, and with all your might. And these words, which I command you this day, shall be in your hearts: and you shall teach them diligently to your children, and shall speak of them when you sit in your house, and when you walk by the way, and when you lie down, and when you rise up. And you shall bind them for a sign upon your hand, and they shall be as frontlets between your eyes. And you shall write them upon the doorposts of your house, and upon your gates.

And it shall come to pass, if you will diligently obey my commandments which I command you this day, to love the Lord your God, and to serve him with all your heart and with all your soul, that I will give the rain of your land in its season, the former rain and the latter rain, that you may gather in your corn, and your wine, and your oil. And I will give grass in your field for your cattle, and you shall eat and be satisfied. Beware, lest your heart be deceived, and you turn aside, and serve other gods, and worship them; and the anger of the Lord be kindled against you, and he shut up the heaven, that there be no rain, and the land yield not her fruit; and you perish quickly from off the good land which the Lord gives you. Therefore you shall lay up these my words in your heart and in your soul; and you shall bind them for a sign upon your hand, and they shall be as frontlets between your eyes. And you shall teach them to your children, speaking of them when you sit in your house, and when you walk by the way, and when you lie down, and when you rise up. And you shall write them upon the doorposts of your house, and upon your gates: that your days may be multiplied, and the days of your children, upon the land which the Lord swore to your fathers to give them, as the days of the heavens above the earth.

And the Lord spoke unto Moses, saying, Speak unto the children of Israel, and bid them make for themselves fringes upon the corners of their garments throughout their generations, and put upon the fringe of each corner a cord of blue: and it shall be a fringe unto you, that you may look upon it, and remember all the commandments of the Lord, and do them; that you go not astray after your own heart and your own eyes, after which you used to go astray: that you may remember and do all my commandments, and be holy unto your God. I am the Lord your God, who brought you out of the land of Egypt, to be your God: I am the Lord your God.

3. True and firm, established and enduring, right and faithful, beloved and precious, desirable and pleasant, revered and mighty, well-ordered and acceptable, good and beautiful is this word unto us for ever and ever. It is true, the God of the universe is our King, the Rock of Jacob, the Shield of our salvation: throughout all generations he endures and his name endures; his throne is established, and his kingdom and his faithfulness endure for ever. His words also live and endure; they are faithful and desirable for ever and to all eternity, as for our fathers so also for us, our children, our generations, and for all the generations of the seed of Israel his servants.

For the first and for the last ages thy word is good and endures for ever and ever; it is true and trustworthy, a statute which shall not pass away. True it is that thou art indeed the Lord our God and the God of our fathers, our King, our fathers' King, our Redeemer, the Redeemer of our fathers, our Maker, the Rock of our salvation; our Deliverer and Rescuer from everlasting, such is thy name; there is no God besides thee.

Thou hast been the help of our fathers from of old, a Shield and Protector to their children after them in every generation: in the heights of the universe is thy habitation, and thy judgments and thy righteousness reach to the farthest ends of the earth. Happy is the man who obeys thy commandments, and takes thy Torah and thy word to his heart. True it is that thou art indeed the Lord of thy people, and a mighty King to plead their cause. True it is that thou art indeed the first and thou art the last, and besides thee we have no King, Redeemer, and Deliverer. From Egypt thou didst redeem us, O Lord our God, and from the house of bondmen thou didst deliver us; all their first-born thou didst slay, but thy firstborn thou didst redeem; thou didst divide the Red Sea and drown the proud; but thou madest the beloved to pass through, while the waters covered their adversaries, not one of whom was left. Wherefore the beloved praised and extolled God, and offered hymns, songs, praises, blessings and thanksgivings to the King and God, who lives and endures; who is high and exalted, great and revered; who brings low the haughty, and raises up the lowly, leads forth the prisoners, delivers the meek, helps the poor, and answers his people when they cry unto him. Praises to the Most High God, blessed is he, and ever to be blessed. Moses and the children of Israel sang a song unto thee with great joy, saying, all of them:

> Who is like unto thee, O Lord, among the mighty ones? Who is like unto thee, glorious in holiness, revered in praises, doing wonders [Ex. 15:11]?

With a new song the redeemed people offered praise unto thy name at the seashore; they all gave thanks in unison, and proclaimed thy sovereignty, and said:

> The Lord shall reign for ever and ever [Ex. 15:18].

Rock of Israel, arise to the help of Israel, and deliver, according to thy promise, Judah and Israel. Our Redeemer, the Lord of hosts is his name, the Holy One of Israel. Blessed art thou, O Lord, who hast redeemed Israel.

FOR THE EVENING:

1. Blessed art thou, Lord our God, King of the universe, who at thy word bringest on the evening twilight, with wisdom openest the gates of the heavens, and with understanding changest times and

variest the seasons, and arrangest the stars in their watches in the sky, according to thy will. Thou createst day and night; thou rollest away the light from before the darkness, and the darkness from before the light; thou makest the day to pass and the night to approach, thou dividest the day from the night, the Lord of hosts is thy name; a God living and enduring continually, mayest thou reign over us for ever and ever. Blessed art thou, O Lord, who bringest on the evening twilight.

2. With everlasting love thou hast loved the house of Israel, thy people; Torah and commandments, statutes and judgments hast thou taught us. Therefore, O Lord our God, when we lie down and when we rise up we will meditate on thy law, and rejoice in the words of thy Torah and thy commandments for ever; for they are our life and the length of our days, and we will meditate on them day and night. Mayest thou never take away thy love from us. Blessed art thou, O Lord, who lovest thy people Israel.

Hear, O Israel . . .

3. True and trustworthy is all this, and it is established with us that he is the Lord our God, and there is none besides him, and that we, Israel, are his people. It is he, our King, who redeemed us from the hand of kings, who delivered us from the grasp of all the tyrants: God, who on our behalf dealt out punishment to our adversaries, and requited all the enemies of our soul; who does great things past finding out and wonders without number; who holds our soul in life, and has not suffered our feet to be moved; who made us tread upon the high places of our enemies, and exalted our horn over all that hate us; who wrought miracles for us and vengeance upon Pharaoh, signs and wonders in the land of the children of Ham; who in his wrath smote all the firstborn of Egypt, and brought forth his people Israel among them to everlasting freedom; who made his children pass between the divisions of the Sea, but sank their pursuers and their enemies in the depths. Then his children beheld his might; they praised and gave thanks unto his name, and willingly accepted his sovereignty. Moses and the children of Israel sang a song unto thee with great joy, saying all of them:

Who is like unto thee, O Lord, among the mighty ones? Who is like unto thee, glorious in holiness, revered in praises, doing wonders [Ex. 15:11]?

Thy children beheld thy sovereign power, as thou didst part the sea before Moses. They exclaimed, This is my God! and said:

The Lord shall reign for ever and ever [Ex. 15:18].

And it is said, *For the Lord has delivered Jacob, and redeemed him from the hand of him that was stronger than he* [Jer. 31:11].

Blessed art thou, O Lord, who hast redeemed Israel.

4. Grant, Lord our God, that we lie down in peace, and raise us again, our King, to life. Spread over us the tabernacle of thy peace, direct us aright through thine own good counsel; save us for thy name's sake, be thou a shield about us; remove from us every enemy, pestilence, sword, famine, and sorrow; remove also satan from before us and from behind us. Shelter us beneath the shadow of thy wings; for thou, O God, art our Guardian and our Deliverer; thou, O God, art a gracious and merciful King. Guard our going out and our coming in unto life and unto peace from this time forth and forevermore. Spread over us the tabernacle of thy peace. Blessed art thou, O Lord, who spreadest the tabernacle of peace over us and over all thy people Israel, and over Jerusalem.

THE WEEKDAY AMIDAH

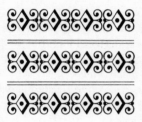

INTRODUCTION

THE AMIDAH *is the most important of the prescribed daily prayers. It must be recited both in the morning and the afternoon services (corresponding to the two daily communal sacrifices, offered in the Temple); in the evening service it is optional, but its recital is, nevertheless, the generally accepted custom. On Sabbaths and festivals the Amidah is recited a fourth time, in the "additional service" (corresponding to the additional sacrifices which were offered on these days; Numbers 28–29); on the Day of Atonement it is recited a fifth time in the late afternoon ("The Concluding Service for the Day of Atonement"). However, although they are considered variant forms of the same prayer, all serving the same liturgical function and all bound by the same rules of recital, the various Amidot differ considerably among themselves in structure and content. The weekday Amidah in the old Palestinian rite (given below), consists of eighteen benedictions (although in rites current today it numbers nineteen—see Birnbaum, pp. 81–95); the Amidah for Sabbaths and festivals, on the other hand, retains only the first three and the last three benedictions, to which it adds, as a fourth, one concerned with the sanctification of the day (e.g., Birnbaum, pp. 265–71, 575–83, 585–95, 655–63; for the single exception from the standard Amidah for Sabbaths and festivals, see "Seven Benedictions in One").*

Some sources suggest that the petitions of the weekday Amidah were omitted on Sabbaths and festivals because if a man were to pray for his needs on Sabbath he would be recalled to his sorrows and anxieties and, as a result, be distressed instead of joyful. However, the Jerusalem Talmud (Shabbat XV, 3, 15b) explicitly states that there is no need to omit on the Sabbath the petition for sustenance in the recital of Grace after meals (see "Grace after Meals"), because it is part of the "fixed form of the benediction"; the same reasoning ought to hold good for the Amidah. Petitions of a national character, moreover, figure prominently in a variety of places in Sabbath and festival prayers (below, e.g., "Benedictions following the Haftarah"). It is more likely therefore, that the Sabbath and festival Amidot were not derived from the weekday one, but antedated it. Fixed community prayers on days of rest had become an established custom long before weekday services were introduced and could not be made to conform when the latter did eventually emerge.

The Eighteen Benedictions for weekdays consist, first, of three devoted to praise, followed by twelve (in current rites, thirteen) that are petitions, and then a final three, the second of which expresses thanksgiving. This structure is considered appropriate to a "servant making requests of his master" (Bab. Berakhot 34a), since "a man should always praise God first and pray [i.e., petition for his needs] afterward" (Bab. Avodah Zarah 7b). Basically, then, the weekday Amidah is a prayer of supplication, but each benediction is concluded in the style of eulogy: "Blessed art thou. . . . " The petitions themselves may be subdivided into two distinct groups: the first six are concerned with general, human, everyday needs, both spiritual and material, while the following five (nowadays, six) give expression to specific national aspirations, all concerned with various aspects of messianic redemption; the last petition is a general plea that our prayers be accepted. The request for redemption in the seventh benediction, therefore, would appear at first glance to be out of place; however, it was originally concerned with the redeeming of individuals or of the community from afflictions of an ephemeral nature, not with salvation in the eschatological sense.

The name Amidah—used mainly by Sephardim—means "standing" and indicates that this prayer must be recited, because of its importance, in a standing position. In Talmudic sources, the Amidah usually

*is simply called "the prayer." The traditional name "Eighteen Bene-
dictions" is no longer strictly appropriate, since a nineteenth benediction came to be added to the weekday Amidah; it certainly does not
fit the Amidot for Sabbaths and festivals. The Amidah is composed in
simple style, a kind of elated prose. Individual benedictions are brief;
many of them consist of two short lines, between which there is a
marked parallelism in the biblical manner, and a concluding eulogy.
In the versions current today a further clause is added to some
benedictions, giving the reason for the worshiper's expectation that his
prayer may be answered, e.g.: ". . . for thou dost pardon and forgive,"
or, ". . . for thou hearkenest in mercy to the prayer of Israel." With
the exception of the first benediction (and some of the conclusions,
e.g., ". . . who healest the sick of his [sic] people Israel"), the entire
prayer addresses God in the second person; this is especially marked in
the berakhah-formula, repeated eighteen (nineteen) times: "Blessed
art thou, O Lord." This mode of address expresses the sense of a
direct, personal relationship between the worshiper and God.*

*No less characteristic is the formulation of the entire prayer (and of
all other prescribed community prayers) in the first person plural,
"we." It is the community which turns to God, praises him, and
presents its needs to him. Even an individual praying at home uses
this style; he, too, considers himself a representative of the community
and puts forward not his own, individual needs (though he may
mention these in addition), but those of the congregation, or, even,
of the people Israel. In each congregational service (except in the
evening), the Amidah is recited twice: first silently by each individual
and then aloud by the reader (originally this was done for the benefit
of those unable to recite). During the repetition by the reader, some
additions are made, notable among them the Kedusha and the Priestly
Blessing (Num. 6:24-26), which is inserted before the last benediction
(in the land of Israel daily; elsewhere only on festivals). As the reader
concludes each benediction, the congregation responds "Amen."*

*There is no reason to assume that the Amidah was originally composed
and instituted by a central authority. Fixed community prayers gradually came into being during the Second Temple period. People would
meet for joint worship, and in the course of time, "orders of prayers"—
which at first differed widely from congregation to congregation—
developed. By the end of this period, the Eighteen Benedictions had*

apparently already become a general custom, though the exact sequence and the content of individual benedictions probably still varied. The seven benedictions for Sabbaths and festivals were already accepted as the norm by the schools of Hillel and Shammai (Tos. Berakhot III, 13). Shortly after the destruction of the Temple the Amidah was "edited" in Yavneh by Rabban Gamliel II and his colleagues. Even then, however, only the order, the general content, and the berakhah-formulas were standardized; the actual wording was left to the individual worshiper or reader. Attempts to reconstruct the "original" text or to ascertain the date when any one section of the Amidah was composed are thus pointless—especially in view of the ruling that benedictions were not to be written down (Tos. Shabbat XIII, 4). Only in the Gaonic period were the definitive versions of the Amidah established and committed to writing; even then, those current in the land of Israel (known to us mainly through the Cairo Genizah) and in Babylonia differed in their wording (though not, on the whole, in their contents). All present-day versions of the Amidah derive from the Babylonian rite.

In the Amidah as it is recited today, the additional, nineteenth, benediction—it actually occupies the fifteenth position—is a petition for the re-establishment of the Davidic kingdom in messianic times. This benediction is invariably missing not only from the Genizah texts of the Eighteen Benedictions but also from the numerous poetic compositions [kerovot] by Palestinian payyetanim that were inserted into the weekday Amidah (on special occasions, as on Purim or Hanukkah). In the Palestinian version of the Amidah (below), the plea for the Davidic kingdom was incorporated in the fourteenth benediction, which calls for the rebuilding of Jerusalem (it is also still referred to in current versions, even though the following benediction takes up the same theme). While probably of Palestinian origin, the separate petition for the restoration of the kingdom of David was not accepted in the standard version adopted by the majority of congregations there (Tos. Berakhot III, 25). In Babylonia, on the other hand, this additional benediction became the general custom.

There is an erroneous statement in the Babylonian Talmud (Berakhot 28b) to the effect that the additional, nineteenth, benediction is the

"*Benediction Concerning the Heretics.*" *There is no reason to doubt the information supplied by the Palestinian Amora, R. Levi, that this benediction was instituted in Yavneh, on the initiative of Rabban Gamliel (indeed, this information is confirmed by a Tannaitic source, given at the bottom of the same page). However, the "Benediction Concerning the Heretics" was not really a new benediction; its author was merely adding a new point to, or enlarging on the meaning of, a benediction previously known as* shel paroshim [*concerning the dissidents*] *or* shel resha'im [*concerning the wicked*]. *He did this by making it apply specifically to heretics, i.e., Jews dissenting from some of the basic tenets of Judaism. In particular, this benediction—in reality, a curse—was probably directed against Judeo-Christians (not sidents*] *or* shel resha'im [*concerning the wicked*]. *He did this by ing to Christianity out of the synagogue (they still prayed there at the end of the first century). The fact that medieval Christian censors viewed this petition as a malediction directed against all Christians accounts for the many changes and "corrections" that were introduced into it over the centuries. Among other such changes, the term* minim [*heretics*] *from which the benediction derived its name was omitted and a variety of other terms substituted for it in most current versions.*

The following is based on the Genizah fragments, first published by Solomon Schechter in Jewish Quarterly Review *(o.s.) X (1898), pp. 656ff. Also Jacob Mann, "Genizah Fragments of the Palestinian Order of Service," Hebrew Union College Annual, II (1925), pp. 269ff. [Jakob J. Petuchowski, ed., Contributions to the Scientific Study of Jewish Liturgy (New York: Ktav Publishing House, 1970), pp. 375ff. and 405ff.].*

THE WEEKDAY AMIDAH

1   Blessed art thou, O Lord,
     Our God and God of our fathers,
     God of Abraham, God of Isaac, and God of Jacob,
     Great, mighty, and awesome God,

God Most High, creator of heaven and earth,
Our shield and shield of our fathers,
Our refuge in every generation.
Blessed art thou, O Lord, shield of Abraham.

2   Thou art mighty—humbling the haughty,
Powerful—calling the arrogant to judgment,
Eternal—reviving the dead,
Causing the wind to blow and the dew to fall,
Sustaining the living, resurrecting the dead—
O cause our salvation to sprout in the twinkling of an eye!
Blessed art thou, O Lord, who revivest the dead.

3   Thou art holy and thy name is awesome
And there is no god beside thee.
Blessed art thou, O Lord, the Holy God.

4   Graciously favor us, our Father, with understanding from thee,
And discernment and insight out of Thy Torah.
Blessed art thou, O Lord, gracious bestower of understanding.

5   *Turn us to thee, O Lord, and we shall return,*
Restore our days as of old (Lam. 5:21).
Blessed art thou, O Lord, who desirest repentance.

6   Forgive us, our Father, for we have sinned against thee,
Erase and blot out our transgressions from before thine eyes,
For thou art abundantly compassionate.
Blessed art thou, O Lord, who forgivest readily.

7   Behold our afflictions and defend our cause,
And redeem us for thy name's sake.
Blessed art thou, O Lord, Redeemer of Israel.

8   Heal us, O Lord our God, of the pain in our hearts,
Remove grief and sighing from us
And cause our wounds to be healed.
Blessed art thou, O Lord, who healest the sick of Israel thy
people.

9   Bless this year for us, O Lord our God,
And may its harvest be abundant.
Hasten the time of our deliverance
Provide dew and rain for the earth [1]

And satiate thy world from thy storehouses of goodness,
And bestow a blessing upon the work of our hands.
Blessed art thou, O Lord, who blessest the years.

10 Blow a blast upon the great *shofar* for our freedom
And raise a banner for the ingathering of our exiles.
Blessed art thou, O Lord, who gatherest the dispersed of thy
people Israel.

11 Restore our judges as of old,
And our leaders as in days of yore,
And reign over us—thou alone.
Blessed art thou, O Lord, Lover of justice.

12 May there be no hope for the apostates,
And speedily uproot the kingdom of arrogance in our own day.
May the Nazarenes [2] and the sectarians perish in an instant.
May they be blotted out of the book of living,
And may they not be written with the righteous (Psalms 69:29).
Blessed art thou, O Lord, who subduest the arrogant.

13 Show abundant compassion to the righteous converts,
And give us a good reward together with those who do your will.
Blessed art thou, O Lord, Stay of the righteous.

14 Have compassion, O Lord, our God, in thine abundant mercy,
On Israel thy people,
And on Jerusalem thy city,
And Zion, the abode of thy glory,
And upon the royal seed of David, thy justly anointed.
Blessed art thou, O Lord, God of David, Rebuilder of Jerusalem.

15 Hear, O Lord, our God, the voice of our prayers,
And have compassion upon us,
For thou art a gracious and compassionate God.
Blessed art thou, O Lord, who hearest prayer.

16 May it be thy will, O Lord, our God, to dwell in Zion,
And may thy servants worship thee in Jerusalem.
Blessed art thou, O Lord, whom we worship with reverence.

17 We thank thee,
Our God and God of our fathers,
For all of the goodness, the lovingkindness, and the mercies

With which thou hast requited us, and our fathers before us.
For when we say, "our foot slips"
Thy mercy, O Lord, holds us up.[3]
Blessed art thou, O Lord, to whom it is good to give thanks.

18   Bestow thy peace
Upon Israel thy people,
And upon thy city,
And upon thine inheritance,
And bless us all, together.
Blessed art thou, O Lord, Maker of peace.

A PARAPHRASE OF THE WEEKDAY AMIDAH

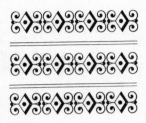

INTRODUCTION

THIS PARAPHRASE *has only recently been reconstructed from a number of fragmentary manuscripts; its author is Saadya Gaon.[1] The text presents a very curious treatment of the Eighteen Benedictions. The order and structure, as well as the individual themes of each of the benedictions, have been preserved, but at the same time radical changes have been introduced. Not the least such change, perhaps, is the hymnic style in which all the benedictions have been rewritten. Even the petitions open with the formula, "Blessed is thy name"; and instead of pleading with God to heal the sick or crush the wicked, they praise him, elaborately, for doing so. In each benediction, one of the great figures of the past whose prayers have been answered is cited paradigmatically (Mishnah Ta'anit II, 4). Then follows the plea that God similarly answer the requests of the worshiper, after which come a biblical quotation and the concluding eulogy. While payyetanim in all periods were in the habit of taking great liberties with the text of the prayers and went so far as to substitute their own wording for the prescribed version, our text goes beyond this, materially altering the nature of the benedictions: petitions are turned into hymns of praise, and, vice versa, petitions are inserted in the first three benedictions, which according to the halakhah must be devoted exclusively to praise. Moreover, in striking contrast to the standard*

37

Amidah versions, which are formulated invariably in the first person plural, all petitions in this paraphrase are expressed in the singular.

There can be no doubt that this composition, which deviates so radically from the basic features characteristic of the standard Amidah, was not intended as a substitute for it; its function must have been to serve in private worship, that is, as a prayer offered by the pious individual who was not content with the standard service but felt the need to recite his own personal prayers in addition. But why, if the function of this composition was to serve the individual's need for optional, non-obligatory prayer, does it imitate so carefully the order, structure, and—in some respects—even the style and form of the Eighteen Benedictions? The answer must be sought in the unique status of the Amidah in Jewish liturgy as "the prayer" par excellence; an individual wishing to assert that his private devotion, offered voluntarily, nevertheless had the standing of proper prayer, would naturally clothe it in the outward garb of the Eighteen Benedictions. This, then, is a pseudo-Amidah in form, and a personal, individual non-obligatory prayer in essence.

Saadya Gaon—the author of this composition—held very strict principles with regard to the forms of the prescribed prayers. He could not possibly have countenanced a prayer formulated in the first person singular as being equivalent to the Amidah. Nor would he have favored a change in the most important distinguishing mark by which obligatory prayers are set apart from spontaneous, individual worship: the berakhah-formula used at the beginning and/or conclusion of each benediction. As the prayer under discussion radically violates these formal rules, it is clear that Saadia can only have intended to use a formula suggestive of the berakhah-formula but not its strict equivalent. In the concluding formulas, for example, it is possible that in the original version abbreviated conclusions were used that would not be considered a berakhah, in the technical, halakhic sense and later copyists erroneously enlarged these into full-fledged formulas.[2]

This composition reflects the tension in Jewish liturgy between formalized, institutionalized prayer and spontaneous, individual piety.

*Not satisfied with limiting themselves to regulated, prescribed prayers,
the pious sought to add more personal, voluntary devotion.*[3] *But such
are the dialectics of conformity and spontaneity in Jewish liturgy that
even such additional prayers, intended as an outlet for individual piety,
strove to retain the outward appearance of obligatory prayer in order
to attain, in the mind of the worshiper, the weight and status of "real"
prayer.*

A PARAPHRASE OF THE WEEKDAY AMIDAH

1. Blessed is thy name, O Lord of hosts, God of Israel, who sittest
over the cherubim, who art the God of Gods and the Lord of Lords,
God compassionate and gracious. . . . God the most High, Maker
of heavens and earth, the great, mighty and revered God, God the
Shield of Abraham, who didst choose Abraham thy friend, and
foundest his heart faithful before thee; as thou didst hear his prayer
at Mount Moriah, so hear thou my prayer for thy sake and for thy
name's sake and for the sake of Abraham thy friend and be thou a
shield about me and protection and refuge and thou be a shield unto
me, shielding me, deliver me as thou passest over me and rescuest me.
But thou, O Lord, art a shield about me and the lifter up of my head
(Psalms 3:4).
Blessed art thou, O Lord, Shield of Abraham.

2. Blessed is thy name, O Lord of hosts, God of Israel, for thou
art God who killest and revivest and in thy hand is the soul of every
living thing, and the breath of all mankind. Thou hast established thy
covenant with Isaac thy servant and as thou didst hear his prayer upon
the altar, so hear my prayer for thy sake and for the sake of thy great
name and for the sake of Isaac thy servant. Revive me and raise me
up upon my feet to walk that I might meditate in thy word. Grant me
that I may be enlightened with the light of the living, for thou revivest
all with the quality of mercy. Send down dew of good will, blessing
and charity to revive the world. *For with thee is the fountain of life,
in thy light do we see light* (Psalms 36:10).
Blessed art thou, O Lord, who quickenest the dead.

3. Blessed is thy name, O Lord of hosts, God of Israel, for thou art God, sanctified in the council of the holy ones, the Holy One and the awesome One that inhabits eternity, whose name is Holy. The Holy One of Jacob, the God of Israel; as thou didst hear his prayer in Beth-el, hear thou my prayer for thy sake, for thy name's sake and for the sake of Israel thy chosen one and sanctify me for thy name's sake as is meet for the sanctity of thy name. Cleanse me to worship thee with a whole heart, in sanctity and in purity. *For thou art holy, thou art enthroned upon the praises of Israel* (Psalms 22:4).

Blessed art thou, O Lord, our holy God.

4. Blessed is thy name, O Lord of hosts, God of Israel, thou art a wise and understanding God, thou hast created all in wisdom and understanding. Thou hast revealed unto us the wisdom of thy Torah through Moses thy chosen one. As thou didst hear his prayer when he stood before thee in the breach, hear thou the prayer of thy servant, the son of thy handmaiden, the poor, the pained, and raise him up upon his feet for thy sake and for the sake of Moses thy chosen one, and give me wisdom and understanding to believe, and grant me to study thy Torah to observe it and to do it. *For the Lord gives wisdom, out of his mouth comes knowledge and discernment* (Prov. 2:6).

Blessed art thou, O Lord, gracious Giver of knowledge.

5. Blessed is thy name, O Lord of hosts, God of Israel, thou art God who takest pleasure in repentance and from the beginning thou hast established a healing for the transgressors, this being repentance. For thou art a guide for the sinners and thou desirest the incense of Aaron thy holy one to make atonement for the people. So hear thou my prayer for thy sake and for thy name's sake and for the sake of thy sanctified priests. Grant me a perfect repentance to return to thee with all my heart and all my soul. Do not let me depart from this world without repentance. *Turn thou us unto thee, O Lord, and we shall return* (Lam. 5:21).

Blessed art thou, O Lord, who delightest in repentance.

6. Blessed is thy name, O Lord of hosts, God of Israel, for thou art God who forgivest and pardonest, good and ready to pardon for

with thee there is forgiveness. Thou hast given a covenant of peace, a covenant of an everlasting priesthood to Phineas thy servant in that he was zealous for thy sake and made atonement for the children of Israel. So hear thou my prayer for thy sake and for thy name's sake and for the sake of Phineas thy servant, and pardon and forgive my sins and my transgressions and my iniquities for they are many. Grant me forgiveness and atonement for I have sinned greatly. *If thou, Lord, shouldest mark iniquities, O Lord, who could stand? For with thee there is forgiveness, that thou mayest be feared* (Psalms 30:3–4).

Blessed art thou, O Lord, who art gracious and dost abundantly forgive.

7. Blessed is thy name, O Lord of hosts, God of Israel, for thou art God who redeemest and savest Israel at all their times of trouble, for in all generations thou art our Redeemer and our Savior for thou didst hear the prayer of Joshua thy servant on the day thou didst hearken unto the voice of a man. So hear thou my prayer for thy sake and for the sake of Joshua thy servant, redeem and release me from all my troubles and hasten redemption for thy people Israel speedily. *Redeem Israel, O God, out of all his troubles* (Psalms 25:22).

Blessed art thou, O Lord, the Redeemer of Israel.

8. Blessed is thy name, O Lord of hosts, God of Israel, for thou art the healer of the sick, the healer of the brokenhearted, thou smitest and healest. Heal me, O Lord, from my sickness and raise me up from my illness, hearken to my prayer and my entreaties, see my pain and my humiliation. As thou didst hear the prayer of Samuel thy servant when he offered up the kine unto thee, so hear thou my prayer for thy sake and for the sake of Samuel thy servant and send healing and mercy to me and to every one who is in need of healing in Israel. Heal, I beseech thee, my illness and the illness of my transgressions and the sorrow of my iniquities for thy name's sake. *Heal me, O Lord, and I shall be healed; save me, and I shall be saved; for thou art my praise* (Jer. 17:14).

Blessed art thou, O Lord, who healest the sick of thy people Israel.

9. Blessed is thy name, O Lord of hosts, God of Israel, for thou art God who blesses the good years and from the blessing of thy goodness all thy creatures will be blessed and will live. As thou didst hear the prayer of David thy servant when he built an altar at the threshing floor of Arnon the Jebusite, so hear thou my prayer for thy sake and for the sake of David thine anointed. Bless me, O Lord of Israel, in all the works of my hands and accept my prayers in all my troubles. Grant me plentitude for my sustenance in blessing, prosperity, mercy, and truth. Grant me blessing whenever I go out and come in. May this year be one of abundant rains, heat, and dew, and successful in the grain and fruit harvest. Speed thou deliverance for thy people Israel. *Let the earth yield her increase; may God, our own God, bless us. And let all the ends of the earth fear him* (Psalms 67:7–8).

Blessed art thou, O Lord, who blessest the years.

10. Blessed is thy name, O Lord of hosts, God of Israel, for thou art God the shepherd of Israel and leadest us as sheep that have no shepherd and thou hast promised us to gather the banished ones of Israel. As thou didst hear the prayer of Solomon thy servant when he built the sanctuary for thy name, so hear thou my prayer for thy sake and for thy name's sake and for the sake of the love of thy sanctuary. *Save us, O Lord our God, and gather us from among the nations, that we may give thanks unto thy holy name, that we may triumph in thy praise* (Psalms 106:47).

Blessed art thou, O Lord, who gatherest the banished ones of thy people Israel.

11. Blessed is thy name, O Lord of hosts, God of Israel, for thou art God who lovest righteousness and judgment. Thou madest known thy righteous ordinances to Israel thy people. Thou hast executed justice and righteousness in Jacob. Thou didst hear the prayer of Elijah thy servant who called thy name, O Lord, the God of Abraham, of Isaac, and of Israel. As thou didst answer him in fire and in rain from heaven, so hear thou my prayer for thy sake and for the sake of Elijah thy servant. Justify me in judgment and do not condemn me. Make my righteousness to go forth as the light, and my night as the noonday. *He loves righteousness and justice; the earth is full of the kindness of the Lord* (Psalms 33:5).

Blessed art thou, O Lord, the King who lovest righteousness and judgment.

12. Blessed is thy name, O Lord of hosts, God of Israel, for thou art God who cuts off the horns of the wicked and of the enemies of Israel thy people, to lift up the horn of Israel in thy kingdom. As thou didst hear the prayer of Elisha thy servant who called thy name and thou didst cause him to prosper wonderfully and he restored to life him that was dead, so hear thou my prayer for thy sake and for thy name's sake and for the sake of Elisha thy servant. Cut off the horn of mine enemies that rise up against me, and appear in the glory of the pride of thy power and thy kingdom upon the whole of thy universe. *Let them be ashamed and affrighted for ever; let them be abashed and perish, that they may know that it is thou alone whose name is the Lord* (Psalms 83:18–19).

Blessed art thou, O Lord, who breakest the wicked and humblest the arrogant.

13. Blessed is thy name, O Lord of hosts, God of Israel, for thou art a righteous God and lovest justice and righteousness. Thou art the confidence of those who trust in thee. As thou didst hear the crying of Jehoshaphat in the war, so hear thou my prayer for thy sake and for thy name's sake. Be thou unto me a trust, a stay, a refuge, and a protection. For thou art our trust and he who causes us to trust, and the trust of our fathers who didst cause them to trust. *In thee did our fathers trust; they trusted, and thou didst deliver them. Unto thee they cried, and escaped; in thee they did trust, and were not ashamed* (Psalms 22:5–6).

Blessed art thou, O Lord, the stay and trust of the righteous.

14. Blessed is thy name, O Lord of hosts, God of Israel, for thou art God who hast chosen Jerusalem; thou hast desired it for thy inhabitation. As thou didst hear the prayer of thy servant Isaiah who called thy name and turned back the sun ten degrees and who consoled with good words, even comforting words concerning Zion and Jerusalem and thy people Israel, so hear thou my prayer for thy sake and for thy name's sake and for the sake of thy servant Isaiah,

and build Jerusalem. *Do good in thy favor unto Zion; build thou the walls of Jerusalem* (Psalms 51:20).

Blessed art thou, O Lord, who rebuildest Jerusalem.

15. Blessed is thy name, O Lord of hosts, God of Israel, for thou art God who causest salvation to flourish for thy people Israel. As thou didst hear the prayer of Hezekiah thy servant when he had been sick and was recovered of his sickness, so hear thou my prayer for thy sake and for thy name's sake and for the sake of Hezekiah thy servant. Speedily make a horn to shoot up unto David and deliver me with a complete deliverance. *O Lord, God, turn not away the face of thine anointed* (II Chron. 6:42).

Blessed art thou, O Lord, who causest the horn of salvation to flourish.

16. Blessed is thy name, O Lord of hosts, God of Israel, for thou art God who hearkenest unto prayer. To thee shall all flesh come. As thou didst hear Jonah's prayer from out of the belly of the fish, out of the belly of the netherworld he cried and thou didst hear his voice, so hear thou my prayer for thy sake and for thy name's sake and bring me up also out of the tumultuous pit, out of the miry clay. We went through fire and through water. Save me and hear my voice. *Out of the depths [have I called thee, O Lord]* (Psalms 130:1).

Blessed art thou, O Lord, who hearkenest unto prayer.

17. Blessed is thy name, O Lord of hosts, God of Israel, for thou art God who acceptest the prayer of those that fear thee and the prayer of the upright who do thy will. As thou didst hear the prayer of Hananiah, Mishael, and Azariah inside the fiery furnace, so hear thou my prayer for thy sake and for thy name's sake and for the sake of thy great compassion, and accept thou our prayers in return for our offerings. *Let the words of my mouth and the meditation of my heart be acceptable before thee, O Lord, my Rock and my Redeemer* (Psalms 19:15).

Blessed art thou, O Lord, who restorest thy Divine Presence unto Zion.

18. Blessed is thy name, O Lord of hosts, God of Israel, for thou art God who acceptest worship. We give thanks and blessing and bow down and prostrate ourselves to thy great name. For as above and below they prostrate themselves before thee, we also will prostrate ourselves before thy glory in the fear of thee. As thou didst hear the prayer of Daniel from the den of lions, so hear thou my prayer for thy sake and for thy name's sake, and deal kindly with us, the good God. And remember unto us thy mercy and restrain thine anger from us and withhold extinction, indignation, wrath, fierce anger, the destroyer and adversary, the evil inclination, stumbling blocks, afflictions, sickness, punishments that are troublesome, cruel, and peremptory which go forth to come upon the world. Save me and ransom me from all these and from all their seasons; and remember unto life all the children of thy covenant and remember us for our well-being and marvelous things. *We will give thanks unto thy name, O Lord, for it is good* (Psalms 54:8).

Blessed art thou, O Lord, whose name is good, and unto whom it is becoming to give thanks.

19. Blessed is thy name, O Lord of hosts, God of Israel, the Lord redeems the soul of his servants; and none of them that take refuge in thee shall be desolate. Regard my supplications and accept my request. Encompass me with peace and bear me tidings of peace. Grant peace unto my limbs for the merits of Daniel and his companions for whom thou hast performed miracles so that the four corners of the universe were stupefied by thy signs and thy wonders which thou didst work unto them. Because of their righteousness grant me relief from my suffering and do not keep thine anger for ever. Let not sin and iniquity impede my prayer. For thou acceptest those that return and showest good will toward them that confess.[4] *The Lord will give strength unto his people; the Lord will bless his people with peace* (Psalms 29:11).

Blessed art thou, O Lord, who blessest thy people Israel with peace.

Let the words of my mouth and the meditation of my heart be acceptable before thee, O Lord, my Rock and my Redeemer (Psalms 19:15).

PRIVATE WORSHIP IN TALMUDIC TIMES

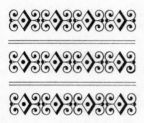

INTRODUCTION

TODAY IT HAS BECOME *rather rare for a Jew to recite individual prayers of his own—inside the synagogue or out—but this was by no means the case at the time when fixed prayers came into being, nor was it the case for a considerable time thereafter. Even within the framework of the set congregational liturgy there was room for individual petitions. Thus the rabbis of the generation of Javneh, for example, debated the precise place for private intercession in the fixed prayers (especially in the Eighteen Benedictions), with the majority advising the interpolation of personal requests at an appropriate place in the Amidah itself (Bab. Avodah Zarah 7b–8a). But there was no objection to private requests being made after the Eighteen Benedictions either; indeed, it became the almost universal custom in Talmudic times to recite such personal prayers at the end of the set service (on weekdays). This personal devotion after "the prayer" is known in Talmudic sources by a variety of names: tahanunim [supplication], "falling on one's face," or simply* devarim [words].

A large number of such prayers, which famous rabbis used to recite (some of them are given below) have been preserved in both talmuds. These, however, may not be entirely representative of the personal prayers of ordinary people. Most rabbis, even in their personal devotions, seem more concerned with national welfare, messianic

47

redemption, and divine assistance in the study and observation of the Torah than with everyday matters and pure and simple material needs. Nevertheless, some of the prayers given below are probably not very different from those recited by simple folk, both in content and in style—the prayer of Rav (which has also been incorporated into the prayerbook; Birnbaum, p. 381) is an instance. The requests offered in such individual prayers would, at times, be of a less than lofty character and express sentiments far from noble: thus we are told that the wife of R. Eliezer, on whom a ban had been imposed by the Sanhedrin under the leadership of Rabban Gamliel, her brother, tried to prevent him from "falling on his face" out of fear that in his personal supplications he would seek vengeance and pray for Rabban Gamliel to be punished. So indeed it happened. For one time, when she did relax her vigilance it was announced immediately afterward that Rabban Gamliel had suddenly died (Bava Metzia 59b).

In our prayerbooks today these private petitions have left their mark in the form of the tahanun which follows the (morning or afternoon) Amidah on weekdays (Birnbaum, p. 103ff.), for the recital of which one "falls on one's face." The prayerbook contains a standardized version of what was originally the individual, spontaneous part of the liturgy (though in this particular section the texts used in different rites differ widely). Another remnant of personal devotion is the brief supplication at the end of the Amidah (Birnbaum, p. 95), based on the prayer of Mar, son of Ravina (see below); the use in this prayer of the first person singular is in itself eloquent testimony to its original character (although the sentence at the end, "He who makes peace . . ." certainly did not originate in private prayer). The confession of sins on Yom Kippur, too, is a survival of the custom of offering personal prayer after fixed community worship, even though, nowadays, the individual uses a set version that is formulated in the we-style.

Even with regard to the set prayers themselves the rabbis objected to a mechanical repetition of the same wording day in and day out. R. Eliazer's protest against the routinization of prayer (Mishnah Berakhot IV, 4) was interpreted by later sages as meaning "that he [the worshiper] should not be like one reading from a letter" (prayers were recited by heart in those days, not from a written text!), or "that he must include something new in it every day." And it is recorded

*that R. Eliazer did in fact recite a new prayer every day, while R.
Abahu coined a new benediction every day (Jerus. Berakhot 8a).*

PRIVATE WORSHIP IN TALMUDIC TIMES

R. Eliazer on concluding his prayer used to say the following: May it
be thy will, O Lord our God, to cause to dwell in our lot, love and
brotherhood and peace and friendship, and mayest thou make our
borders rich in disciples and prosper our latter end with good prospect
and hope, and set our portion in Paradise, and provide us with a good
companion and a good impulse in thy world, and may we rise early
and obtain the yearning of our heart to fear thy name, and mayest
thou be pleased to grant the satisfaction of our desires!

R. Johanan on concluding his prayer added the following: May it be
thy will, O Lord our God, to look upon our shame, and behold our
evil plight, and clothe thyself in thy mercies, and cover thyself in thy
strength, and wrap thyself in thy lovingkindness, and gird thyself
with thy graciousness, and may the attribute of thy kindness and
gentleness come before thee!

R. Zera on concluding his prayer added the following: May it be thy
will, O Lord our God, that we sin not nor bring upon ourselves shame
or disgrace before our fathers!

R. Hiyya on concluding his prayer added the following: May it be thy
will, O Lord our God, that our Torah may be our occupation, and
that our heart may not be sick nor our eyes darkened!

Rav on concluding his prayer added the following: May it be thy
will, O Lord our God, to grant us long life, a life of peace, a life of
good, a life of blessing, a life of sustenance, a life of bodily vigor, a

life in which there is fear of sin, a life free from shame and confusion, a life of riches and honor, a life in which we may be filled with the love of the Torah and the fear of Heaven, a life in which thou shalt fulfill all the desires of our heart for good!

Rabbi [i.e., R. Judah, the Prince] on concluding his prayer added the following: May it be thy will, O Lord, our God and God of our fathers, to deliver us from the impudent and from impudence, from an evil man, from evil hap, from the evil impulse, from an evil companion, from an evil neighbor, and from the destructive satan, from a hard lawsuit and from a hard opponent, whether he is a son of the covenant or not a son of the covenant!

R. Safra on concluding his prayer added the following: May it be thy will, O Lord our God, to establish peace among the celestial family, and among the earthly family, and among the disciples who occupy themselves with thy Torah whether for its own sake or for other motives, and may it please thee that all who do so for other motives may come to study it for its own sake!

R. Alexandri on concluding his prayer added the following: May it be thy will, O Lord our God, to station us in an illumined corner and do not station us in a darkened corner, and let not our heart be sick nor our eyes darkened! (According to some, however, this was the concluding prayer of R. Hamnuna, and R. Alexandri on concluding his prayer used to add the following: Sovereign of the Universe, it is known full well to thee that our will is to perform thy will, and what prevents us? The yeast in the dough [i.e., the evil impulse] and the subjection to foreign powers. May it be thy will to deliver us from their hand, so that we may return to perform the statutes of thy will with a perfect heart!)

Rava on concluding his prayer added the following: My God, before I was formed I was not worthy [to be formed], and now that I have been formed I am as if I had not been formed. I am dust in my lifetime, all the more in my death. Behold I am before thee like a vessel full of shame and confusion. May it be thy will, O Lord my God, that I sin no more, and the sins I have committed before thee wipe out in thy great mercies, but not through evil chastisements and diseases! This was the confession of R. Hamnuna Zuta on the Day of Atonement.

Mar, the son of Ravina, on concluding his prayer added the following: My God, keep my tongue from evil and my lips from speaking guile. May my soul be silent to them that curse me and may my soul be as the dust to all. Open thou my heart in thy law, and may my soul pursue thy commandments, and deliver me from evil hap, from the evil impulse and from an evil woman and from all evils that threaten to come upon the world. As for all that design evil against me, speedily annul their counsel and frustrate their designs! *May the words of my mouth and the meditation of my heart be acceptable before thee, O Lord, my rock and my redeemer* (Psalms 19:15)!

Bab. Berakhot 16b–17a

SEVEN BENEDICTIONS IN ONE

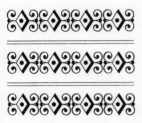

INTRODUCTION

THE FOLLOWING PRAYER, *recited on Friday nights after the silent Amidah, is undoubtedly a radical abbreviation of the Amidah for Sabbath. It consists of the greater part of the first benediction (in its Palestinian version); of a middle section which contains, in semi-poetic form, abbreviated references to each of the seven benedictions, the phrasing of which is based in most cases on their concluding formulas (again in their ancient Palestinian wording), and, finally, the concluding section of the fourth benediction of the Sabbath Amidah, devoted to "the sanctification of the day" (see "The Weekday Amidah"). It raises, however, several problems. Since it is recited aloud by the reader, this composition is apparently meant to serve in place of the repetition of the Amidah. But no repetition of the Amidah is ever found in the evening service, either on weekdays or on festivals (as the recital of the Amidah in the evening is itself optional, no provision was required to repeat it for those who could not recite it on their own—see "The Weekday Amidah"). Moreover, while shortened versions of the Amidah were in use on certain occasions, an abbreviation of the entire Amidah to one single benediction is quite unheard of and has no parallel.*

The source of this strange custom has been preserved in the Jerusalem Talmud (Berakhot VIII, 1; 11a): "They have the custom over there [Babylonia] that where no wine is available, the reader passes before the ark [to recite aloud the Amidah] and says one benediction comprising seven and concludes with [Blessed art Thou] who hallowest Israel and the Sabbath day."

On the eve of Sabbaths and festivals a "sanctification" [Kiddush]—similar in content to the fourth benediction of the Amidah—was to be (and still is) recited at home, over a cup of wine, before the festive meal (Birnbaum, pp. 289, 597, 665). Where no wine was available, the "sanctification" was recited, instead, in the synagogue in the form of the Amidah; since the recital of the Amidah was not obligatory in the evening, an abbreviated form was used, in which stress was laid mainly on the benediction concerning "the sanctification of the day." Such, apparently was the custom in Babylonia ("over there") where, in contrast to Palestine, wine was scarce. No similar provision was made for the eve of festivals, because apparently even Babylonian Jews made a special effort to obtain a cup of wine for such relatively rare occasions.

A further problem has to do with the wording of this composition, which as we have seen, points plainly to Palestinian origin. Why would a prayer such as this come to be composed in Palestine, where wine was plentiful and no substitute for the Kiddush was required? The answer lies in the non-obligatory nature of the evening Amidah. It was felt that on the Sabbath eve, at least some brief form of the Amidah should be recited, containing "the sanctification of the day" which in all other Sabbath services constitutes the core of the Amidah. Whereas the original function of this composition, then, was to provide an abbreviated Amidah for Sabbath eve, it was eventually employed for a different purpose in Babylonia, where a substitute form of Kiddush was required.[1]

SEVEN BENEDICTIONS IN ONE

Blessed art thou, O Lord our God and God of our fathers, God of Abraham, God of Isaac and God of Jacob, the great, mighty and awesome God, the most High God, Creator of heaven and earth.

He with his word was a shield to our forefathers, and by his bidding will revive the dead; the holy God, like whom there is none; who gives rest to his people on his holy Sabbath day, because he took pleasure in them to grant them rest. Him we will serve with fear and awe, and daily and constantly we will give thanks unto his name in the fitting form of blessings.[2] He is the God to whom thanksgivings are due, the Lord of peace, who hallows the Sabbath and blesses the seventh day, and in holiness gives rest to a people sated with delights, in remembrance of the creation.

Our God and God of our fathers, accept our rest; sanctify us by thy commandments, and grant our portion in thy Torah, satisfy us with thy goodness, gladden us with thy salvation; purify our hearts to serve thee in truth; and in thy love and favor, O Lord our God, let us inherit thy holy Sabbath; and may Israel, who hallow thy name, rest thereon. Blessed art thou, O Lord, who hallowest the Sabbath.

THE ADDITIONAL AMIDAH FOR NEW YEAR

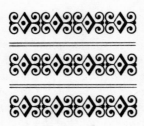

INTRODUCTION

INVARIABLY THE AMIDOT *for Sabbath and festivals consist of seven benedictions: they have the first and last three in common with the weekday Amidah, whereas the fourth, intermediate, benediction is devoted to the "sanctification of the day" (see "The Weekday Amidah"). The sole exception is the Additional [musaf] Amidah on the New Year, which has three intermediate benedictions: after "the sanctification of the day" there follow a benediction devoted to "remembrance" and another on the theme of the shofar. All three deal in various ways with the significance of the day, for the first day of the seventh month, known today as Rosh Ha-shanah (New Year), is designated in the Torah "a memorial [or remembrance] proclaimed by the blast of the shofar" (Lev. 23:24) and as "a day of blowing the shofar" (Num. 29:1); and in the prayers themselves it is invariably referred to as "this day of remembrance, a day of blowing the shofar."*

According to the custom reflected in the Mishnah, the shofar was sounded not, as it is today, prior to the musaf, but during its recital, in three series of three tones each, (Mishnah Rosh Ha-shanah IV: 5, 9). Therefore, three suitable occasions had to be provided in the

57

*Amidah for sounding the shofar, and hence the three benedictions
expressing the special character of the day.*

*The Mishna (ibid.) mentions an additional special prayer for the
New Year Amidah,[1] devoted to the Kingdom of God. Where this
additional prayer was to be inserted—in the third or in the fourth
benediction of the Amidah—was a matter of debate among the sages,
not one of whom ever suggested that a separate tenth benediction be
given over to it. One might draw the conclusion that by the time
the prayer concerning "the Kingdom of God" became customary, the
framework of nine benedictions had already been firmly established.[2]
But it appears more likely that all three special benedictions—concerned with the Kingdom of God, remembrance, and the shofar
respectively—in fact were a very ancient "order of prayers" in their
own right, providing the three occasions required for the blowing of
the shofar.[3] Eventually, when the recital of the Amidah became the
established custom on all festivals, these three benedictions were
incorporated into it. Since, however, one of the seven benedictions of
the Amidah (devoted to "the sanctification of the day") already provided an eminently suitable occasion for sounding the shofar, only two
of the original three benedictions were retained intact; the third was
combined with one of the benedictions of the ordinary festival
Amidah.*

*According to the final ruling of the halakhah, the prayer concern-
ing the Kingdom is combined with the fourth benediction, the
sanctification of the day; but it appears that the rejected alternative
view, that it be inserted into the third benediction, has nevertheless
left its mark. The impressive prayer, almost hymnic in character,
"Now, Lord our God, impose thine awe . . ." (see below), inserted
into the third benediction, is evidently an alternative opening of the
prayer for "the Kingdom of God," as can be seen readily from a
comparison of its contents with the introduction to that prayer in the
fourth benediction. Even though it seems superfluous, in view of the
equivalent prayer in the fourth benediction, the retention of two
equivalent prayers, originally alternatives, one beside the other, is
quite common in Jewish liturgical practice.[4]*

*Each of the three special compositions—concerned with the King-
dom, remembrance, and the shofar—is made up, according to the*

Mishnah (Rosh Ha-shanah IV, 6), of a selection of no fewer than ten Bible verses referring to the topic. In present-day custom there come first three verses from the Pentateuch, then three from Psalms, followed by three from the Prophets, and one more from the Pentateuch. The concluding "Kingdom" verse is the first verse of the Shema, which, though it does not contain the word "king," is considered to express "the acceptance of the yoke of the kingdom of Heaven" (see "The Shema and its Benedictions"). Nothing is said in the Mishnah (ibid., but cf. Mishnah Ta'anit II, 3–4) of any introduction or conclusion to these groups of biblical passages; not even the concluding formulas are mentioned. Their existence is obviously presupposed since these compositions are clearly defined as benedictions in the liturgical sense.

The composition given below, known as tekiata de[-bey]Rav is in use in all present-day rites (though we know of alternative ones in poetic form, some of them preserved in the Ashkenazi mahzor). It is written in elated, rhythmic prose and makes impressive use of the biblical type of parallelism. Each of its three constituent parts has the same basic structure: a declarative prologue—a kind of affirmation of faith, leading up to the first of the Bible passages; the Bible passages themselves, concluding with verses of a messianic nature (from the later Prophets); an epilogue—a prayer of supplication, concerned, explicitly or implicitly, with messianic redemption. (The concluding verse from the Pentateuch is separated from the preceding nine and is embodied within the epilogue). The entire composition follows a single pattern and is of one piece—the work, apparently, of a single author, of the first or second century C.E. (who may have made use of a more ancient composition in the introduction to the "Kingdom" verses).[5]

The first prologue (which begins in the middle of the fourth benediction, after "the sanctification of the day"), "It is our duty to praise," affirms that Israel alone among all nations recognizes God as the Creator and the Master of the world; it expresses the hope that he will one day establish his kingdom over all the earth and all peoples will submit to his rule. After the Bible verses, the last (or next to last) of which contains the promise, "the Lord shall be king over all the earth," there follows, in the original version, the epilogue, containing a fervent petition that God soon implement this prophecy and establish his kingdom over the whole universe. (This epilogue embodies also the concluding section of "the sanctification of the day," and the concluding eulogy refers, naturally, to both themes.)

The prologue to the "remembrance" verses develops the idea that he who remembers all is also the judge of all—individuals and nations alike. Toward the end it cites the Flood as an example of an awesome judgment, as well as God's love for Noah, whose seed he increased "like the dust of the earth and his offspring like the sand of the sea" (in Scripture these promises were actually made to Abraham, but they are transferred here, in a kind of Midrash, to Noah, the father of reborn mankind). This provides the transition to the first of the Bible verses, Genesis 8:1.[6] The epilogue again follows naturally on the messianic promises from the later prophets, such as, "I will remember my covenant with you in the days of your youth and I will establish with you an everlasting covenant"; there follow supplications that God may remember us for good, grant us salvation, and remember the covenant. Here the "remembrance" is interpreted more in the national than in the universal sense; the motif of judgment recedes and prominence is given to the remembrance of the covenant with the Patriarchs and the binding of Isaac (the version before us combines two alternative originals, one emphasizing "the remembrance of all forgotten things"—i.e., all hidden sins—and the other the remembrance of the covenant or the binding of Isaac).[7]

Lastly, the prologue to the shofar verses deals with the revelation from Sinai, to which all three Pentateuch verses refer. The epilogue takes up the prophetic passages concerning the ingathering of the exiles. Whereas the prologues and epilogues of the first two sections strike an emphatically universal note (as does the prayer "Now, Lord our God, impose thine awe . . ." in the third benediction) in the third section, the prologue refers to the giving of the Torah to Israel and the epilogue refers to the exclusively national aspect of redemption. This shift of emphasis may be due to the specific content of the biblical passages with which the opening and concluding parts link. However, as we know from alternative poetic compositions on this theme, the choice of the Bible verses themselves was largely within the discretion of the author of the prayer. In the work of the ancient liturgical poets Yose ben Yose and Eleazar Ha-Kaliri the entire emphasis is on the Jews and their salvation—hence the author of our composition may have wished to stress as well the universal aspect of both judgment and redemption, while retaining the usual emphasis on Israel's unique position (in the present but not in the messianic

future) as the only people affirming belief in the one God and his
sovereignty over all his creatures.

THE ADDITIONAL AMIDAH FOR NEW YEAR

1. Blessed art thou, Lord our God and God of our fathers, God of Abraham, God of Isaac, and God of Jacob, the great, mighty and awesome God, the most high God, who bestowest lovingkindnesses, and art Master of all things; who rememberest the pious deeds of the Patriarchs, and in love wilt bring a redeemer to their children's children for thy name's sake.

Remember us unto life, O King, who delightest in life, and inscribe us in the book of life, for thine own sake, O living God.

O King, Helper, Guardian, and Shield. Blessed art thou, O Lord, the Shield of Abraham.

2. Thou, O Lord, art mighty for ever, thou revivest the dead, thou art mighty to save.

Thou sustainest the living with lovingkindness, revivest the dead with great mercy, supportest the falling, healest the sick, loosest the bound, and keepest thy faith to them that sleep in the dust. Who is like unto thee, Lord of mighty acts, and who resemblest thee, O King, who causest death and revivest, and causest salvation to spring forth?

Who is like unto thee, Father of mercy, who in mercy rememberest thy creatures unto life?

Thou art faithful to revive the dead. Blessed art thou, O Lord, who revivest the dead.

3. Thou art holy, and thy name is holy, and holy beings praise thee daily.

Now, Lord our God, impose thine awe upon all thy works, and thy dread upon all thou hast created, that all works may fear thee and all creatures prostrate themselves before thee, that they may all form a single band to do thy will with a perfect heart, even as we know, Lord our God, that dominion is thine, strength is in thy hand, and might in thy right hand, and that thy name is to be feared above all that thou hast created.

Give then glory, O Lord, to thy people, praise to them that fear thee, hope to them that seek thee, and speech to them that wait for thee, joy to thy land, gladness to thy city, a flourishing horn unto David thy servant, and a clear shining light unto the son of Jesse, thine anointed, speedily in our days.

Then shall the just see this and be glad, and the upright shall exult, and the pious triumphantly rejoice, while iniquity shall close her mouth, and wickedness shall be wholly consumed like smoke, when thou makest the dominion of arrogance to pass away from the earth.

And thou, O Lord, shalt reign, thou alone, over all thy works on Mount Zion, the dwelling place of thy glory, and in Jerusalem, thy holy city, as it is written in thy holy words, *The Lord shall reign for ever, thy God, O Zion, unto all generations, Praise the Lord* (Psalms 146:10).

Thou art holy and thy name is awesome, and there is no god beside thee, as it is written, *And the Lord of hosts is exalted in judgment, and the holy God is sanctified in righteousness* (Isa. 5:16). Blessed art thou, O Lord, the holy King.

4. Thou hast chosen us from all peoples; thou hast loved us and taken pleasure in us, and hast exalted us above all tongues; thou hast sanctified us by thy commandments, and brought us near unto thy service, O our King, and called us by thy great and holy name.

And thou hast given us in love, O Lord our God, this Day of Remembrance, a day of blowing the shofar; a holy festival, as a memorial of the exodus from Egypt.

But on account of our sins we were exiled from our land, and removed far from our country, and we are unable to fulfill our obligations in thy chosen house, that great and holy temple which was called by thy name, because of the hand that has been stretched out against thy sanctuary. May it be thy will, O Lord our God and God of our fathers, merciful King, that thou mayest again in thine abundant compassion have mercy upon us and upon thy sanctuary, and speedily rebuild it and magnify its glory. Our father, our king, do thou speedily make the glory of thy kingdom manifest upon us; shine forth and exalt thyself upon us in the sight of all living; bring our scattered ones among the nations near unto thee, and gather our dispersed from the ends of the earth. Lead us with exultation unto Zion thy city, and unto Jerusalem the place of thy sanctuary with everlasting joy; and there we will prepare before thee the offerings that are obligatory for us, the continual offerings according to their order, and the additional offerings according to their enactment; and the additional offerings of this Day of Remembrance, we will prepare and offer unto thee in love according to the precept of thy will, as thou hast prescribed for us in thy Torah through the hand of Moses thy servant, by the mouth of thy glory, as it is said:

And in the seventh month, on the first day of the month, you shall have a holy convocation; you shall do no servile work: it shall be a day of blowing the shofar unto you. And you shall offer a burnt-offering for a sweet savor unto the Lord; one young bullock, one ram, seven he-lambs of the first year without blemish (Num. 29:1–2). And their meal-offering and their drink-offerings as has been ordained; three tenth parts of an ephah for each bullock; and two tenth parts for the ram, and one tenth part for each lamb, with wine according to the drink-offering thereof, and two he-goats wherewith to make atonement, and the two continual offerings according to their enactment; beside the burnt-offering of the New Moon and the meal-offering thereof, and the continual burnt-offering and the meal-offering thereof, and their drink-offerings, according to their ordinance, for a sweet savor, an offering made by fire unto the Lord.

It is our duty to praise the Master of all things, to ascribe greatness to him who formed the world in the beginning, since he has not made us like the nations of other lands, and has not placed us like other families of the earth, since he has not assigned unto us a portion as unto them, nor a lot as unto all their multitude. For they bow before those that are vain and of no purpose, and pray unto a god that cannot save.[8] But we bend the knee and bow and acknowledge before the supreme King of kings, the Holy One, blessed be he, who stretched forth the heavens and laid the foundations of the earth, the seat of whose glory is in the heavens above, and the abode of whose might is in the loftiest heights. He is our God; there is none else: in truth he is our King; there is none beside him: as it is written in his Torah, *And you shall know this day, and lay it to your heart, that the Lord he is God in heaven above and upon the earth beneath: there is none else* (Deut. 4:39).

We therefore hope in thee, O Lord our God, that we may speedily behold the glory of thy might, when thou wilt remove the abominations from the earth, and the idols will be utterly cut off, when the world will be perfected under the kingdom of the Almighty, and all the children of flesh will call upon thy name, when thou wilt turn unto thyself all the wicked of the earth. Let all the inhabitants of the world perceive and know that unto thee every knee must bend, every tongue must swear. Before thee, O Lord our God, let them bow and fall; and unto thy glorious name let them give honor; let them all accept the yoke of thy kingdom and do thou reign over them speedily, and for ever and ever. For the kingdom is thine, and to all eternity thou wilt reign in glory; as it is written in thy Torah, *The Lord shall reign for ever and ever* (Ex. 15:18).

And it is said, *He has not beheld iniquity in Jacob, neither has he seen perverseness in Israel: The Lord his God is with him, and the trumpet shout for a King is among them* (Num. 23:21). And it is said, *And he became King in Jeshurun, when the heads of the people were gathered, the tribes of Israel together* (Deut. 33:5). And in thy holy words it is written, saying, *For the kingdom is the Lord's, and he is ruler over the nations* (Psalms 22:29). And it is said, *The Lord reigns; he is clothed in majesty; the Lord is clothed, he has girded himself with strength; the world also is firm, that it cannot be moved* (Psalms 93:1). And it is said, *Lift up your heads, O you gates, and be you lifted up, you everlasting doors, that the King of glory may come in. Who is the King of glory? The Lord, strong and mighty, the Lord mighty in battle. Lift up your heads, O you gates; lift them up, you everlasting doors that the King of glory may come in. Who then is the King of glory? The Lord of hosts, He is the King of glory* (Psalms 24:7–10). And by the hands of thy servants, the Prophets, it is written, saying: *Thus says the Lord, the King of Israel and his Redeemer, the Lord of hosts: I am the first and I am the last; and beside me there is no God* (Isa. 44:6). And it is said, *And saviors shall come up on mount Zion to judge the mount of Esau, and the kingdom shall be the Lord's* (Obad: 21). And it is said, *And the Lord shall be King over all the earth; in that day shall the Lord be One and His name one* (Zech. 14:9). And in thy Torah it is written saying, *Hear, O Israel: the Lord our God, the Lord is One* (Deut. 6:4).

Our God and God of our fathers, reign thou in thy glory over the whole universe, and be exalted above all the earth in thy honor, and shine forth in the splendor and excellence of thy might upon all the inhabitants of thy world, that whatsoever has been made may know that thou hast made it, and whatsoever has been created may understand that thou hast created it, and whatsoever has breath in its nostrils may say, the Lord God of Israel is King, and his dominion rules over all. Sanctify us by thy commandments, and grant our portion in thy Torah; satisfy us with thy goodness, and gladden us with thy salvation: O purify our hearts to serve thee in truth, for thou art God in truth, and thy word is truth, and endures for ever. Blessed art thou, O Lord, King over all the earth, who sanctifiest Israel and the Day of Remembrance.

5. Thou rememberest what was wrought from eternity and art mindful of all that has been formed from of old: before thee all secrets are revealed and the multitude of hidden things from the beginning; for there is no forgetfulness before the throne of thy glory, nor is there anything hidden from thy eyes. Thou rememberest every deed that has been done; not a creature is concealed from thee; all things are manifest and known unto thee, O Lord our God, who lookest and seest to the end of all generations. For thou wilt bring the appointed time of remembrance when every spirit and soul shall be visited, and the multitudinous works be remembered with the innumerable throng of thy creatures. From the beginning thou didst make this thy purpose known, and from aforetime thou didst disclose it. This day, on which was the beginning of thy work, is a memorial of the first day, for it is a statute for Israel, a decree of the God of Jacob. On it also sentence

is pronounced upon the lands—which of them is destined to the sword and which to peace, which to famine and which to plenty; and each separate creature is visited, and recorded for life or for death. Who is not visited on this day? For the remembrance of every creature comes before thee, each man's deeds and destiny, his works and ways, his thoughts and schemes, his imaginings and achievements. Happy is the man who forgets thee not, and the son of man who strengthens himself in thee; for they that seek thee shall never stumble, neither shall any be put to shame who trust in thee. The remembrance of all works comes before thee, and thou enquirest into the doings of them all. Of Noah also thou wast mindful in thy love, and didst visit him with a promise of salvation and mercy, when thou broughtest the waters of the flood to destroy all flesh on account of their evil deeds. So his remembrance came before thee, O Lord our God, to increase his seed like the dust of the earth, and his offspring like the sand of the sea: as it is written in thy Torah, *And God remembered Noah, and every living thing, and all the cattle that were with him in the ark: and God made a wind to pass over the earth, and the waters subsided* (Gen. 8:1). And it is said, *And God heard their groaning, and God remembered his covenant with Abraham, with Isaac, and with Jacob* (Ex. 2:24). And it is said, *Then will I remember my covenant with Jacob; and also my covenant with Isaac, and also my covenant with Abraham will I remember; and I will remember the land* (Lev. 26:42). And in thy holy words it is written saying, *He has made a memorial for his wondrous works: the Lord is gracious and full of compassion* (Psalms 111:4). And it is said, *He has given food unto them that fear him: he will ever be mindful of his covenant* (ibid., 5). And it is said, *And he remembered for them his covenant, and repented according to the multitude of his mercies* (ibid., 106: 45). And by the hands of thy servants, the Prophets, it is written saying, *Go and cry in the ears of Jerusalem, saying, Thus says the Lord, I remember for you the affection of your youth, the love of your bridal state; how you went after me in the wilderness, in a land that was not sown* (Jer. 2:2). And it is said, *Nevertheless, I will remember my covenant with you in the days of your youth, and I will establish with you an everlasting covenant* (Ezek. 16:60). And it is said, *Is Ephraim a precious son unto me? Is he a caressed child? As often as I speak of him, I earnestly remember him; therefore my heart yearns for him, I will surely have compassion upon him, says the Lord* (Jer. 31:20).

Our God and God of our fathers, let us be remembered by thee for good: grant us a visitation of salvation and mercy from thy heaven, the heavens of old; and remember unto us, O Lord our God, the covenant and the kindness and the oath which thou didst swear unto Abraham our father on Mount Moriah: and may the binding with which Abraham our father bound his son Isaac on the altar appear before thee, how he overbore his compassion in order to perform thy will with a perfect heart. So may thy compassion overbear thy anger against us; in thy great goodness may the fierceness of thy wrath turn aside from thy people, thy city and thy inheritance. Fulfill unto us, O Lord our God, the word in which thou hast promised us in thy Torah through the hand of Moses thy servant, from the mouth of thy glory, as it is said, *But I will remember unto them the covenant of their ancestors, whom I brought forth out of the land of Egypt in the sight of the nations, that I might be their God: I am the Lord* (Lev. 26:45). For thou art he who remembers from eternity all forgotten things, and before the throne of whose glory there is no forgetfulness. O remember the binding of Isaac this day in mercy unto his seed. Blessed art thou, O Lord, who rememberest the covenant.

6. Thou didst reveal thyself in a cloud of glory unto thy holy people in order to speak with them. Out of heaven thou didst make them hear thy voice and wast revealed unto them in clouds of purity. The whole world trembled at thy presence, and the works of creation were in awe of thee, when thou didst thus reveal thyself, O our King, upon Mount Sinai to teach thy people the Torah and commandments, and didst make them hear thy majestic voice and thy holy utterances out of flames of fire. Amid thunders and lightnings thou didst manifest thyself to them, and while the *shofar* sounded thou didst shine forth upon them; as it is written in thy Torah, *And it came to pass on the third day, when it was morning, that there were thunders and lightnings, and a thick cloud upon the mount, and the sound of the shofar exceeding loud: and all the people that were in the camp trembled* (Ex. 19:16). And it is said, *And the sound of the shofar waxed louder and louder; Moses spoke, and God answered him by a voice* (ibid., 19). And it is said, *And all the people perceived the thunderings and the lightnings, and the sound of the shofar, and the mountain smoking: and when the people saw it, they trembled and stood afar off* (ibid., 20:15). And in thy holy words it is written,

saying, *God is gone up with a shout, the Lord with the sound of a shofar* (Psalms 47:6). And it is said, *With trumpets and sound of shofar shout joyously before the King, the Lord* (ibid., 98:6). And it is said, *Blow the shofar on the New Moon, at the beginning of the month, for our day of festival: for it is a statute for Israel, a decree of the God of Jacob* (ibid., 81:4–5). And it is said, *Praise the Lord, praise God in his sanctuary, praise him in the firmament of his power. Praise him for his mighty acts: praise him according to his abundant greatness. Praise him with the blast of the shofar: praise him with the harp and the lyre. Praise him with the timbrel and dance: praise him with stringed instruments and the pipe. Praise him with the clear-toned cymbals: praise him with the loud-sounding cymbals. Let everything that has breath praise the Lord. Praise the Lord* (ibid., 150: 1–6). And by the hands of thy servants, the Prophets, it is written saying, *All you inhabitants of the world, and you dwellers on the earth, when an ensign is lifted up on the mountains, see, and when the shofar is blown, hear* (Isa. 18:3). And it is said, *And it shall come to pass on that day, that a great shofar shall be blown; and they shall come who were lost in the land of Assyria, and they that were dispersed in the land of Egypt; and, they shall worship the Lord in the holy mountain at Jerusalem* (ibid., 27:13). And it is said, *And the Lord shall be seen over them, and his arrow shall go forth as the lightning: and the Lord God shall blow the shofar, and shall go with the whirlwinds of the south. The Lord of hosts shall be a shield unto them* (Zech. 9:14–15). So be a shield unto thy people Israel with thy peace.

Our God and God of our fathers, sound the great shofar for our freedom, lift up the ensign to gather our exiles; bring our scattered ones among the nations near unto thee, and gather our dispersed from the ends of the earth. Lead us with exultation unto Zion thy city, and unto Jerusalem the place of thy sanctuary with everlasting joy; and there we will prepare before thee the offerings that are obligatory for us, as is commanded us in thy Torah through the hand of Moses thy servant, from the mouth of thy glory, as it is said, *And in the day of your gladness, and in your set feasts, and in the beginnings of your months, you shall blow with the trumpets over your burnt-offerings, and over the sacrifices of your peace-offerings; and they shall be to you for a remembrance before your God: I am the Lord your God* (Num. 10:10). For thou hearest the sound of the shofar and givest heed to the trumpet blast, and there is none like unto thee. Blessed art thou, O Lord, who in mercy hearest the sound of the trumpet of thy people Israel.[9]

CONCLUDING SERVICE FOR DAY OF ATONEMENT

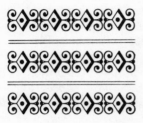

INTRODUCTION

IN PRESENT LITURGY *the Day of Atonement is alone in having five separate services, each containing the Amidah (as compared with four services on Sabbaths and festivals, and three on weekdays see "The Weekday Amidah"). The special "concluding" service [ne'ilah] takes place at dusk at the end of the day. In ancient times a ne'ilah service was held on other occasions as well, especially on public fast days (cf., Mishnah Ta'anit IV, 1, 4); its name (lit., "closing [of the gates]") indicates that it was held just before the closing of the Temple gates for the night. The Amidah of the ne'ilah service does not differ greatly from the other Amidot preceding it; however, in the brief petitions inserted into the two first and the two last benedictions, both on the New Year and on the Day of Atonement, the formula, "inscribe us in the book of life," and its equivalents (cf., "The Additional Amidah for the New Year"), are exchanged for "seal us into the book of life"— indicating that with the day drawing to its end, the divine decree is about to be made final. In the repetition of the Amidah by the reader, a number of special poetic compositions (differing in various rites) are added; at the conclusion of the entire service, the first verse of the Shema is proclaimed solemnly and a single blast of the shofar designates the end of the day.*

In the silent Amidah the only addition is the prayer given below,

71

which is, however, not recited as part of the Amidah itself, but follows after the concluding eulogy of the last benediction (and after the "short" confession of sins), instead of the "long" confession, which occupies the same place in all other Amidot of the Day of Atonement. It emphasizes God's willingness to accept repentance; for—as the prophet Ezekiel states repeatedly—God desires repentance rather than the death of the wicked. Coupled with humble recognition of our utter weakness as human beings, this last-minute appeal to God's compassion fittingly reflects the consciousness of the worshiper that the Day of Atonement—the one occasion when man may seek complete forgiveness and begin his life all over again—is rapidly drawing to its close.

CONCLUDING SERVICE FOR DAY OF ATONEMENT

Thou givest a hand to transgressors, and thy right hand is stretched out to receive the penitent; thou hast taught us, O Lord our God, to make confession unto thee of all our sins, in order that we may cease from the violence of our hands, that thou mayest receive us into thy presence in perfect repentance, even as fire-offerings and sweet savors, for thy words' sake which thou hast spoken. Endless would be the fire-offerings required for our guilt, and numberless the sweet savors for our trespasses; but thou knowest that our latter end is the worm, and hast therefore multiplied the means of our forgiveness. What are we? What is our life? What is our piety? What our righteousness? What our helpfulness? What our strength? What our might? What shall we say before thee, O Lord our God and God of our fathers? Are not all the mighty men as nought before thee, the men of renown as though they had not been, the wise as if without knowledge, and the men of understanding as if without discernment? For most of their works are void, and the days of their lives are vanity before thee, and the preeminence of man over the beast is nought, for all is vanity.

Thou hast distinguished man from the beginning, and hast recognized his privilege that he might stand before thee; for who shall say unto thee, What dost thou? and if he be righteous what can he give thee?

But thou of thy love hast given us, O Lord our God, this Day of Atonement to be the season of pardon and forgiveness for all our iniquities, that we may cease from the violence of our hands, and may return unto thee to do the statutes of thy will with a perfect heart. In thine abounding compassion, have mercy upon us, for thou delightest not in the destruction of the world, as it is said, *Seek the Lord, while he may be found, call upon him while he is near* (Isa. 55:6). And it is said, *Let the wicked forsake his way, and the man of iniquity his thoughts; and let him return unto the Lord, and he will have mercy upon him; and to our God for he will abundantly pardon* (ibid., 7). But thou art a God ready to forgive, gracious and merciful, slow to anger, plentiful in kindness, and abounding in goodness; thou delightest in the repentance of the wicked, and hast no pleasure in their death; as it is said, *Say unto them: As I live, says the Lord God, I have no pleasure in the death of the wicked; but that the wicked turn from his way and live: turn, turn from your evil ways; for why will you die, O house of Israel?* (Ezek. 33:11). And it is said, *Have I any pleasure at all in the death of the wicked, says the Lord God, and not rather that he should return from his way, and live?* (ibid., 18:23). And it is said, *For I have no pleasure in the death of him that dies, says the Lord God; Wherefore turn yourselves and live* (ibid., 32). For thou art the pardoner of Israel and the forgiver of the tribes of Jeshurun in every generation, and beside thee we have no King who pardons and forgives.

THE KEDUSHAH

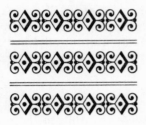

INTRODUCTION

THE NAME KEDUSHAH [*sanctification*] *is commonly used to designate the prayers which embody the description of the angelic choirs, based upon Isaiah 6:3 and Ezekiel 3:12. There are three such prayers, inserted in the first benediction (Yotzer or) before the Shema in the morning service (cf., "The Shema and Its Benedictions"); in the third benediction of the Amidah, when recited aloud by the reader ("The Weekday Amidah"); and in the prayer, beginning u-va le-tzion go'el (Birnbaum, p. 131). In each of these prayers a different form is used. In the last, the two biblical verses, followed by Exodus 15:18, are quoted by themselves, without any introduction or framework (though each is accompanied by its Aramaic targum [translation]). In the Yotzer-benediction, the quotations from Isaiah and Ezekiel are part of a description of the homage paid to God every day by the angelic hosts; a brief connecting passage between the two attributes the former verse to the seraphim, while "the ofanim and the holy Hayot" respond with the latter. The Kedushah inserted into the Amidah is the most elaborate as well as the most varied. Some rites use only one form of the Kedushah in all the Amidot (e.g., the Yemenite rite, derived from the order of prayers laid down by Maimonides). Most, however, have a special, enlarged form of the Kedushah for musaf on Sabbaths and festivals; while in all other Amidot, the passages from*

Isaiah and Ezekiel are followed by one more verse (Psalms 146:10); in musaf this verse is preceded by the first verse of the Shema (Deut. 6:4) and by the last words of the concluding verse of the Shema, "I am the Lord your God" (Num. 15:41). This form of the Kedushah, incorporating the Shema, was also the one employed in the ancient Palestinian rite (where it was recited, however, only in the morning service on Sabbaths and festivals).

In all forms of the Kedushah as inserted into the Amidah the prayer opens with an introduction, such as "Let us sanctify thy name in the world even as they [the angels] sanctify it in the highest heavens, as it is written by the prophet: 'They keep calling to one another, Holy, holy, holy is the Lord of hosts; the whole earth is full of his glory' "; in musaf the version given below is used (Sephardim as well as Hasidim have different introductory formulas). The sentences connecting the Bible verses also differ: on weekdays they are very short and simple (Birnbaum, p. 83); in the Sabbath morning service they are very much enlarged, poetical in tone and containing a fervent prayer for the coming of the Kingdom of God (Birnbaum, p. 351); in the musaf service (cf., below) a semi-poetical version is also used, which links the various parts by the device known as shirshur, viz., the concluding phrase of a sentence being repeated as the opening phrase in the next, e.g., ". . . the whole earth is full of his glory—His glory fills the universe . . ." The arrangement of the Kedushah in the Amidot is responsive; the opening as well as the connecting clauses are chanted by the reader, while the Bible verses are spoken by the entire congregation.

The differences among the various forms of the Kedushah are not mere matters of style. The introductions to the Kedushah used in the Amidah make it plain that we, i.e., the congregation of worshipers, representing Israel, are sanctifying God's name, as do the angels in heaven; the Kedushah is no longer the special form of worship peculiar to the angels, but has been "adopted" by Israel, whose praise offered on earth is the counterpart to that of the heavenly beings. The underlying conception here appears to be that Israel's Kedushah is more important than that of the angels and takes precedence over it; this is, indeed, stated explicitly in the Talmud: "The ministering angels do not say their praise above, until Israel have said theirs down below" (Bab. Hullin 91b). This notion probably underlies even the Kedushah of Yotzer; it is because the angels must wait, as it were, for the Kedushah recited by Israel, that the latter pronounce it at the beginning of the morning service. (In the Yotzer this idea is present only by implication, whereas in the Amidah it is fully spelled out.) Moreover, in all forms of the Kedushah, as recited in the Amidah, a third verse follows the two angelic verses of praise, and this third verse is pronounced by Israel: "The Lord shall reign forever, your God, O Zion, for all generations!" With this verse of praise, Israel actually joins the heavenly choirs and adds its voice to those of the Seraphim and the Hayot. But it is in the Kedushah of musaf that the idea of Israel's direct participation in the heavenly song of praise finds its most striking expression, when to the angelic hymns is added the first verse of the Shema: "Hear, O Israel, the Lord is our God, the Lord is One"—a form of praise which only Israel, not the angels, can pronounce, and which is understood to signify the proclamation of God's Kingdom (see "The Shema and Its Benedictions"). It is in response to this intervention by Israel—not to the song of the angels preceding it—that God himself at last makes his voice, too, heard in the heavenly drama, proclaiming: "I am the Lord, your God."

There can be no doubt that the Kedushah prayers and the ideas expressed in them stem from a type of Jewish mysticism, known as merkavah [i.e., "chariot," meaning the divine throne] mysticism, which has been preserved mainly in the later Hekhalot-literature, but the beginnings of which belong to early Rabbinic Judaism. Merkavah mystics aspired to ascend to the heavens and ultimately to the divine throne; the angelic hymns served as the vehicle of their "ascent." [1] Although this type of mysticism was firmly anchored in Rabbinic Judaism, the rabbis took the view that such esoteric lore and practices had to be limited to initiates (cf., Mishna Hagigah II, 1) and it may be assumed that their introduction into the synagogue service was at first opposed in some quarters. Some form of the Kedushah, nevertheless, was already in use in the second century C.E. (Tos. Berakhot I, 9), and by the fourth or fifth century we have definite testimony to the use of the Kedushah in the Amidah. The early Palestinian liturgical poets (payyetanim), from Yannai (fifth or sixth century) on, make the Kedushah the centerpiece of their liturgical compositions and elaborate upon it in fervent hymns. There are no grounds for considering the Kedushah a Babylonian creation, but it is true that while in Palestine the Kedushah was accepted only in the morning Amidah of Sabbaths and festivals (and that of the Yotzer benediction, too, was recited only on Sabbaths and festivals), in Babylonia it spread to all Amidot (except the evening one) and both forms of Kedushah came to be recited also on weekdays.[2] In this, as in all other matters, present-day custom follows the Babylonian pattern.

THE KEDUSHAH

READER: We will reverence and sanctify thee in words of the holy Seraphim, who hallow thy name in the sanctuary, as it is written by thy prophet, *and they called one unto the other and said:*

CONGREGATION: *Holy, holy, holy is the Lord of hosts: the whole earth is full of his glory* (Isa. 6:3).

READER: His glory fills the universe; his ministering angels ask one another, Where is the place of his glory? Those over against them say, *Blessed—*

CONGREGATION: *Blessed be the glory of the Lord from his place* (Ezek. 3:12).

READER: From his place may he turn in mercy and be gracious to the people who, evening and morning, twice every day, proclaim the unity of his name, saying in love, *Hear—*

CONGREGATION: *Hear, O Israel: the Lord our God, the Lord is One* (Deut. 6:4).

READER: One is our God; he is our Father; he is our King; he is our Deliverer; and he in his mercy will let us hear a second time, in the presence of all living [his promise], *To be your God.*

CONGREGATION: *I am the Lord your God* (Num. 15:41).

READER: And in thy holy Scriptures it is written, saying,

CONGREGATION: *The Lord will reign for ever, your God, O Zion, unto all generations. Praise the Lord* (Psalms 146:10).

READER: Through all generations we will declare thy greatness, and to all eternity we will proclaim thy holiness, and thy praise, our God, shall not depart from our mouth for ever, for thou art a great and holy God and King. Blessed art thou, O Lord, the holy God.

THE KADDISH

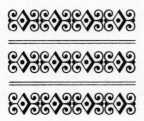

INTRODUCTION

BEST KNOWN AS *the mourner's prayer, the Kaddish in its various forms appears frequently in synagogue-prayers in a variety of functions.[1] The mourner's Kaddish is recited toward the end of each service, after the Alenu prayer (Birnbaum, p. 137); this, at least, is its original location, but in most congregations it is now repeated again after various psalms at the end of the service (e.g., Birnbaum, pp. 139–51; 217–49). However, two different forms of the Kaddish serve as integral parts of the precribed liturgy itself: the "complete" Kaddish, recited after each of the Amidot (though in some cases other prayers intervene cf., Birnbaum, pp. 133; 183; 275; 361; 405, etc.) and the "half Kaddish," recited generally between different units of the service as a kind of transitional prayer, for instance, between the morning psalms and the Shema (cf., Birnbaum, p. 69) or between the evening Shema and its benedictions and the Amidah (cf., Birnbaum, p. 199; for other occasions of the recital of the "half Kaddish," cf., Birnbaum, pp. 117; 123; 159; 389). The "half-Kaddish" consists only of the first two sections, while in the "complete" Kaddish the following is added, "May the prayers and supplications of the whole house of Israel be accepted by their Father who is in heaven; and say, Amen." Yet another form of the Kaddish is the "Kaddish of the Sages" [Kaddish de-rabbanan], recited after the reading in public, or the congregational study, of chapters from the Mishnah or the like, and this has an additional prayer for peace and sustenance for the rabbis and their disciples (cf., Birnbaum, pp. 45–47). Lastly, a Kaddish in which the first section is greatly elaborated into a detailed prayer for messianic redemption— the one given below—is used in most rites only after a burial (cf., Birnbaum, pp. 737–39) or on the occasion of the completion of an entire Talmudic tractate, studied communally; in the Yemenite rite (which follows the order of prayers of Maimonides) this form is used as the regular "Kaddish of the Sages."*

The sections common to all types of Kaddish contain an elaborate hymn of praise. The opening phrases, however, "May his great name be magnified and sanctified," have clear messianic associations (see Ezekiel, chapter 38 and especially verse 23), and the eschatological theme is taken up again in the prayer for the establishment of the Kingdom of God, which in the Sephardi rites is followed by a request for the coming of the Messiah: "May he establish his Kingdom and may he let flourish his salvation and may he bring near [the time of] his Messiah." The theme of messianic redemption thus appears to be an organic part of the opening of the Kaddish; hence the text given below would seem to have preserved one of its original versions, of which the other, more common, forms are but condensations.

In style the Kaddish is utterly different from most of the synagogue liturgy. Not only is it one of the rare prayers preserved in Aramaic—all the basic prayers like the Amidah, the Shema, etc., were composed in Hebrew—but it also uses appellations and epithets of God not found elsewhere in the liturgy, e.g., "The Holy One, blessed be he," or "[Our] Father, who is in heaven," while the epithets commonly used in other prayers, especially the Tetragrammaton (usually rendered: Lord) and "our God" are lacking. In the first section, God is referred to as "He," and no name or epithet is used at all. The entire prayer—even the petitions—is formulated in the third person; no address of God in the second person occurs. Each section does conclude with an address to the congregation, though, inviting a response: "And say, Amen"—another feature not found in synagogue prayers.

All these features of both style and content are, however, fully in harmony with the original function of the Kaddish, which came into being not as part of the synagogue service—it is not mentioned as part of the synagogue liturgy either in the Mishnah or in the Talmud—but as a concluding prayer after the public sermon (cf., Bab. Sotah 49a; Yalkut Shim'oni: Proverbs, §951). Most such prayers, quite a few of which have been preserved ("May the merciful Father . . . ," Birnbaum, p. 121; "May his Kingdom soon be revealed . . . ," ibid.; "Magnified and hallowed . . . ," Birnbaum, p. 367; "May he help, shield and save . . . ," ibid.; "May salvation arise from heaven . . . ," Birnbaum, p. 377), address God in the third person, use appellations like the ones in the Kaddish, and are concerned, among other things, with petitions for messianic redemption in general and the establishment of the Kingdom of God in particular. All these characteristics stem directly from the function these prayers served, as conclusions to public sermons. The appellations used are the ones employed most frequently in the homilies of the rabbis; the sermons themselves did not address God but spoke of him and his deeds in the third person; and they concluded, most frequently, with words of consolation from the later Prophets concerning the messianic redemption. Moreover, at least, some of these prayers were formulated, like the sermons themselves, in the Aramaic vernacular. And often the rabbi who delivered the sermon would conclude by asking divine blessings on all who engage in the study and the teaching of the Torah; to such prayers the audience was called upon to express its consent by responding, "Amen." [2]

Of all the various versions of the Kaddish in the present-day liturgy, the one closest to the original function is undoubtedly the "Kaddish de-rabbanan." However, from at least the sixth century on, the Kaddish also appears in the synagogue liturgy, as it does today, after the Amidah, before barekhu, and so forth. As a mourner's prayer the Kaddish became customary only at a very late date, the thirteenth century, in the Ashkenazi rite. It is not entirely clear what prompted the choice of the Kaddish for this purpose; there is certainly nothing in the text that lends support to the popular conception of the Kaddish as a prayer for the soul of the departed. A legend, found only in very late sources, tells that R. Akivah succeeded in alleviating the sufferings of a dead sinner by teaching his son to recite the Kaddish (according to some versions, in others he teaches him to recite barekhu). It seems likely that the Kaddish was selected as the mourner's prayer chiefly because it was understood as an acknowledgment of divine justice; by reciting this magnificent hymn of praise, the bereaved proclaims, that in spite of his loss, he will not rebel against God but will lead the congregation in singing His praise. In the version given below the Kaddish also gives expression to the hope of a revival of the dead in times to come; and even though not explicit in the ordinary versions, this motif, allied by association to the prayer for the Kingdom of God, may have played its part in turning the Kaddish into a mourner's prayer.

THE KADDISH

May his great name be magnified and sanctified in the world that is to be created anew, when he will revive the dead, and raise them up unto life eternal, rebuild the city of Jerusalem, and establish his temple in the midst thereof, and uproot all alien worship from the earth and restore the worship of the true God. May the Holy One, blessed be he, establish his kingdom and his glory during your life and during your days, and during the life of all the house of Israel, speedily and at a near time; and say Amen.

CONGREGATION: Let his great name be blessed for ever and to all eternity.

Blessed, praised and glorified, exalted, extolled and honored, magnified and lauded be the name of the Holy One, blessed be he; though he be high above all blessings and hymns, praises and consolations, which are uttered in the world; and say Amen.

May there be abundant peace from heaven, and life for us and for all Israel; and say Amen.

He who makes peace in his high places, may he make peace for us and for all Israel; and say Amen.

BENEDICTIONS FOLLOWING THE HAFTARAH

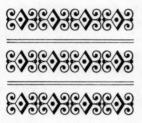

AFTER THE READING *from the Torah, a section from the Prophets* *[haftarah: conclusion] is read out in the morning services of Sabbaths* *and festivals (and in the afternoon services of fast days). This custom* *is undoubtedly ancient (Luke 4:16ff.; Acts 13:15ff.). A benediction* *is recited before the prophetic reading, and after it a series of four* *benedictions. The benedictions after the haftarah constitute a whole* *"order of prayers" in themselves. Only the first of them refers directly* *to the prophetic reading; the second is, in effect, a prayer for the* *rebuilding of Jerusalem; the third is a petition for the reestablishment* *of the Davidic kingdom in messianic times; the fourth is a peculiar* *form of "sanctification of the day."*

Scholars have noted a certain analogy of structure and content *among these benedictions and the Eight Benedictions recited in* *Temple times by the High Priest on the Day of Atonement after his* *reading from the Torah (Mishnah Yoma VII, 1; cf., also Sotah VII,* *7–8). In both cases the benedictions do not appear to serve merely the* *function of "benedictions after the reading," but rather to be part of* *the main order of prayer of the day. If this is correct, both must have* *originated at a time when the present-day Amidah of musaf (which* *follows after the reading from the Torah and Prophets) was not yet* *customary; the series of benedictions discussed here served the function of the Amidah, namely, the main Sabbath or Festival prayer, as is demonstrated especially by the presence (also in the benedictions of the High Priest) of a benediction devoted to "the sanctification of the day."* [1] *The inclusion of the petitions for the building of Jerusalem and for the coming of the messianic king among the benedictions after the haftarah is due probably to the custom, prevalent especially in the ancient Palestinian rite, to choose for the prophetic readings some of the prophecies of consolation containing a messianic message; hence these petitions take up themes expressed, or at least suggested, by the prophetic passage itself.*

It has been pointed out that the phrase, "Let no stranger occupy David's throne; let others no longer possess themselves of his glory," appears to presuppose that at present "strangers" have, indeed, usurped David's throne. [2] *Such an allusion could only fit the era of the Hasmoneans, whose kingdom was considered illegitimate because they were of priestly, not Davidic, descent. It would then appear that the benediction as we have it must have been formulated in the second or first century* B.C.E.

BENEDICTIONS FOLLOWING THE HAFTARAH

Blessed art thou, O Lord our God, King of the universe, Rock of all worlds, righteous through all generations, O faithful God, who sayest and doest, who speakest and fulfillest, whose words are all truth and righteousness. Faithful art thou, O Lord our God, and faithful are thy words, and not one of thy words shall return void, for thou art a faithful and merciful God and King. Blessed art thou, O Lord, God, who art faithful in all thy words.

Have mercy upon Zion, for it is the home of our life, and save her that is grieved in spirit speedily, even in our days. Blessed art thou, O Lord, who makest Zion joyful through her children.

Gladden us, O Lord our God, with Elijah the prophet, thy servant, and with the kingdom of the house of David, thine anointed. Soon may he come and rejoice our hearts. Let no stranger occupy his throne; let others no longer possess themselves of his glory; for by thy holy name thou didst swear unto him, that his light would not be quenched for ever. Blessed art thou, O Lord, the Shield of David.

For the Torah, for the divine service, for the prophets, and for this Sabbath day, which thou, O Lord our God, hast given us for holiness and for rest, for honor and for glory—for all these we thank and bless thee, O Lord our God: blessed be thy name by the mouth of every living being continually and for ever. Blessed art thou, O Lord, who sanctifiest the Sabbath.

GRACE AFTER MEALS

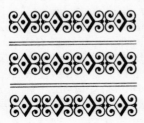

INTRODUCTION

EVEN THOUGH GRACE *is a domestic prayer it has many striking features in common with the fixed synagogue liturgy. In contrast to other benedictions recited before or after partaking of food and drink, which consist of one benediction and are usually brief and to the point, "Grace after Meals" is an entire "order of prayers," and it takes up a variety of subjects besides the thanksgiving for food itself. Grace consists of a series of four separate and elaborate benedictions, of which the fourth ("who art good and doest good") is variously stated to have been introduced in Yavneh or after the defeat of Bar-Kokhba and the fall of Bethar, when permission was granted to bury the fallen. The "Amen" spoken after the third benediction indicates that this used to be the conclusion of the entire prayer, as does the fact that the fourth benediction opens with the berakhah-formula instead of concluding with it, in accordance with the rule for a benediction forming part of a series. What follows after "Mayest thou never deprive us of any good thing" is no longer part of Grace as prescribed and differs greatly in each of the rites.*

The first benediction is devoted to thanksgiving for food, and is of a universal character. The second adds thanks for "the good land" which God has given Israel (Deut. 8:10); but, in keeping with the

89

ruling of various Talmudic sages it also mentions the covenant of circumcision, the Exodus, and the giving of the Torah to Israel—all national concerns not directly connected with thanksgiving for food. The third benediction—the only one that is a petition—is identical both in content and in style to the (Palestinian) benediction for the rebuilding of Jerusalem in the Amidah (cf., "The Weekday Amidah"), to which is added, appropriately, a plea that God sustain and feed us. Moreover, in the manner typical of the Amidah and other synagogue prayers, mention is made of "the sanctity of the day" on Sabbaths and festivals. There can be no doubt then that the occasion of reciting Grace after the two or three daily meals was turned into a full-fledged prayer-service in miniature, concerned, like all other communal prayers, with the needs of the community and Israel as a whole.

The "Invitation to Grace" which precedes the first benediction whenever a meal is partaken in a company of at least three is a peculiar feature; it becomes more elaborate when the group has ten members, and even more so when it has a hundred (Mishnah Berakhot VII, 3; the Mishnah also offers formulas to be used in a company of a thousand or of ten thousand). This invitation, though not formulated in the standard berakhah-style, is nevertheless regarded by some old sources as a liturgical berakhah in the strict sense. The gradation of the formula according to the number of participants is another curious feature to which no parallel exists in the synagogue service (cf., Mishnah Berakhot ibid., end).

There can be little doubt that Grace itself as well as the "Invitation to Grace" goes back to earliest times. Very likely its origin must be sought in the large community meals which were customary in the Second Temple period; such meals are known to us also from the Dead Sea Scrolls. The elaborate form of Grace, including the "invitation," probably was originally limited to community meals of ten or more participants; its extension to ordinary domestic meals appears to be a later development, but one antedating Tannaitic times.[1]

GRACE AFTER MEALS

LEADER: Let us say Grace!

COMPANY: Blessed be the name of the Lord henceforth and forever.

LEADER: Let us bless our God whose food we have eaten.

COMPANY: Blessed be our God whose food we have eaten and through whose goodness we live.

LEADER: Blessed be he and blessed be his name.

1. Blessed art thou, Lord our God, King of the universe, who sustainest the whole world with goodness, kindness, and mercy. He gives food to all creatures, for his mercy endures forever. Through his abundant goodness we have never yet been in want; may we never be in want of sustenance for his great name's sake. For he is God who sustains all, doest good to all, and provides food for all the creatures he has created. Blessed art thou, O Lord, who dost sustain all.

2. We thank thee, Lord our God, for having given a lovely, good, and spacious land to our fathers as a heritage; for having brought us forth from the land of Egypt and freed us from the house of slavery; for thy covenant which thou hast sealed in our flesh; for thy Torah which thou hast taught us; for thy laws which thou hast made known to us, for the life, grace and kindness thou hast bestowed on us; and for the sustenance thou grantest us daily, at every season, at every hour.

For everything, Lord our God, we thank thee and bless thee; be thy name forever blessed by all as it is written: *And you shall eat and be satisfied, and bless the Lord your God for the good land he has given you* (Deut. 8:10). Blessed art thou, O Lord, for the land and the sustenance.

3. Have compassion, Lord our God, on Israel thy people, on Jerusalem thy city, on Zion the abode of thy glory, on the royal house

of David thine anointed one, and on the great and holy Temple that bears thy name. O God, our Father, tend and nourish us; sustain and maintain us; grant us deliverance. Speedily, Lord our God, grant us relief from all our troubles. Lord our God, O make us not dependent on the gifts and loans of men but rather on thy full, open and generous hand, that we may never be put to shame and disgrace.

Rebuild Jerusalem the holy city speedily in our days. Blessed art thou, O Lord, who in his mercy rebuildest Jerusalem. Amen.

4. Blessed art thou, Lord our God, King of the universe, O God, thou art our Father, our King, our Creator, our Redeemer, the Holy One of Jacob, the Shepherd of Israel, the King who art good and doest good to all. Thou bestowest favors on us continuously; thou doest ever confer on us kindness and mercy, relief and deliverance, prosperity and blessing, life and peace and all goodness. Mayest thou never deprive us of any good thing.

May the Merciful One reign over us forever and ever.
May the Merciful One be worshiped in heaven and on earth.
May the Merciful One be praised for countless generations; may he be glorified among us forever and ever; may he be honored in us to all eternity.
May the Merciful One grant us a respectable livelihood.
May the Merciful One break the yoke from our neck; may he lead us securely into our land.
May the Merciful One send abundant blessings upon this house and upon this table at which we have eaten.
May the Merciful One send us Elijah the Prophet—of blessed memory—to bring us the good tidings of deliverance and comfort.
May the Merciful One bless the master of this house and the mistress of this house, their entire family and all that is theirs.
May he bless us and all that is ours; may he bless us all alike with a perfect blessing even as our forefathers Abraham, Isaac, and Jacob were blessed in every way; and let us say, Amen.
May they in heaven plead for all of us that we may have enduring peace. May we receive a blessing from the Lord, righteousness from the God of our salvation,[2] may we find grace and good favor in the sight of God and man.[3]

May the Merciful One make us worthy of the days of the Messiah and of the life in the world to come.

He gives great salvation to his king, and shows mercy to his anointed, to David and to his seed forever (Psalms 18:51).

He who creates peace in his high places, may he create peace for us and for all Israel; and say, Amen.[4]

LITANIES FOR TABERNACLES

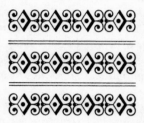

INTRODUCTION

THE AUTUMN FESTIVAL of *Tabernacles is the occasion for prayers for rain and is held to be "the time of judgment concerning the water" (Mishnah Rosh Ha-shanah I, 2). The litanies recited on this festival, in all of which the congregational response hosha-na (an abbreviated form of the biblical* hoshia-na *[O Save!]) is repeated in each line, were also, at least originally, prayers for rain specifically or for general prosperity in the new agricultural year about to start.*[1] *In most, however, the object of the prayer for "salvation" is not stated explicitly, while in some (comparatively late ones) other objects of supplication appear, such as the Temple or the people of Israel. In Number 3, given below—composed by the sixth-century payyetan Eliezer Ha-Kaliri—we have, in fact, a comprehensive farmer's prayer, in which all types of crops and produce are enumerated, together with the specific dangers from which each of them might be saved.*

Numbers 1, 2, and 4 given below (as well as a few others extant) are piyyutim by unknown authors.[2] *They represent a curious type of composition, which is distinguished by the following features of style and form:*

a. They are made up of 22 short, stereotyped, lines, each of

95

which contains—*apart from the response hosha-na*—*only two or three other words (appellations of God and the like); in each line these words are exchanged for other, equivalent ones.*

b. They use a form of alphabetical acrostic, are arranged in a simple rhythm (based on an equal number of words in each line) and some (e.g., Numbers 1 and 2) contain a primitive type of rhyme, achieved through the use of the same grammatical suffix at the end of each line.

c. They have none of the stylistic features characteristic of the piyyut in general; nor do they possess any internal structure whatsoever. Each line simply reiterates the basic content in different words. Were the poems not limited by the acrostic form to the twenty-two letters of the Hebrew alphabet, each composition might be either considerably shorter or considerably longer.[3]

This extremely primitive type of "poetry" is, in effect, produced by a simple mechanical technique and came into being, presumably, by way of improvisation. Hence it is most surprising that such accomplished poets as Ha-Kaliri or Saadya (tenth century), both of whom are noted for the highly complex structure of their compositions, should have composed many hoshanot of this type with only slight improvements or variations. It is true that Ha-Kaliri (in Number 3 below) specifies different objects in each line and, moreover, attempts to double the acrostic (though not consistently in all lines); nevertheless the monotonous repetition of short lines, which could theoretically go on forever, remains the dominant feature. We must conclude that no radical changes could be introduced in this pattern because even by Ha-Kaliri's time the prototype was already well-established and hallowed by tradition. Indeed, all the formal elements of which these compositions are made are known to us from the time of the Second Temple, though not in this particular combination or applied in such stereotyped manner. The hoshanot are a form of litany, a category of prayer found among many different peoples and cultures and used almost invariably in connection with religious processions.[4] The hoshanot came into being in connection with the processions around the Temple altar on Tabernacles (cf., Mishna Sukkah IV, 5), and thus they represent one of the earliest forms of post-biblical poetry known to us.[5]

LITANIES FOR TABERNACLES

1   *O save*
    For thy sake, our God
    For thy sake, our Creator
    For thy sake, our Redeemer
    For thy sake, O thou who
        seekest us.

2   *O save*
    For the sake of thy truth
    For the sake of thy covenant
    For the sake of thy greatness
    For the sake of thy teaching
    For the sake of thy majesty
    For the sake of thy troth
    For the sake of the memory
        of thee
    For the sake of thy mercy
    For the sake of thy goodness
    For the sake of thy unity
    For the sake of thine honor
    For the sake of thy wisdom
    For the sake of thy kingdom
    For the sake of thine eternity
    For the sake of thy mystery
    For the sake of thy strength
    For the sake of thy splendor
    For the sake of thy
        righteousness
    For the sake of thy holiness
    For the sake of thy
        compassion
    For the sake of thy presence
    For the sake of thy praise.

3   *O save*
    The earth from the curse
    Our cattle from sterility
    Our threshing floor from the
        locust
    Our corn from fire
    Our substance from mis-
        adventure
    Our food from destruction
    The olives from falling
    The wheat from the grass-
        hopper
    Our sustenance from the
        worm
    Our vines from the cater-
        pillar
    The vineyard from the
        cankerworm
    The autumn fruit from blight
    Our produce from crickets
    Our souls from terror
    Our plenty from corruption
    Our flocks from disease
    Our fruit from the blasting
        wind
    Our sheep from the plague
    Our harvest from ruin
    Our abundance from lean-
        ness
    The barley from mildew
    The crop from the palmer-
        worm.

4   God of spirits   O save
    Searcher of hearts   cause us to prosper
    Strong Redeemer   answer us in the day that we call

    Speaker of righteousness   O save
    Thou that art clad in glory   cause us to prosper
    Trusty and gracious   answer us in the day that we call

    Pure and upright   O save
    Thou who pitiest the poor   cause us to prosper
    Good and bountiful Lord   answer us in the day that we call

    Diviner of thoughts
    Mighty and resplendent   O save
    Thou that art clothed in   cause us to prosper
      righteousness   answer us in the day that we call

    King of eternities
    Thou that art girt with light
      and majesty   O save
    Thou who supportest the   cause us to prosper
      falling   answer us in the day that we call

    Helper of the poor   O save
    Redeemer and Deliverer   cause us to prosper
    Everlasting Rock   answer us in the day that we call

    Holy and revered   O save
    Merciful and compassionate   cause us to prosper
    Keeper of the covenant   answer us in the day that we call

    Stay of the perfect
    Sovereign of eternity   O save
    Thou who art perfect in thy   cause us to prosper
      ways   answer us in the day that we call

NOTES

INTRODUCTION

1. The original German edition of this standard work was published in Munich in 1921; the first English edition appeared in London in 1933.
2. Thus, "*And to serve him with all your heart* [Deut. 11:13]: what is the service [avodah] that is performed in the heart? This is prayer!" (Bab. Ta'anit 2b). And, "Just as the service of the altar is called *avodah*, so is prayer called *avodah*" (Sifre Deut. 41).
3. Apparent exceptions are in reality vestiges of the private, individual prayers, some of which were ultimately incorporated into the prayerbook (see the chapter, "Private Worship in Talmudic Times").
4. A variety of Talmudic dicta extol the value and significance of the congregational responses, which are the core and essence of the service. "Nothing is greater before the Holy One, blessed be he, than the *Amen* which Israel say in response" (Deut. Rabba VII); "to him who responds *Amen* with all his strength, the gates of the Garden of Eden will open" (Bab. Shabbat 119b); "he who responds *Amen* is greater than he who recites the benediction" (Bab. Berakhot 53b).
5. See Joseph Heinemann, "The Formula *melekh ha-olam*," *Journal of Jewish Studies* XI (1960), pp. 177–79.
6. See Joseph Heinemann, *Prayer in the Period of the Tanna'im and Amora'im* [Hebrew] (Jerusalem: 1966), p. 120.
7. In Louis Finkelstein, ed., *The Jews—Their History, Culture and Religion* (Philadelphia: Jewish Publication Society, 1949), p. 865.

THE BREATH OF EVERY LIVING BEING

1. Cf., M. H. Goshen-Gottstein; *Textus* III (1963), pp. 156–58.

THE SHEMA AND ITS BENEDICTIONS

1. Geza Vermes, "Pre-Mishnaic Jewish Worship and the Phylacteries from the Dead Sea," *Vetus Testamentum* IV (1959), pp. 65ff.

THE WEEKDAY AMIDAH

1. During the rainy season a request for rain must be made in this benediction, while in the second benediction the clause is inserted, "causing the wind to blow and the rain to fall." The manuscript published by Schechter—which has the one but not the other—is inconsistent.
2. Hebrew: *natzerim*; apparently the Judeo-Christians are meant.
3. Psalm 94:18, transposed into the plural.

A PARAPHRASE OF THE WEEKDAY AMIDAH

1. See Menahem Zulay, *The Poetical School of Rav Saadya Gaon* [Hebrew] (Jerusalem: Schocken Books, 1964), pp. 242–57.
2. Joseph Heinemann, "Sa'adya Ga'on's Attitude to Changes in the Forms of Prayers" [Hebrew] *Bar-Ilan Annual* I (1963), pp. 220–33 (English summary, pp. xlvii–l).
3. Shalom Spiegel, "On Medieval Jewish Poetry," in *The Jews . . .* Louis Finkelstein, ed. (Philadelphia: Jewish Publication Society, 1949), p. 539.
4. This strophe does not conform to the structural pattern evident throughout the whole composition.

SEVEN BENEDICTIONS IN ONE

1. Cf., Joseph Heinemann, "One Benediction Comprising Seven," *Révue des Etudes Juives* CXXV (1966), pp. 101ff.
2. "In the fitting form of blessings" [*me'eyn ha-berakhot*] is a corruption of *me'on ha-berakhot*—"the abode [or: source] of blessings," as is evident from a number of ancient sources and from the Yemenite version. "The abode of blessings and the Lord of peace" was one of the concluding formulas, current in the ancient Palestinian rite, of the last benediction of the Amidah.

ADDITIONAL AMIDAH FOR NEW YEAR

1. See Joseph Heinemann, "Malkhuyot, Zikhronot ve-Shofarot," *Maayanot: High Holiday Volume* (Jerusalem: World Zionist Organization, 1968), pp. 546–69, especially 547, *n.*6. Leon J. Liebreich, "Aspects of the New Year Liturgy," *Hebrew Union College Annual* XXXIV (1963), pp. 125ff. Herman Kieval, *The High Holy Days* I (New York: The Burning Bush Press, 1959), pp. 152–63.

2. See Louis Finkelstein, "The Development of the *Amidah*," *Jewish Quarterly Review*, n.s. XVI (1925–26), pp. 1–18, *n*.43.
3. See Adolph Buchler, *Types of Jewish Palestinian Piety* (London: Jews' College Publications, 1922), pp. 236–40.
4. See Leon J. Liebreich, "The Insertions in the Third Benediction of the Holy Day Amidoth," *Hebrew Union College Annual* XXXV (1964), pp. 79ff.; especially 94ff. and the bibliography cited there.
5. See Joseph Heinemann, "Prayers of Beth Midrash Origin," *Journal of Semitic Studies* V (1960), pp. 264ff.; especially 277ff.
6. See Leon J. Liebreich, *Hebrew Union College Annual* XXXIV (1963), pp. 166–67.
7. Ibid., pp. 144ff.
8. This clause was deleted by medieval Christian censors from most Ashkenazi prayerbooks.
9. There follow the three concluding benedictions of the Amidah; the wording is the same as every day, except for the insertion in the last and next-to-last of brief petitions asking to be inscribed in the book of life (Birnbaum, p. 663). In the original Ashkenazi rite, the last benediction has the old Palestinian conclusion (see "The Weekday Amidah" and Birnbaum, ibid.).

THE KEDUSHAH

1. See Gershom G. Scholem, *Jewish Gnosticism, Merkabah Mysticism and Talmudic Tradition* (New York: The Jewish Theological Seminary of America, 1960).
2. Cf., Ismar M. Elbogen, *Der jüdische Gottesdienst in seiner geschichtlichen Entwicklung* [Hebrew] Joseph Heinemann, ed. (Tel Aviv: Dvir Company, 1972), pp. 52–53.

THE KADDISH

1. See David de Sola Pool, *The Kaddish*, 3rd edition (New York: The Union of Sephardic Congregations, Inc., 1964).
2. See Heinemann, "Prayer," pp. 264ff.

BENEDICTIONS FOLLOWING THE HAFTARAH

1. Cf., Heinemann, "Prayer," pp. 143–44; Kaufmann Kohler, "The Origin and Composition of the Eighteen Benedictions" *Hebrew Union College Annual* I (1924), pp. 392–93; Leon J. Liebreich, s.v. "Liturgy, Jewish," in Encyclopaedia Britannica, 1965 edition, pp. 140–41.
2. See Viktor Aptowitzer, *Parteipolitik der Hasmonäerzeit im rabbinischen und pseudoepigraphischen Schrifttum* (Wien: Kohut Foundation, 1927), pp. 50ff.

GRACE AFTER MEALS

1. See Joseph Heinemann, "Birkhath Ha-Zimmun and Havurah Meals," *Journal of Jewish Studies* XIII (1962), pp. 23–29.
2. Adapted from Psalm 24:5.
3. Adapted from Proverbs 3:4.
4. Concerning the style of the concluding section, cf., "The Kaddish"; and Heinemann, "Prayers," pp. 264–80.

LITANIES FOR TABERNACLES

1. See Jakob J. Petuchowski, " 'Hoshi'ah na' in Psalm 118:25—A Prayer for Rain," *Vetus Testamentum* V (1955), pp. 266ff.
2. Number 4 is used today in the Ashkenazi rite on Simhat Torah, the festival concluding Tabernacles; but there can be no doubt that it belongs to the same category of hosha-na litanies, even though it uses three alternating responses of which hosha-na is but one.
3. Of Number 1 only four lines have been preserved. In Number 4 the last letter of the alphabet is repeated three times; a total of twenty-four lines (divisible by three) is required there, for the sake of the three alternating responses.
4. See James Hastings, s.v. "Litany" in *Encyclopaedia of Religion and Ethics*, 1915 edition, VIII, pp. 78ff.
5. See Heinemann, "Prayer," pp. 88–98 [*Tarbiz* XXX (1961), pp. 357–69].

SUGGESTIONS FOR FURTHER READING (*in English*)

Abrahams, Israel. A *Companion to the Authorized Daily Prayerbook* (London: Eyre and Spottiswoode, 1922 and New York: Hermon Press, 1966).

Goldschmidt, Daniel. "Liturgy," in *Encyclopaedia Judaica*. Vol. 11, pp. 392–402.

Heinemann, Joseph. "Amidah," in *Encyclopaedia Judaica*. Vol. 2, pp. 838–45.

Idelson, A. Z. *Jewish Liturgy and Its Development* (New York: Schocken Books, 1967).

Kieval, Herman. *The High Holy Days* I (New York: The Burning Bush Press, 1959).

Millgram, Abraham E. *Jewish Worship* (Philadelphia: Jewish Publication Society, 1971).

Petuchowski, Jakob J. *Understanding Jewish Prayer* (New York: Ktav Publishing House, 1972).

———., ed. *Contributions to the Scientific Study of Jewish Liturgy* (New York: Ktav Publishing House, 1972).

PART TWO

SERMONS

INTRODUCTION

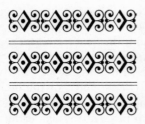

WITH THE CONQUEST of the Near East by Alexander the Great in the fourth century B.C.E., and the consequent spread of Hellenism, the Jews in the Land of Israel became exposed to a variety of outside influences and were forced to take a stand on a great many religious and spiritual issues. The Roman conquest three centuries later, which eventually resulted in the destruction of the Temple and the loss of political independence, undermined Jewish self-confidence still further; a mood approaching despair took hold in numerous circles. At the same time the religious establishment had to face the challenge of various sectarian groups like the Dead Sea Sect and the Judeo-Christians.

Through sermons and homilies, the rabbis—the spiritual leaders of the era—tried, on the whole, successfully, to give guidance and spiritual encouragement to a perplexed Jewry, to provide answers to the problems of the times, to refute the arguments of both internal and external opponents, and to strengthen the conviction that the Torah was still a valid way of life and the future of the Jewish people and of Judaism still assured. The subject matter of their sermons was derived for the most part from aggadah, that body of material—consisting of legends, biblical commentaries, popular sayings, parables, and the like—which in a sense represents the theology of the rabbis. This theology was unsystematic in character, often presented, as the occasion demanded, in the form of narratives designed for the popular audience.

The preachers succeeded in making the Bible an unceasing source of new meaning and inspiration. Through creative philology and sometimes daring methods of interpretation, they overcame exegetical difficulties and imparted fresh significance to biblical stories and biblical heroes, whom they transformed into ideal types. Shifts of emphasis took place, novel interpretations were offered of the biblical text. The Bible itself, for example, was found to be the source of the rabbis' own authority in the community, in place of the old leadership of priests and prophets; the great heroes of the past, such as the Patriarchs, Moses, and David, were seen as typical "disciples of the wise," prefigurations of the rabbis themselves. To take another example: the binding of Isaac was no longer presented as a demonstration of Abraham's absolute obedience to God's will but as a prototype of martyrdom, with the spotlight now focused on Isaac and his willingness to give up his life for the sanctity of God. Again after the destruction of the Temple in 70 C.E., when atonement for sin could no longer be obtained through sacrifice, acts of lovingkindness were proclaimed as possessing the same remissive quality. And when the old biblical faith in a this-wordly reward for a righteous life could no longer satisfy a people sunk in disaster and persecution, the rabbis unhesitatingly substituted belief in a reward in the hereafter.

To enhance the beauty and effectiveness of his sermon, a preacher would take a biblical story and embellish and amplify it, make use of folktales and parables, employ dramatization and various other rhetorical devices. The entertainment value of a sermon was frequently no less salient than its overt burden of moral and religious edification— indeed, the Jewish preachers of Talmudic times were sometimes criticized for being too theatrical, more interested in the quality of their performance than in imparting religious truth. Small wonder that people came in droves to hear these sermons, especially when the preacher was well-known. People were drawn even from outlying villages, and made special arrangements beforehand to permit them to travel beyond the Sabbath limit of 2,000 cubits (Mishnah Eruvin III, 5).

The rabbis contrasted the synagogues and houses of study, where sermons were usually delivered, to the invidious attractions of the circus and the theater of the Hellenistic Roman world. Remarkably enough, they succeeded in making most people prefer the former:

"They that sit in the gate talk of Me" (Psalms 69:13) was given two different interpretations: " . . . those are the Gentiles who sit in their theaters and circuses . . . scoffing Me," and ". . . those are Israel who sit in the synagogues and houses of study . . ." (Lamentations Rabba, Proem 17). The audience at a sermon actively expressed its approval or disapproval, reacting now with laughter and satisfaction, now with indifference if a preacher failed to arouse interest. The preacher for his part adapted the level of his discourse to the audience; in addressing simple people he had recourse to very graphic, even ribald, images.[1] The popularity of the aggadic sermon emerges clearly from the following statement of the third-century Amora, R. Issaac Nappaha, himself a famous preacher: "In days of old when the *perutah* [a small coin] was easy to come by, a man desired to hear words of Mishnah and of Talmud; but now, when the *perutah* is no longer easily found, and when, moreover, we suffer from the Kingdom [i.e., Roman rule], a man desires to hear words of Scripture and words of aggadah" (Pesikta de Rav Kahana, Buber, ed., 101b).

Sermons were delivered, whenever possible, on every Sabbath and on other special occasions, including fast days (cf., Mishnah Ta'anit II, 1), especially on the Ninth of Av. They were based in large part on the Torah section read that day, the *seder* (of the so-called Triennial Cycle) on an ordinary Sabbath and the special pericopes read on festivals. On special Sabbaths (for example, before and after the Ninth of Av), the homily might be drawn from the reading from the Prophets. The exact hour of the sermon varied. It is known that sermons were delivered on Friday night (Leviticus Rabba IX, 9), on Sabbath morning after the reading from Scripture (Luke 4:16ff.), or on Sabbath afternoon (Yalkut Shim'oni, Prov. § 964). It appears that many sermons (of the proem-type, discussed below) were given before the Scriptural reading and served as an introduction to it; such sermons were no doubt rather brief.

If the preacher was one of the great sages, he would make his appearance only after the whole audience had assembled; in the meantime, younger rabbis, acting as auxiliary preachers, would keep the people occupied (Gen. Rabba XCVIII, 11). The preacher made use of a *turgeman* (interpreter), whose task it was to broadcast the sermon in a loud voice that could be heard by all sections of the audience. This was not so much a practical device—for some of the preachers at least must have had voices powerful enough to make themselves heard—as it was a token of respect. Although preachers as a rule took proper care in the preparation of their sermons, it was not unheard of for members of the audience to address questions to which inexperienced preachers sometimes were unable to reply (Gen. Rabba LXXXI, 2).

The Rabbinic editors of the classical Midrashim that have come down to us, especially of the so-called homiletical Midrashim,[2] undoubtedly drew upon material that had first been used in public sermons delivered on Sabbaths and festivals. This is not to say, however, that the Midrashic homilies are identical with the sermons as they were actually preached in public. It appears that the later compilers of the Midrashim made use of a variety of actual sermons, in full or in part, from which they fashioned a new entity that might be called a "literary homily." Consequently, we do not know very much, certainly far less than would at first appear, about the forms of the public sermon itself. Nevertheless, some types can be identified with certainty.

One rhetorical form found frequently in the Midrash, the proem (*petihta*), undoubtedly had its origin in the sermon. The proem opens with a quotation from Scripture, taken not from the text read on the day in question but usually from the Hagiographa. From this remote verse the preacher proceeds to evolve a chain of expositions and interpretations, until, at the very end, he arrives at the first (or second) verse of the seder of the day. Quite often the opening passage chosen is an unexpected one, its connection with the lesson for the day not at all obvious; this is done to arouse the curiosity of the audience. Sometimes the connection between the opening and the concluding verses is established by means of a play on words or similar rhetorical device. Nearly always, the opening verse expresses a general idea which is subsequently illustrated by the specific example provided by the contents of the pericope. Some scholars think such proems served originally as the opening sections of the sermon, or, more likely, were complete sermons in themselves. The peculiar upside-down structure of the proem, which inevitably concludes with the beginning of the weekly lesson, seems to indicate that the sermon was delivered before the reading from Scripture and served as an introduction to it.[3]

The proem was by no means the only type of sermon. A question posed by a member of the audience often served as the taking-off point for a sermon. (This custom is reflected in homilies, especially in the Midrashim of the Tanhuma group, that open with a halakhic question, preceded by the formula *yelammedenu rabbenu* ["May our master teach us"], or the like.) The challenge to the preacher lay not so much in finding the answer—for the questions usually referred to well-known halakhot—but in improvising a way to link both the question and the answer with the real subject matter of the sermon, the Bible reading for the day; this type of sermon, too, invariably concludes with the first verse (or verses) of the Scriptural lesson. It is possible that the question posed to the preacher was known to him beforehand and planted.

A single example has been preserved of a sermon which opens with a halakhic question and concludes not with the beginning of the scriptural lesson but with the answer to the question. It stands to reason that this must have been a customary pattern, too, at some time.

There were also sermons that opened with a kind of benediction, praising God for the gift of the Torah, and proceeding to the specific theme to be developed. Others took for their point of departure a verse from the weekly portion itself. A different and less frequent pattern has the first verse of the pericope followed immediately by a reference to a verse from another place, in the light of which the first verse is interpreted, e.g.: " 'Then came Amalek' . . . this verse is to be explained in connection with the passage in Job, where it is said 'Can the rush shoot up without mire . . .' " (Mekhilta, Amalek, beginning).

Midrashic homilies often conclude on a messianic note, contrasting the troubles of "this world" with the joys of "the world to come." These probably represent perorations of actual sermons. Other sermons ended in a prayer expressing gratitude to God for the Torah or, more frequently, requesting the speedy advent of redemption. An example of such a concluding prayer is the Kaddish.

In different times and places, then, sermons exhibited a variety of structures and forms. Midrashic homilies, however, are constructed in a more or less uniform pattern: after a series of proems there follows "the body of the sermon" (the structure of which is not clearly defined) and finally the peroration, which strikes the messianic note in most cases. (In Midrashim of the Tanhuma type, these sections are preceded by an opening passage that poses a halakhic question.) These homilies must be considered creations of the editors of the Midrashim, who made use of a number of sections, especially proems, drawn from different sermons and combined in a new structure—the "literary homily." [4] The homily does *not* reflect a single sermon as it was actually preached in public, since no preacher would have used an entire consecutive series of independent preambles simply to arrive over and over again at the same point he had reached with the first one.

The following texts were chosen for their literary value and their specific subject matter. At the same time, they serve to illustrate the different forms and patterns of the sermon and the homily in Talmudic times. At least some of them may be considered perfect representations of the rabbinic art of the sermon at its best.

THE WORDS OF THE TORAH GROW AND INCREASE

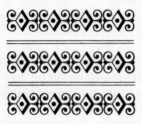

INTRODUCTION

R. ELEAZAR B. AZARIAH, *the author of this sermon, was a member of the first generation of the Sages of Yavneh, at the end of the first century* C.E. *Hence this homily—undoubtedly a genuine sermon, delivered orally before an audience—is one of the earliest extant (though our text may have preserved no more than an outline of it). The framework of the story in the Babylonian Talmud (Hagigah) clearly establishes the occasion of the sermon (even though the full text also refers to two other homilies, and all three cannot have been delivered on the same Sabbath); the closely knit structure and the variety of rhetorical devices typical of oral delivery similarly attest to the homily's having originated as a sermon. The most striking such device is the three parallel lines:*

some pronouncing unclean	*and others pronouncing clean*
some prohibiting	*and others permitting*
some declaring unfit	*and others declaring fit*

These lines possess a clearly marked rhythm, each contains a thesis and antithesis, and the whole series is repeated, with slight variations, no fewer than three times (in the manuscript version). Other stylistic means employed by the preacher include rhetorical questions ("Should a man say: . . . how then shall I learn Torah?") and the admonition,

113

addressed individually, as it were, to each member of the audience (the Hebrew text uses the second person singular): "Therefore make your ear like the hopper . . ."

According to the reading presented here, this sermon is structured in the proem pattern: it opens with Ecclesiastes 12:11 concerning the "words of the wise" and conclude with Exodus 20:1 "And God spoke all these words" (after which follow a few concluding lines). Hence it may be assumed that this sermon was delivered on the Sabbath on which Exodus 20—the account of the revelation from Sinai—was read. The homily is about the authority to be granted "the words of the wise," and the difficult problem caused by the frequent controversies among the Sages particularly acute at Yavneh, where the task was undertaken of arriving at a decision in the numerous differences of opinion between the houses of Hillel and Shammai. But why should a sermon that aims at elucidating the revelation chapter of Exodus open, intentionally, with a verse concerning "the words of the wise"? It does so because it is primarily concerned with the intricate relationship between the written Torah revealed by God himself at Sinai, and the oral Torah, proclaimed and transmitted by the sages of each generation. Over against the divine revelation stands this Torah of human origin, which evolves and changes and is full of contradictions and differences of opinion. How can there be two Torahs? And what authority can the Torah of the Sages claim for itself? On these complex and involved matters the preacher takes his stand in a dialectical, perhaps somewhat paradoxical, manner. His contention is this: not only are the two Torahs one and the same, but only through "the words of the wise," which grow and increase does the Torah remain viable, dynamic, and full of meaning; in spite of changes and permutations, the oral Torah as well as the written one is given from one shepherd. Moreover, it is thanks to "the words of the wise" that the Torah is "the Torah of life," which "directs those who study it to the paths of life." Proof of this contention (not made explicit in the version given here), lies in Exodus 20:1: And God spoke all these words—the words of the written, as well as those of the oral, Torah.

It seems likely that some further expositions of R. Eleazar, preserved separately elsewhere (Pal. Sanhedrin X, 1, 28a), were originally an integral part of this sermon: "The words of the wise are like a goad [kedarvonot]—like the ball with which young girls play [kadur banot];

like the ball which is thrown from one hand and caught by the other,
so Moses received the Torah at Sinai and passed it on to Joshua, and
Joshua passed it on to the elders, and so forth (cf., Mishnah Avot
I, 1)." The same source follows with some interpretations of the three
different Hebrew words for "goad." These expositions complement
and elaborate upon the ideas of the sermon by stressing the impor-
tance of tradition—handed like a ball from generation to generation—
from which, ultimately, even the conflicting "words of the wise" of
the present generation derive their unchallenged authority.

THE WORDS OF THE TORAH GROW AND INCREASE

Once R. Johanan b. Beroka and R. Eleazar Hisma went to R. Joshua
at Peki'in. He said to them: What new teaching was there at the
house of study today? They replied: We are your disciples and your
waters do we drink.[a] He said to them: Even so, it is impossible for a
study session to pass without some new teaching. Whose Sabbath [or:
week] was it? It was the Sabbath of R. Eleazar [b] b. Azariah. And what
was the theme of his sermon today? . . .

He [R. Eleazar b. Azariah] opened his discourse: *The words of the*
wise are as goads and as nails well planted are the words of masters
of assemblies, which are given from one shepherd (Eccles. 12:11).

---

[a] *your waters do we drink:* We are the ones who benefit from your
teaching, but there is nothing we can teach you.

---

[b] *the Sabbath of R. Eleazar:* After Rabban Gamliel had been removed from the presidency of the academy, and subsequently, been
reinstated (Bab. Berakhot 28a), he and his successor, R. Eleazar, used
to take turns delivering the sermons.

Why are the words of the Torah likened to a goad? To teach you that just as the goad directs the heifer along its furrow to bring forth life to the world, so the words of the Torah direct those who study them from the paths of death to the paths of life. But [you might think that] just as the goad is movable [c] so the words of the Torah are movable; therefore the text says: "nails." But [you might think that] just as the nail neither diminishes nor increases,[d] so too the words of the Torah do neither diminish nor increase; therefore the text says: "well planted"; just as a plant grows and increases, so the words of the Torah grow and increase.[e]

The masters of assemblies: these are the disciples of the wise, who sit in assemblies and study the Torah, some pronouncing unclean and others pronouncing clean, some prohibiting and others permitting, some declaring unfit and others declaring fit. Should a man say: Since some pronounce unclean and others pronounce clean, some prohibit and others permit, some declare unfit and others declare fit—how then shall I learn Torah? [f] Therefore the text says: All of them *are given from one shepherd.* One God gave them, one leader proclaimed them from the mouth of the Lord of all creation, blessed be He; for it is written: And God spoke all these words [g] (Ex. 20:1). Therefore

---

[c] *movable:* Liable to change.

---

[d] *neither diminishes nor increases:* The reading has been amended according to the parallel in Tos. Sotah VII, 1.

---

[e] *grow and increase:* Through the teachings and interpretations of the wise.

---

[f] *Should a man say, etc.:* The reading is given according to MS Munich.

---

[g] *all these words:* That is, including the—apparently novel—teaching of the wise.

make your ear like the hopper and acquire a perceptive heart to understand the words of those who pronounce unclean and the words of those who pronounce clean, the words of those who prohibit and the words of those who permit, the words of those who declare unfit and the words of those who declare fit.

He [R. Joshua] said to them: The generation in which R. Eleazar b. Azariah lives is not orphaned.

Bab. Hagigah 3a–b

THE SIN OF MOSES AND THE SIN OF DAVID

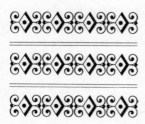

INTRODUCTION

SIFRE TO DEUTERONOMY *is one of the "Tannaitic Midrashim," which —though possibly edited at a later date—contain material not later than the early third century* C.E. *There are many indications that in this passage a sermon, as preached in public, has been preserved. Thematically, all its various constituent parts are concerned with a single complex of ideas: sin-prayer-forgiveness. In the foreground appear the two great figures of Moses and David, who are compared and contrasted to one another. In the first section, Moses appears superior to David both because his sin is less grave than David's and because he does not desire to conceal it, insisting, on the contrary, that it be "written down" in the Torah. Even so, these "two good leaders" appear jointly in the following section as models for future generations: despite their great meritoriousness, they ask to be pardoned for their transgressions as an act of grace. Parables, which make up a considerable part of this homily, are a common characteristic of public sermons.*

If the last section, quoted below, may be considered part of the same sermon, then the homily as a whole concludes with a quotation of the first verse of the weekly pericope; and since it opens with another quotation from Proverbs, it may be an example—one of the few from the Tannaitic period—of the proem pattern of the public sermon. But we cannot rule out the possibility that this sermon represents a different pattern—found not infrequently in the Tannaitic Midrashim—in which the preacher opens his discourse with the first verse of the weekly lesson and immediately links it with a verse from the Hagiographa that serves as an exposition to it.[1]

THE SIN OF MOSES AND THE SIN OF DAVID

And I besought the Lord at that time, saying (Deut. 3:23), this is what is meant by the verse: *The poor uses entreaties*[a]; *but the rich answers impudently* (Prov. 18:23). Israel had two good leaders, one was Moses and the other was David, King of Israel. Moses said to the Holy One, blessed be He: "Lord of the universe, let my transgression be written down after my death lest people say: 'it appears that Moses falsified the Torah[b] or said something he was not commanded to say.'" This is like a king who decreed: Anyone who eats unripe figs grown during the Sabbatical year is to be led around the central square.[c] A woman of good family plucked and ate unripe figs grown

---

[a] *The poor uses entreaties:* Refers to Moses; the second half of the verse is not expounded here. Elsewhere (Deut. Rabba II, 4) it is interpreted as referring to God.

---

[b] *it appears that Moses falsified the Torah:* He suppressed the details of his own transgression.

---

[c] *unripe figs, etc.:* According to Saul Lieberman (*Greek in Jewish Palestine*, New York, 1942, pp. 162 ff.) the "eating of unripe figs" is a figurative expression, signifying illicit intercourse between a bridegroom and his betrothed before the marriage has been formally legalized. While premature and, therefore, forbidden—just as the actual

in the Sabbatical year and they led her around the square. She said: "I beg of you, your majesty, publish my sin lest the people of the city think that I was found guilty of adultery or witchcraft; when they see unripe figs hanging 'round my neck they will know the true reason for my being led around the square." Thus Moses said to the Holy One, blessed be He: "Let the sin which I have committed be written down after my death." The Holy One, blessed be He replied: "I shall indeed write that it was only because of the water," for we read: *Because you rebelled against My commandment in the wilderness of Zin, in the strife of the congregation* (Num. 27:14). R. Simeon tells a parable of a king who went about with his son in his carriage. He came to a narrow place and the carriage overturned on top of his son; his eye was blinded, his hand severed and his leg broken. Whenever the king came to this same place he was wont to say: "Here my son was hurt, here his eye was blinded, here his hand was severed, here his leg was broken." Likewise, the Lord three times mentions "the waters of strife," "the waters of strife," "the waters of strife," as if to say: Here I killed Aaron, here I killed Moses.[d] Hence it is said: *Their judges are thrown down by the sides of the rock* (Psalms 141:6).[e]

---

eating of unripe figs is forbidden in the Sabbatical year, when only fit produce may be consumed—this transgression, naturally, is far less severe than the sin of adultery. It was the custom to lead a transgressor—adorned with objects indicating the character of his transgression—around a public square.

In corresponding texts, we find this parable, with some variations, either referring to Moses' sin alone (with the element of impatience, involved in the hitting of the rock, being the point of comparison) or else for a comparative evaluation of the sins of Moses and David respectively; David, by implication, is like "a woman found guilty of adultery."

---

[d] *Here I killed Aaron . . . Moses:* Here I decreed that they should die.

---

[e] *Their judges are thrown down:* Moses and Aaron were punished because of the rock.

David said to God: "Let not the sin which I have committed be written down after my death," to which the Lord replied: "This will not benefit you, for people will say: 'Because He loved him He forgave him.' " This is like a man who borrowed a thousand measures of wheat a year from the king. Everyone used to say: "Is it possible that he can repay a thousand measures of wheat a year? If the king does not seize his property, he must have granted him remission." Once he delayed payment and did not return any part of his debt; the king entered his house, seized his sons and his daughters and put them up for sale in the slave market. Then everyone knew that the king had not granted him a remission. So all the retribution meted out to David was multiplied,[f] for we read: *And he shall restore the lamb fourfold* (II Sam. 12:6). R. Haninah says: "Fourfold"—that means four times four: sixteen times. Also the Prophet Nathan reproved him for this deed. David replied: *I have sinned against the Lord* (ibid.: 13), to which the prophet answered him: *The Lord also has put away your sin; you shall not die* (ibid.), and he says: *Against thee, thee only, have I sinned, and done that which is evil in Thy sight* (Psalms 51:6).

Israel had two good leaders: One was Moses and the other was David, King of Israel, who could have demanded forgiveness[g] for the whole world on account of their good deeds; and yet, all they asked of the Almighty was that He grant them pardon as an act of grace. Now if those able to demand forgiveness on account of their good deeds only asked the Holy One, blessed be He, that He grant them pardon as an act of grace, how much more must one who is merely one out of the millions of the pupils of their pupils request the Holy One, blessed be He, that He grant him pardon merely as an act of grace.

Another interpretation: *And I besought the Lord*—There are ten

---

[f] *So all the retribution . . . was multiplied* to demonstrate that God exacted full retribution for sins.

---

[g] *who could have demanded forgiveness:* Even though they had each committed one sin, their good deeds were so numerous they far outweighed their transgressions.

expressions for prayer: [h] Cry out, cry, groan, distress, lamentation, intercession, falling down, praying, entreaty, standing up, placate, beseech: "Cry out" in Egypt, for we read: *And it came to pass in the course of those many days that the king of Egypt died; and the children of Israel sighed by reason of the bondage, and cried out for help* (Ex. 2:23); "cry"—as it says: *And their cry under bondage came up to God* (ibid.); "groaning"—*And God heard their groaning* (ibid.: 24); "distress"—*In my distress I called upon the Lord* (Psalms 18:7); "lamentation"—*Neither lift up lamentation for them* (Jer. 7:16); "intercession"—*Neither make intercession to Me* (ibid.); "falling down"—*And I fell down before the Lord as at the first* (Deut. 9:18); "praying"—*And I prayed unto the Lord* (ibid.: 26); "entreaty"— *And Isaac entreated the Lord for his wife* (Gen. 25:21); "standing up"—*Then stood up Phinehas and interposed* (Psalms 106:30); "placating"—*But Moses set himself to placate the Lord* (Ex. 32:11); "beseech"—*And I besought the Lord*

Sifre Deuteronomy Va-ethanan, beginning.

[h] *ten expressions for prayer:* Our text actually enumerates twelve.

GOD TRIES THOSE THAT FEAR HIM

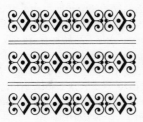

INTRODUCTION

THIS PROEM to Genesis 22—the story of the akedah [the "binding of Isaac"]—is based on a series of verbal links and similarities in sound between the opening verse from the book of Psalms and the text in Genesis: "them that fear thee" has its counterpart in Genesis 22:12: "for now I know that you are a God-fearing man"; while the roots of the Hebrew words for banner [nes] and "to be displayed" [noses] are almost identical with the keyword of Genesis 22:1: And God tried [nissah] Abraham. This forms the basis for an ingenious play on words: God "tries" or tests Abraham in order to "lift him up" [n-s-'] and make him renowned for his exemplary fear of God. In this manner, the preacher replies to a series of theological problems—not all stated explicitly—which the akedah and similar stories were liable to raise in the minds of the audience: Why did God need to test Abraham time and again ("In ten trials was Abraham tried"—Mishnah Avot V, 3)? Did He not know Abraham's righteousness and could He not have foreseen that Abraham would emerge triumphantly from his tenth trial just as he had from the nine preceding ones? The answer is suggested in our homily. The trials of the righteous are required not for the sake of God, who knows what is in their hearts, but for the sake of men; Abraham's righteousness had to be demonstrated

125

conclusively to the world at large, to justify the great rewards promised to him and his descendants.

The questions and answers raised by the preacher are meant to relate not only to Abraham and the events of the remote biblical past, but to the condition of the Jewish people at the time of the Aggadists as well. Why do the people of Israel, Abraham's descendants and no less righteous then he, suffer such oppression and tribulation at the hands of "the wicked [Roman] empire"? Their trials, too, this proem suggests, are meant to prove their merit and to justify the rewards that will accrue to them at the time of redemption.

GOD TRIES THOSE THAT FEAR HIM

Thou hast given a banner to them that fear Thee, that it may be displayed because of the truth. Selah (Psalms 60:6): this means exaltation upon exaltation, greatness upon greatness, in order to lift them up in the world, to exalt them in the world, like a ship's banner. And for what reason? *Because of the truth. Selah:* In order that God's justice may be glorified in the world. For if one should say: Whom He wishes to make rich, He makes rich, to make poor, He makes poor; whom He desires, He makes King; when He wished, He made Abraham rich, and when He wished He made him King; you can answer him and say: Can you do what Abraham did? *Abraham was a hundred years old, when his son Isaac was born unto him* (Gen. 21:5). Yet after all this suffering[a] it was said to him: *Take now your son, your only son . . . and offer him there, for a burnt-offering . . .* (ibid., 22:2), and he did not refuse. Hence: *Thou hast given a banner to them that fear Thee, that it may be displayed* —this is what is written: *And God tried Abraham* (ibid., 22:1).

Genesis Rabba LV, 1

[a] *after all this suffering:* This long and patient waiting for the birth of his only son.

THE TABERNACLE AND THE DIVINE PRESENCE

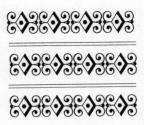

INTRODUCTION

THIS HOMILY *is a proem to the reading of Num. 7:1 ff., which is the portion for the Sabbath of Hanukkah (according to the custom underlying the Pesikta; whereas today this is the reading for the first day of Hanukkah).*

The opening verse from Song of Songs, 5:1, "I am come into my garden, my sister, my bride," certainly must have come as a surprise to the audience; what possible connection might it have with the biblical passage describing the setting up of the Tabernacle by Moses? Here again the link is established, on one level, by a play on words: "bride" [kallah] and "completion" ("on the day that Moses brought to completion [kallot] the setting up of the Tabernacle") are similar in sound. But this outward and rather farfetched connection is merely the foundation for a whole edifice of ideas: the setting up of the Tabernacle symbolizes the marriage union of God and Israel, as a consequence of which the Divine Presence comes to dwell again on earth. As the preacher elaborates in detail, the Presence had originally dwelled among men, but the iniquities of successive generations had caused its gradual removal; this process was then reversed by a succession of righteous generations that slowly returned the Presence from the seventh heaven to the sixth, from the sixth to the fifth, and so on. With the erection of the Tabernacle—the

*outward expression of the covenant between God and His people—
this process reached its culmination, in the return of the Divine bridegroom to His bridal chamber. Thus primordial harmony and the
union between God and mankind were reestablished. Not every link
in this chain of daring ideas is fully spelled out in the sermon; but
all are implicit in the powerful imagery.*

THE TABERNACLE AND THE DIVINE PRESENCE

I am come into my garden, my sister, my bride (Song 5:1). R. Azariah, citing R. Judah bar R. Simon, told the parable of a king who
became so angry at his wife that he deposed her and cast her out
of his palace. After a time, when he was willing to bring her back,
she said: "Let him first do something new for my sake, then let him
bring me back." Thus in the past the Holy One would accept offerings from above, as it is said [of Noah's offering] *the Lord smelled
the sweet savor* (Gen. 8:21). Now, however, He will accept offerings
from below: *I am come into my garden, my sister, my bride.*
R. Haninah said, The Torah [incidentally] teaches etiquette—a
groom is not to enter the bridal chamber until his bride gives him
leave: *Let my beloved come into his garden* (Song 4:16), and only
then, *I am come into my garden.*

R. Tanhum, the son-in-law of R. Eleazar ben Avina, citing R. Simeon
ben Yosne, said: it does not say, "I am come into a garden" but
I am come into my garden [*ganni*], i.e., my bridal chamber [*gin-
nuni*], the place where from the beginning the Divine Presence was
implanted; for originally the root of the Presence was fixed in the
regions of the earth below, as it is said, *They heard the voice of
the Lord God walking in the garden* (Gen. 3:8).

R. Abba bar Kahana said: The text implies that God, in anger
after Adam had sinned, was hastening to walk away [a] from him to

---

[a] *hastening to walk away:* This meaning is ascribed to the Hebrew *mithalekh,* which appears instead of the expected form, *me-
halekh.*

go up [to heaven]. Thereupon *Adam and his wife hid themselves* (ibid.), as R. Aivu explained: in that instant Adam's stature was diminished to no more than a hundred cubits.

R. Isaac said: It is written, *The righteous shall inherit the earth, and dwell thereon in eternity* (Psalms 37:29). And where will the wicked dwell? Are they to fly about in the air? *Shall . . . dwell thereon in eternity* means that the righteous will cause the Divine Presence to dwell [b] on earth.

Originally, then, the root of the Presence was fixed in the regions of the earth below. After Adam sinned, the Presence removed itself to the first heaven. The generation of Enosh arose: they sinned; the Presence removed itself from the first heaven to the second. The generation of the flood arose: they sinned; the Presence removed itself from the second heaven to the third. The generation of the dispersion of the races of man arose: they sinned; the Presence removed itself from the third heaven to the fourth. The Egyptians in the days of our father Abraham arose: [c] they sinned; the Presence removed itself from the fourth heaven to the fifth. The Sodomites arose: they sinned; the Presence removed itself from the fifth heaven to the sixth. The Egyptians in the days of Moses arose: from the sixth heaven to the seventh.

Over against these wicked men, seven righteous men arose and caused the Presence to come back to earth. Our father Abraham arose: by his merit he caused the Presence to come back from the seventh heaven to the sixth. Isaac arose: by his merit he caused the Presence to come back from the sixth heaven to the fifth. Jacob

---

[b] *will cause . . . to dwell:* This meaning is extracted through a change of vocalization in the word *yishkenu.*

---

[c] *in the days of . . . Abraham arose:* Chronologically the seven righteous men do not coincide with the seven generations of the wicked.

arose: by his merit he caused the Presence to come back from the fifth heaven to the fourth. Levi arose: by his merit he caused the Presence to come back from the fourth heaven to the third. Kohath arose: by his merit he caused the Presence to come back from the third heaven to the second. Amram arose: by his merit he caused the Presence to come back from the second heaven to the first. Moses arose: by his merit he caused the Presence to come back to the earth. Hence *And it came to pass on the day that Moses brought to completion the setting up of the Tabernacle* (Num. 7:1).

Pesikta de Rav Kahana I, 1

THE LEPER AND THE TEMPLE

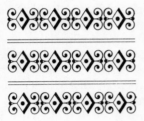

INTRODUCTION

THIS PROEM *to the reading of Lamentations on the Ninth of Av,
the anniversary of the destruction of the Temple, opens with a passage, not only utterly unexpected, but at first sight offensive and
very nearly blasphemous: verses in the book of Leviticus (13:45 ff.)
that describe the leper and his impurity are interpreted allegorically
to be referring to the Temple. Only at the end of the sermon does
the preacher make a verbal link—between the continuation of the
law of the leper; "all the days wherein the plague is in him he shall
be unclean . . . he shall dwell alone" (ibid., 46), and "How does
the city dwell alone" (Lam. 1:1)—to reveal the foundation for the
comparison of the fate of Zion, polluted by idolatry and doomed,
to the disgrace and isolation of the leper. Before this connection is
established, the allegory is a shocking one—an affect intended by
the preacher who wished to provoke his audience into thought.
This is a perfect example of the way in which the element of the
unexpected can play an important part in the structure of the proem,
building up a tension that is resolved only at the end.*

*It should be noted that the allusion to the law of the leper
functions in two opposing ways here. At the beginning to demonstrate the guilt of the people in having polluted the Temple and
causing its destruction; at the end to provide yet another proof-text*

for an underlying message of comfort and consolation: the period of disgrace and suffering will only last exactly as long as the period of transgression.

THE LEPER AND THE TEMPLE

R. Alexandri [a] opened his discourse. *And the leper in whom the plague is* (Lev. 13:45): *"the leper"* refers to the Temple; *in whom the plague is*—this is idol-worship which defiles like the plague, (as it is said, "And they profaned My sanctuary and defiled it"). *His clothes shall be rent:* these are the priestly garments; *the hair of his head shall go loose:* as it is said, *And the covering of Judah was laid bare* (Isa. 22:8): that which should have been covered,[b] He disclosed. *And he shall cover his upper lip:* When Israel was exiled among the nations of the world, not one of them was able to bring a word of Torah out of his mouth. *And shall cry, "Unclean, unclean":* this is the destruction of the First and Second Temples.[c]

---

[a] *R. Alexandri:* Of course, he cannot be considered the author of the proem in its entirety, since his exposition is quoted at the end in his name.

---

[b] *that which should have been covered:* Possibly the Holy of Holies, which was uncovered and laid bare at the time of the Destruction.

---

[c] *of the First and Second Temples:* The Aggadists often claim that Scripture hints at events much later than the text in question.

R. Jose ben Halafta said: Whoever knows how many years Israel worshiped idols also knows when the son of David will come; [d] and we have three verses to support this statement. The first is, *And I will visit upon her the days of the Baalim,*[e] *wherein she offered unto them* . . . . (Hos. 2:15). The second is, *And it came to pass that, as He called, and they would not hear; so shall they call,*[f] *and I will not hear* (Zech. 7:13). The third is, *And it shall come to pass that you shall say, "Wherefore has the Lord our God done all these things to us?* . . . *Like as you have forsaken Me* . . . *so shall you serve strangers in a land that is not yours"* (Jer. 5:19).

R. Johanan and R. Simeon ben Lakish both commented on this matter. R. Johanan said: This point may be derived from *because, even because* (Lev. 26:43), indicating measure for measure. R. Simeon ben Lakish said: It may be derived from *Your land, strangers devour it against you* (Isa. 1:7): i.e., corresponding to what you have done, strangers shall devour it. R. Alexandri derived it from this verse, *All the days wherein the plague is in him he shall be unclean* . . . *he shall dwell alone* . . .[g] (Lev. 13:46). *How does the city dwell alone* . . . (Lam. 1:1).

Lamentations Rabba, Proem XXI

[d] *Whoever knows how many years etc.:* For the total number of years of punishment and exile, after which the Messiah will come, will be equal to the number of years Israel worshiped idols.

[e] *the days of the Baalim:* That is, the exact number of days.

[f] *As he called* . . . *so shall they call:* The same period of time.

[g] *All the days* . . . *dwell alone:* Israel will "dwell alone" in exile for an amount of time corresponding to all the days in which it was polluted by idol-worship.

THE BONES OF JOSEPH

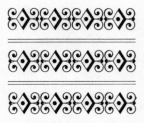

INTRODUCTION

THE INDIVIDUAL *expositions and heterogeneous interpretations of which this homily consists—most of which have also been preserved as separate units elsewhere—have been welded together into a larger, organic entity which develops a number of interconnected themes. This entity undoubtedly was the creation of a preacher, and certainly not the work of the editor of the Mekhilta, who, like the author of the other halakhic midrashim, did no more than collect all the expositions he could find and arrange them according to the order of the verses, making no attempt at integration.*

The sermon opens with what appears to have been the beginning of the weekly portion (or, if the lesson began, as it now does, with Exodus 13:17, its third verse), without any preamble. This gives the preacher the opportunity to praise Moses' eagerness to perform acts of piety—of which his care for Joseph's coffin is but one example— and to apply to him the verse, "The wise in heart takes on commandments." The Hebrew term mitzvot *can mean deeds of merit as well as specific commandments: hence this verse applies no less to Joseph, who, it is claimed, observed the entire Ten Commandments. Skillfully the two exemplary figures of Moses and Joseph are associated with each other in a number of ways. If Moses himself undertook the care of Joseph's remains, this was no more than just for Joseph had done the same for his father, Jacob; and Moses, in turn, was to receive his own suitable reward when God Himself saw to his burial. But why was it that throughout the forty years of Israel's wandering, Joseph's coffin [aron] accompanied the ark [aron] of Him that lives eternally? "Because he who lies in this coffin observed all that is written on the Tablets, that lie in the ark— to teach you that with what measure a man metes, it is measured unto him."*

The phrases found in Exodus 13:19 are expounded one by one: "for he had straightly sworn the sons of Israel" and, lastly, "God will surely remember you." But again these various elements are linked together organically.

The expositions concerning the oath extracted by Joseph of "the sons of Israel," i.e., his brothers, are woven into the fabric of the sermon by what precedes them: after it has been demonstrated that Joseph observed the Ten Commandments, a number of additional commandments observed by him are enumerated, e.g., "You shall not hate your brother in your heart," "You shall not take vengeance," etc., all of which illustrate his forgiveness and generosity toward his brothers in spite of what they had done to him. The concluding phrase, "God will surely remember you," is utilized by the preacher in order to work up to what is a frequent pattern of sermonic peroration. "He did remember you in this world, and He will also remember you in the world to come" are words of comfort and consolation, referring to the future redemption of Israel, by which even the "remembrance" in Egypt, the first redemption, will be overshadowed.

Among the foremost elements which lend this sermon its appeal are the vivid, dramatic descriptions of Moses' desperate search for Joseph's coffin, a quest which succeeds thanks to the mysterious figure of the ancient Serah, who alone "survived from that generation"; the miraculous means employed to raise the heavy coffin from the depths of the Nile; the lively scene in which "the nations of the world" express their wonder at the sight of the two arks accompanying the Israelites in the wilderness. The dramatic quality of the story is underlined by the jeopardy in which the entire exodus from Egypt is placed at the last moment when Joseph's coffin cannot be found and then cannot be lifted from the waters. Moses' address to Joseph has a note of despair: "The oath to redeem his children,

*which God swore to our father Abraham, has reached its fulfillment
. . . do not delay us, for because of you we are delayed"*; for the
two oaths—God's, to redeem Israel, and Israel's, to take the bones
of Joseph out of Egypt—appear at this moment to be irreconcilable.

Among the distinguishing marks of the sermon, delivered orally
before a live audience, are repetitive phrases like *"Joseph than whom
none of his brothers was greater, acted meritoriously . . . . Moses,
than whom no one in Israel was greater, acted meritoriously . . ."*;
the frequent questions—some of them rhetorical—*"But how did
Moses know where Joseph was buried?"*, *"What are these two arks?"*,
etc.; the direct address to the audience: *"And do not be surprised at
this!"*; and the like. While it is not an invariable rule that a live
sermon must present a continuous text, uninterrupted by mention
of the names of individual teachers who are the authors of its constituent parts, the more fully integrated sermons nevertheless tend
to do so; this homily gains in compactness if the two comments
reported in the name of R. Nathan—probably additions to the
original sermon, made perhaps by the editor of the Mekhilta—are
omitted.

THE BONES OF JOSEPH

And Moses took the bones of Joseph with him (Ex. 13:19). This
proclaims the wisdom and the piety of Moses. For all Israel were
busy with the booty while Moses busied himself with the duty of
looking after the bones of Joseph. Of him Scripture says: *The wise
in heart takes on commandments* (Prov. 10:8).[a] But how did Moses
know where Joseph was buried? It is told that Serah, the daughter
of Asher, survived from that generation and she showed Moses the
grave of Joseph. She said to him: The Egyptians put him into a
metal coffin which they sank in the Nile. So Moses went and stood

---

[a] *takes on commandments*: Prefers *mitzvot*, meritorious deeds,
to material gain.

by the Nile. He took a pebble [b] and, throwing it into the Nile, he cried out and said: "Joseph, Joseph, the oath to redeem his children, which God swore to our father Abraham, has reached its fulfillment. Give honor to the Lord, the God of Israel, and do not delay us, for because of you we are delayed. But if not, we shall be cleared of guilt regarding your oath." Immediately Joseph's coffin came to the surface, and Moses took it. And do not be surprised at this! Behold it says: *But as one was felling a beam, the axe head fell into the water . . . and the man of God said: "Where fell it?" and he showed him the place. And he cut down a stick, and cast it in and made the iron float* (II Kings 6:5–6). Now, if Elisha, the disciple of Elijah, could make the iron come to the surface, how much more could Moses, the master of Elijah, do so!

[R. Nathan says: They had buried him in the capital of Egypt in the mausoleum of the kings, as it is said: *And they embalmed him, and he was put in a coffin in Egypt* (Gen. 50:26).] This is to teach you that with what measure a man metes, it is measured unto him. Miriam waited for her brother a while, as it is said: *And his sister stood afar off* (Ex. 2:4). And in the wilderness God caused the ark, the Divine Presence, the priests, the Levites, all Israel, and the seven clouds of glory to wait for her, as it is said: *And the people journeyed not till Miriam was brought in again* (Num. 12:15). Joseph, than whom none of his brothers was greater, acted meritoriously in burying his father, as it is said: *And Joseph went up to bury his father . . . and there went up with him . . . .* (Gen. 50:7–9). Whom can we find greater and more honored than Joseph with whom no less a person than Moses busied himself.

Moses, than whom no one in Israel was greater, acted meritoriously in busying himself with the bones of Joseph, as it is said: *And Moses took the bones of Joseph with him.* Whom can we find greater and more honored than Moses, who was attended to by God Himself, as it is said: *And He buried him in the valley* (Deut. 34:6). And, what is more, with Jacob there went up the servants of Pharaoh and the elders of his house, while with Joseph there went up the ark, the Divine Presence, the priests, the Levites, all Israel, and the seven

[b] *He took a pebble*: Another reading—A tablet of gold on which the Tetragrammaton was engraved.

clouds of glory. Furthermore, the coffin of Joseph went alongside the ark of the Eternal.ᶜ And the nations of the world would say to the Israelites: "What are these two arks?" And the Israelites would say to them: "The one is the ark of the Eternal, and the other is a coffin with a dead body in it." The nations then would say: "What is the importance of this coffin that it should go alongside the ark of the Eternal?" And the Israelites would say to them: "The one lying in this coffin has fulfilled that which is written on what lies in that ark." On the tablets lying in this ark is written: *I am the Lord your God* (Ex. 20:2). And of Joseph it is written: *For, am I in the place of God?* ᵈ (Gen. 50:19). On the tablets in this ark is written: *You shall have no other gods before Me* (Ex. 20:3), and of Joseph it is written: *For I fear God* (Gen. 42:18). It is written: *You shall not take the name of the Lord your God in vain* (Ex. 20:7), and of Joseph it is written: *As Pharaoh lives* (Gen. 42:15). It is written: *Remember the Sabbath day* (Ex. 20:8), and of Joseph it is written: *And kill the beasts and prepare* (Gen. 43:16), which can only mean "preparing" for the Sabbath, as it is said: *And it shall come to pass on the sixth day that they shall prepare* (Ex. 16:5). It is written: *Honor your father* (Ex. 20:12), and of Joseph it is written: *And Israel said unto Joseph: "Do not your brethren feed the flock in Shechem? Come, and I will send you unto them." And he said to him: "Here am I"* (Gen. 37:13)—he knew that his brothers hated him and yet he would not disobey his father's orders. It is written: *You shall not murder* (Ex. 20:13), and Joseph did not murder Potiphar. It is written: *You shall not commit adultery* (ibid.)—he did not commit adultery with Potiphar's wife. It is written: *You shall not steal* (ibid.) —he did not steal, as it is said: *And Joseph gathered up all the money . . . and Joseph brought the money into Pharaoh's house* (Gen. 47:14). It is written: *You shall not bear false witness against your neighbor* (Ex. 20:13), and Joseph never told his father what his brothers had done to him. Now, if he would not tell his father even

---

ᶜ *the Eternal*: Literally, "He who lives for ever."

ᵈ *Am I in the place of God?*: Implies his belief in the One God.

things that were true about his brothers, how much less would he tell against them what was false! It is said: *You shall not covet* (Ex. 20:14)—he did not covet Potiphar's wife. It is written: *You shall not hate your brother in your heart* (Lev. 19:17),[e] and of Joseph it is said: *And he comforted them, and spoke kindly unto them* (Gen. 50:21). It is written: *You shall not take vengeance, nor bear any grudge* (Lev. 19:18), and of Joseph it is written: *And as for you, you meant evil against me; but God meant it for good* (Gen. 50:20). It is written: *That your brother may live with you* (Lev. 25:36), and of Joseph it is written: *And Joseph sustained his father and his brethren* (Gen. 47:12).

For he had straightly sworn the sons of Israel. This means he had made them swear for themselves and also that they would impose the oath upon their children.

[R. Nathan says: Why did he impose the oath upon his brothers rather than upon his sons? He thought, if I impose the oath upon my sons the Egyptians might not let them fulfill it. And if they said to the Egyptians: "Our father has carried his father out," the Egyptians might answer them: "Your father was a king." Therefore he imposed the oath upon his brothers and not upon his sons.] Joseph said to them: "My father came down here of his own free will and yet I took him back. I came down here against my will. I impose an oath upon you that you bring me back to the place from whence you stole me." And they did so, for it is said: *And the bones of Joseph which the children of Israel brought up out of Egypt, buried they in Shechem* (Josh. 24:32).[f]

---

[e] *You shall not hate,* etc.: Up to this point, the preacher has demonstrated that Joseph observed the entire Ten Commandments ("written on what lies in that ark"); now he adds several other commandments that have a special bearing on Joseph's relationship to his brothers (preparatory to the introduction of the brothers—"the sons of Israel"—in the following paragraph).

---

[f] *in Shechem:* The place from which he had been "stolen" (Gen. 37:13ff.).

God will surely remember you (ibid.).[g] He did remember you in Egypt, and He will also remember you at the sea. He did remember you at the sea, and He will also remember you in the wilderness. He did remember you in the wilderness, and He will also remember you at the rivers of Arnon. He did remember you in this world, and He will also remember you in the world to come.

Mekhilta of R. Ishmael, ad. loc.

[g] *will surely remember you:* In the Hebrew, the root *p-q-d* is repeated twice (for emphasis); hence the following interpretation, which assumes two "remembrances," one in the past and one in the future.

THE SOUL OF MAN IS THE LAMP OF THE LORD

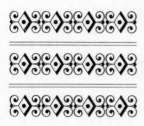

INTRODUCTION

THIS CLASSIC EXAMPLE *of a sermon by the famous Palestinian homilist R. Tanhum bar Abba (fourth century C.E.) has been preserved only in the Babylonian Talmud; it may have undergone slight changes, such as the introduction of some Talmudic terminology (e.g., "there is no difficulty") and the attribution of some constituent expositions to Babylonian teachers (the names of individual sages may not have appeared at all in the original sermon). The framework of the homily, the question asked of R. Tanhum at the beginning to which he replies at the end, leaves no doubt that we have here an actual sermon, though probably in an abbreviated form. A question posed by the audience was frequently the starting point of a sermon; in many cases the preacher replies to such a question immediately and then proceeds to link his answer by a series of expositions to the beginning of the weekly reading from the Torah. In this homily, however—the only one of the type extant—the answer comes at the end of the entire discourse, and the Scriptural reading is not referred to at all (unless we assume that the homily is connected with a reading from the prophets, dealing with one of the incidents concerning David or Solomon).*

The halakhic question, concerning the permissibility of extinguishing a burning lamp on the Sabbath if it will benefit a sick person, is used by the preacher to spin a complex discussion of life and death and their respective values. He quotes three verses, two from Ecclesiastes (ascribed to Solomon) and one from Psalms (ascribed to David), which sharply contradict each other; the entire discourse is devoted to resolving these contradictions. The discussion does not confine itself to the theoretical level but it focuses on dramatic incidents from the lives of David and Solomon. The answers are dialectical: the merit of the dead outweighs that of the living; yet a corpse is of less value than a live dog; only in life can man engage in the study of Torah and observe the Commandments, hence even a short hour of life is precious and irreplaceable. While developing this existential paradox of man's life and death, the preacher also manages incidentally to extol, as the supreme value, the study of Torah—which delivers man from death.

In his opening R. Tanhum startlingly addresses a direct question to Solomon, accusing him of contradicting both himself and David, his father. In the course of developing his exposition, the preacher presents two major, dramatic episodes from the lives of David and Solomon: the story of the entry of the Ark in the days of Solomon and the account of David's death. In both episodes, the two heroes appear in juxtaposition, and they serve, indirectly, the purpose of comparative evaluation (in which, undoubtedly, David emerges the superior figure). Each of the two accounts is highly dramatic; and various links connect them both with each other and with the sermon as a whole. The different elements and ideas introduced one by one gradually converge and prepare us for the conclusion: the living are superior to the dead, for while alive, men can engage in the study of the Torah, but even for the greatest of men, once dead, we must not desecrate the Sabbath—while to save a dog's life the Sabbath can be desecrated. Hence, as long as man is alive, anything should be done to prolong his life, even if only for a short while! At the end, the practical conclusion is spelled out in full through a vivid simile, based on Proverbs 20:27, which takes the place of the formal reason given in other sources for the rule that saving life supersedes the Sabbath. This simile makes its rhetorical point brilliantly—despite the fact that it is logically defective (the problem being not whether a lamp may be allowed to go out but whether it may be extinguished).

Four separate strands are woven together in this sermon: the halakhic question and its reply; the discourse on the relative value of life and death; the narratives from the lives of David and Solomon;

and the attempt to resolve the contradictions in the biblical verses. Employing a variety of rhetorical and literary devices the preacher succeeds in integrating all these different elements—an outstanding example of the sermon as art.

THE SOUL OF MAN IS THE LAMP OF THE LORD

This question was asked before R. Tanhum of Nawe: What about extinguishing a burning lamp for the sake of a sick man on the Sabbath? Thereupon he commenced and said: You, Solomon, where is your wisdom and where is your understanding? It is not enough for you that your words contradict the words of your father David, but they are self-contradictory! Your father David said: [a] *The dead praise not the Lord* (Psalms 115:17); while you said: *Wherefore I praised the dead which are already dead* (Eccles. 4:2), but yet again you said, *For a living dog is better than a dead lion* (ibid., 9:4). Yet there is no difficulty. As to what David said, *The dead praise not the Lord*, this is what he meant: Let a man always engage in Torah and good deeds before he dies, for as soon as he dies he is restrained from the Torah and good deeds, and the Holy One, blessed be He, finds nothing to praise in him. And this is what R. Johanan said, What is meant by the verse, *Among the dead [I am] free* (Psalms 88:6)? Once a man dies he becomes free of the Torah and good deeds. And as to what Solomon said, *Wherefore I praised the dead which are already dead*— When Israel sinned in the wilderness, Moses stood before the Holy One, blessed be He, and spoke many prayers and supplications before Him, but he was not answered. Yet when he exclaimed, *Remember Abraham, Isaac, and Israel, thy servants!* (Ex. 32:13), he was immediately answered. Did not then Solomon well say, *wherefore I praised the dead which are already dead?*

Another interpretation: in worldly affairs, when a king of flesh

---

[a] *Your Father David said:* In the Book of Psalms of which David is supposed to be the author.

and blood issues a decree, it is doubtful whether it will be obeyed or not; and even if you say that it is obeyed, it is obeyed during his lifetime but not after his death. Whereas Moses our Teacher decreed many decrees and enacted numerous enactments, and they endure for ever and unto all eternity. Did then not Solomon well say, *wherefore I praised the dead*, etc.?

Another interpretation: *wherefore I praised*, etc., is in accordance with Rav Judah's dictum in Rav's name, viz.: What is meant by, *Show me a token for good that they which hate me may see it, and be ashamed* (Psalms 86:17)? David prayed before the Holy One, blessed be He, "Sovereign of the Universe! Forgive me for that sin!" [b] "It is forgiven," replied He. "Show me a token in my lifetime," he entreated. "In your lifetime I will not make it known, but I will make it known in the lifetime of your son Solomon." For when Solomon built the Temple, he wanted to take the Ark into the Holy of Holies, whereupon the gates stuck to each other. Solomon uttered twenty-four prayers, yet he was not answered. Then he opened [his mouth] and exclaimed, *Lift up your heads, O you gates, and be you lifted up, you everlasting doors, that the King of glory may come in* (Psalms 24:7). They rushed upon him to swallow him [c] up, crying, *Who is the King of glory?* He answered: *The Lord, strong and mighty* (ibid., 8). Then he repeated, *Lift up your heads, O you gates; lift them up, you everlasting doors that the King of glory may come in. Who then is the King of glory? The Lord of hosts, He is the King of glory, Selah* (ibid., 9ff.); yet he was not answered. But as soon as he prayed, *O Lord God, turn not away the face of Thine anointed; remember the good deeds of David Thy servant* (II Chron. 6:42), he was immediately answered. In that hour the faces of all David's enemies turned black like the bottom of a pot, and all Israel knew that the Holy One, blessed be He, had forgiven him that sin. Did then not Solomon well say, *wherefore I praised the dead which are already dead?* And thus it is written, *On*

[b] *For that sin:* The sin he committed with Bathsheba.

[c] *They rushed upon him to swallow him:* They believed that by "King of glory" he was referring to himself.

*the eighth day he sent the people away, and they blessed the king,
and went unto their tents joyful and glad of heart for all the goodness
that the Lord had shown unto David his servant, and to Israel his
people* (I Kings 8:66). *And they went unto their tents* means that
they found their wives clean; *joyful,* because they had enjoyed the
luster of the Divine Presence; *and glad of heart,* because their wives
conceived and each one bore a male child; *for all the goodness that
the Lord had shown unto David his servant,* that He had forgiven him
that sin; *and to Israel his people,* for He had forgiven them the sin
of the Day of Atonement.[d]

And as to what Solomon said, *for a living dog is better than a
dead lion*—that is as Rav Judah said in Rav's name, viz.: what is
meant by the verse, *Lord, make me to know mine end, and the
measure of my days, what it is; let me know how short-lived I am*
(Psalms 39:5)? David said before the Holy One, blessed be He,
"Sovereign of the Universe! *Lord, make me to know mine end.*" "It
is a decree before Me," He replied, "that the end of a mortal is not
made known." "*And the measure of my days what it is*"—"it is a
decree before Me that a person's span [of life] is not made known."
Let me know how short-lived I am. He said to him: "You will die on
the Sabbath." "Let me die on the first day of the week!"[e] "The reign
of your son Solomon shall already have become due, and one reign
may not overlap another even by a hairbreadth." "Then let me die on
the eve of the Sabbath!" He said, "*For a day in your courts is better
than a thousand* (Psalms 84:11): better the one day that you sit and
engage in study than the thousand burnt-offerings which your son

---

[d] *the sin of the Day of Atonement:* On the occasion of the dedica-
tion of the Temple, a feast was held for fourteen days in the seventh
month (I Kings 8:2, 65), which, if it is assumed to have started on
the first of the month, must have included the Day of Atonement,
which then would not have been observed that year as a fast (cf., Bab.
Moed Katan 9a).

---

[e] *on the first day of the week:* On the Sabbath, the dead can
neither be attended to nor buried; see below.

Solomon is destined to sacrifice before Me on the altar." Every Sabbath day he would sit and study all day. On the day that his soul was to be at rest, the angel of death stood before him but could not prevail against him, because Torah did not cease from his mouth. "What shall I do to him?" asked he. Now there was a garden before his house; so the angel of death went, ascended, and rustled in the trees. David went out to see; as he was ascending the stairs, they broke under him. Thereupon he became silent and his soul had repose. Then Solomon sent to the house of study: "My father is dead and lying in the sun; and the dogs of my father's house are hungry; [f] what shall I do?" They sent back: "Cut up a carcass [g] and place it before the dogs, and as for your father, put a loaf of bread or a child upon him [h] and carry him away." Did then not Solomon well say, *for a living dog is better than a dead lion?*

And as for the question which I asked before you [i]—a lamp is called a lamp, and the soul of man is called a lamp: [j] better that the lamp of flesh and blood be extinguished than the lamp of the Holy One, blessed be He.

Bab. Shabbath 30a–b

[f] *the dogs . . . are hungry:* They may therefore devour the corpse.

[g] *cut up a carcass:* Ordinarily not permitted on the Sabbath.

[h] *put a loaf . . . upon him:* Only in this fashion—for the sake of the loaf of bread, as it were—may a corpse be moved on the Sabbath.

[i] *which I asked before you:* Actually—Which you asked before me. According to Rashi (ad loc.), this circumlocution is an expression of humility on the part of R. Tanhum.

[j] *the soul of man is called a lamp:* As it is said, "The soul of man is the lamp of the Lord" (Prov. 20:27); this proof text has, apparently, been omitted through a scribal error.

SIN AND ATONEMENT

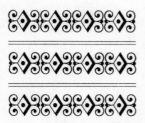

INTRODUCTION

THIS HOMILY *follows the pattern, characteristic of the* Tanhuma-Yelammedenu *Midrashim, of beginning with a question addressed to the preacher. The sermon opens with the reply to the question, and then the preacher proceeds with a variety of aggadic expositions until he arrives at the opening verse of the weekly Torah reading, with which he concludes. In our case, it would have been possible to make a direct connection between the halakhah concerning fast days proclaimed for the sake of rain and the text of Genesis 19:24, "Then the Lord caused to rain," by the association of ideas (though in the Hebrew two different words for rain are used); but the preacher, while probably assuming that this association would be taken note of by his audience, does not develop it. Instead he embarks on a less direct course: fast days are devoted to prayer and repentance, the purpose of which is to avert the threat of disaster (e.g., drought); and Abraham's prayer for Sodom would also have prevented the punishment decreed, if the people of Sodom had only repented. This complex of ideas the homilist illustrates first by the story of the golden calf, in which all the elements mentioned are present: sin, fasting, repentance, atonement. But, since the people of Sodom persisted in their wickedness, the preacher continues: "See how beautiful is repentance . . . but if the Holy One, blessed be He, warns him the first, the second, and the third time and he does not repent, He calls him to account . . .", and then enlarges upon Abraham's prayer for Sodom, which, although powerful, could not prevent retribution from coming.*

SIN AND ATONEMENT

Let our teacher teach us: When a law court has decreed a fast for the community [to pray] for rain to come,[a] and it came that same day, do they have to complete the fast? Our rabbis taught: If they fasted and the rain came before sunrise, they do not complete the fast; if after sunrise, they are to complete it, thus R. Meir. While R. Judah says: If before midday, they do not complete it; if after midday, they are to complete it. Whence do the later generations derive their Scriptural authority for fasting on Monday and Thursday? When Israel committed that deed,[b] Moses ascended on Thursday and descended on Monday; whence do we know this?

R. Levi said: He ascended on Thursday, and from Thursday to Thursday and to Thursday makes fifteen days, and from Friday to Friday and to Friday makes thirty days, and from Sabbath to Sabbath is eight, this makes thirty-eight days, and Sunday and Monday make forty. This is why the Sages decreed that they are to fast on Monday and Thursday, the days of Moses' ascent and descent. At the end of forty days they fasted and cried as did Moses. The Holy One, blessed be He, was filled with compassion for them and made this day into a day of atonement for their sins; this is the Day of Atone-

---

[a] *for rain to come:* If any calamity befell the community—especially drought—fast days were decreed. When a series of such fasts is decreed, they are held on consecutive Mondays and Thursdays.

---

[b] *committed that deed:* Made the golden calf.

ment of which we read: *For on this day shall atonement be made for you* (Lev. 16:30). See how beautiful is repentance, said the Holy One, blessed be He: *Return unto Me, and I will return unto you* (Mal. 3:7); for if a man has committed many sins and he returns to the Holy One, blessed be He, He considers him as though he had not sinned, for it is written: *None of his transgressions that he has committed shall be remembered against him; for his righteousness that he has done he shall live* (Ezek. 18:22). And if the Holy One, blessed be He, warns him the first, second, and third time and he does not repent, He calls him to account, for we read: *Lo, all these things does God work, twice, yea thrice, with a man* (Job 33:29); when He derives no pleasure from him, He immediately calls him to account. This is proved by the following case: When the Holy One, blessed be He, wanted to overthrow Sodom and its sister towns and Abraham begged mercy for them, thinking that perhaps there was hope for them, it is written: *And Abraham drew near, and said: Wilt Thou indeed sweep away the righteous with the wicked?* (Gen. 18:23). What does "and he drew near" mean?

R. Joshua says, "and he drew near" is an expression meaning battle, as it is written: *So Joab and the people that were with him drew near unto the battle* (II Sam. 10:13).

R. Nehemiah says, "and he drew near" is nothing but an expression for prayer, for it is written: *And it came to pass at the time of the offering of the evening offering, that Elijah the prophet came near* (I Kings 18:36); and the Sages say, "And he drew near" is nothing but an expression for entreaty, for we read: *Then Judah came near unto him* (Gen. 44:18). Abraham said to the Holy One, blessed be He, *Wilt Thou indeed sweep away the righteous with the wicked?*, and he begged mercy for them until he had gone down from fifty to ten and when he found no merit for them, the Divine Presence withdrew from him, for we read: *And the Lord went His way, as soon as He had left off speaking to Abraham* (Gen. 18:33). And right away retribution came upon them. Whence do we know this? From what we have read in the lesson of the day: *Then the Lord caused to rain upon Sodom . . .* (Gen. 19:24).

Tanhuma, S. Buber, editor, Va-yera 16

THE SECRET OF THE LORD

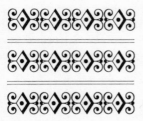

INTRODUCTION

THIS IS ANOTHER *example of a sermon that opens with a halakhic question addressed to the preacher; but in this one no immediate link suggests itself between the question and the beginning of the Torah lesson of the day. The preacher develops an instructive discourse, but it does not appear to lead him any nearer to the required transition to Genesis 18:17. His major theme is the prohibition against writing down the oral Torah (which also includes the Targum, the translation of the Scriptural readings into Aramaic). The reason he finds, unexpectedly, is the fact that this Torah is the mystery and secret of God, revealed only to His chosen people; the written Torah, on the other hand, especially in its Greek translation, has been appropriated as well by other nations and religions, who proclaim, on the strength of it: "We are Israel." The preacher here is undoubtedly voicing a polemic against Pauline Christianity, with its claim that the Church represents "Israel according to the spirit," having inherited the position of chosenness formerly held by the Jews (Romans 2:28–29; 4:1ff; Galatians 3:26–29). This claim, he implies, is discredited by the fact that the Gentiles, and the Christians among them, are ignorant of the oral Torah—God's true mystery.*

This discourse has brought us no closer to the lesson of the day: "Shall I hide from Abraham that which I am doing?" To reach his goal, the homilist needs a connecting link, which he finds in Psalms 25:14: "The secret of the Lord is with them that fear Him." This verse forms the conclusion of the first section, where it serves as a proof text that God has revealed His true mystery to none but Israel; and at the same time it provides the transition to the Scriptural account of God's prior revelation to Abraham of His intention to destroy Sodom.

THE SECRET OF THE LORD

Let our teacher teach us: May the person who translates for the reader of the Torah ^a look at the written text? Our rabbis taught: The translator is forbidden to look at the text,^b and the reader is forbidden to direct his eyes anywhere except at the Torah, for the Torah was given in writing, as we read: *And I will write upon the tables* (Ex. 34:1), but the person who translates in public is forbidden to look at the Torah. R. Judah ben Pazzi said: It is stated explicitly, *Write these words* (ibid.: 27); this refers to the Bible which was given in writing. *For after the tenor [lit., "by the mouth"] of these words* (ibid.), this refers to the translation which has been ordained to be made by word of mouth. R. Judah bar Simon said: *I have made a covenant with you and with Israel* (ibid.), through writing and by word of mouth *I have made a covenant with you;* and if you exchange the oral

---

^a *translates for the reader of the Torah:* At the time of the public reading from the Torah (and the prophets) the text had to be rendered also into Aramaic, the common language of the people. The reader and the translator were two different persons; the translation was not written down, but rendered by heart.

---

^b *forbidden to look at the text:* To make it clear that the Aramaic translation is not inscribed in the Torah scroll.

for the written and the written for the oral, I have not made a covenant with you. R. Judah Halevi, the son of R. Shalom, said: Moses requested that the Mishnah be written down too, but the Holy One, blessed be He, foresaw that in days to come the nations of the world would translate the Torah and read it in Greek and would say: "We are Israel." Therefore the Holy One, blessed be He, told Moses: *I shall write for him many things of My law* (Hos. 8:12), therefore *they shall be accounted as a stranger's* (ibid.). Why is that so? Because the Mishnah is God's own secret and He reveals His secret only to the righteous, as we read: *The secret of the Lord is with them that fear Him* (Psalms 25:14). And so one finds even at the time when the Holy One, blessed be He, was angry with Sodom on account of their wicked deeds and the Holy One, blessed be He, desired to overthrow Sodom, He did not seal their verdict until He had consulted with Abraham. Whence do we know this? From what we have read in the lesson of the day: *Shall I hide from Abraham that which I am doing?* (Gen. 18:17).

Tanhuma, S. Buber, editor, Va-yera 6

ABRAHAM AND SARAH IN EGYPT

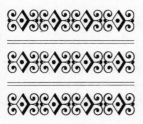

INTRODUCTION

THIS HOMILY *is an example of a sermon pattern which opens (after quoting the first verse or verses of the weekly portion) with words of praise and thanksgiving to God for His lovingkindness toward Israel or the righteous, or for His gift of the Torah and the Commandments. Usually, the preacher focuses attention on his main theme in this opening formula.*

A striking feature of this particular homily is the attempt it makes at retelling the biblical story in an edited version. In fact, most of it is simply a paraphrase of the biblical account, enriched and made more dramatic through the addition of dialogue (e.g., between Abraham and the customs officers, between Sarah and God, etc.); the dramatic impact is also strengthened through having Sarah participate actively in the punishment of Pharaoh. But of greater consequence for the changed character of the story are the additions, omissions, and subtle comments of the homilist, all aimed at making an otherwise dubious narrative more palatable to the audience. Why, if he is aware of the grave danger threatening Sarah in Egypt because of her beauty, does Abraham do nothing to prevent it? Is it conceivable that Abraham could instruct Sarah to tell a lie, in order "that it may be well with me for your sake, and that my soul may live because of you?" How can he abandon Sarah to her fate and even accept gifts as she is taken in to Pharaoh's house (Gen. 12:16: "And he dealt well with Abram for her sake; and he had sheep and oxen . . .")? Moreover, would not both Abraham and Sarah have prayed to God in their distress? And, finally, while we are told that the Lord plagued Pharaoh and his house (ibid.: 17), the Bible does not say explicitly that these plagues prevented Sarah from being dishonored.

All these questions and doubts are removed, in one way or another, in the preacher's retelling of the story. The objectionable lie is deleted; so is the verse referring to Abraham's reward. Both Abraham and Sarah are depicted praying to God fervently in their misfortune. Abraham cannot have foreseen the danger for he is unaware of Sarah's beauty until he sees her reflection in the river while they are entering Egypt. In consequence, he makes desperate efforts to hide her from the Egyptians; far from seeking to acquire riches, he is prepared to pay exorbitant customs fees to prevent the officers from opening the chest in which Sarah is concealed. We are no longer left in the dark as to Sarah's fate: God answers her prayer and proclaims: By your life, no evil shall touch you and your husband. Moreover, the angel prevents Pharaoh from even taking off her shoe or touching her clothing. And not only does the narrative in its new form remove all objections and qualms, but it gains considerably in dramatic force and in the capacity to entertain.

The story as retold in our homily has striking similarities with an ancient "midrash" on the same subject in the Genesis Apocryphon [1] *found among the Dead Sea Scrolls. There, too, we find omissions of objectionable details as well as additions and elaborations (including an almost lyrical description of Sarah's beauty); and, most striking of all, in the Genesis Apocryphon as in our homily, Abraham and Sarah are compared with the cedar and the palm tree—undoubtedly on the basis of Psalms 92:13, quoted at the conclusion of our homily. (The sentences enclosed in square brackets represent material that appears to have been added to the original sermon.)*

ABRAHAM AND SARAH IN EGYPT

And there was a famine in the land (Gen. 12:10). Before this it is stated: *Now the Lord said unto Abram* (ibid.: 1). Blessed be the name of the King of Kings, the Holy One, blessed be He, who desired to test this righteous man in order to make his good deeds known to the world. Immediately, a famine came upon the world which overtook the Land of Israel. Abraham told his wife Sarah: "There is famine in the country." [Our Sages said there had never been such a famine in the world.] He told her: "It is good to dwell in Egypt, let us go there because it is amply supplied with bread and meat." The two of them went forthwith.

When they reached the gate of Egypt and stood by the Nile, our father Abraham saw Sarah's reflection in that river like the rising sun. [From this our Sages taught that compared with Sarah, all women are as a monkey compared with humans.] He said to her: *Behold, now I know that you are a fair woman to look upon.* (ibid.: 11). [From this you learn that until then he had not known her in the way men know women.] He said: "Egypt is steeped in lechery, as it is written: *Whose flesh is as the flesh of asses, and whose issue is like the issue of horses* (Ezek. 23:20); so I shall put you inside a chest and lock you in because I am afraid for myself, *and it will come to pass, when the Egyptians shall see you, that they will say: This is his wife; and they will kill me, but you they will keep alive* (Gen. 12:12)." Having done so, he proceeded to cross; the customs officers gathered 'round and asked him: "What are you carrying in that chest?" He answered: "Barley." They said: "No, it is wheat." He replied: "Charge the duty on wheat." Said they: "It is pepper." He said: "Charge the duty on pepper." They said: "But it is minted gold." Thus pressing upon him, they opened the chest and saw her bright as the shining sun. They told him: "This is no woman for a commoner," *And the princes of Pharaoh saw her, and praised her to Pharaoh* (ibid.: 15). When Abraham saw this he began to weep and pray to God, saying: "Lord of the universe, is this then the reward for the trust which I have put in Thee? And now act for the sake of Thy compassion and Thy mercy and do not put my trust

to shame." And also Sarah cried out and said: "Lord of the universe,
I did not know anything, but because he told me that Thou said unto
him, 'Get out of your country,' I had trust in Thy words and now I
remain all alone, without my father, my mother, and my husband.
Shall that wicked one come and have his will of me? Act for the
sake of Thy great name and for the sake of my trust in Thy words."
The Holy One, blessed be He, answered her: "By your life, no evil
shall touch you or your husband." This is what is written: *There shall
no mischief befall the righteous; but the wicked are filled with evil*
(Prov. 12:21), and I shall make an example of Pharaoh and his house
as it is written: *And the Lord plagued Pharaoh and his house with
great plagues because of* [lit., "upon the word of"] *Sarai Abram's wife*
(Gen. 12:17). What is the meaning of "upon the word of Sarai"?
At that instant an angel descended from heaven, a rod in his hand,
and as Pharaoh was about to take off her shoe, he struck him upon
his hand. When he was about to touch her clothing, he struck him.
The angel took counsel with Sarah with regard to every single stroke.
How do we know? Because it is written: "Upon the word of Sarai"; it
does not say "on account of Sarai," and not "concerning," and not
"for the sake of," and not "because of Sarai," but "upon the word
of Sarai." When Sarah told the angel to strike Pharaoh, he struck him
and when she told him to wait a little, he did so. Also the prefects
and the ministers and all the members of his household were struck
at the same time as he, for we read: *And the Lord plagued Pharaoh
and his house with great plagues*, greater than any plagues which had
ever come upon or will ever come upon human beings. The words,
"and his house," are meant to include the slaves, walls, pillars, vessels,
and everything else so as to fulfill that which is written: *There shall no
mischief befall the righteous; but the wicked are filled with evil*. But
of Abraham it is said: *The righteous shall flourish like the palm tree;
he shall grow like a cedar in Lebanon* (Psalms 92:13).

Tanhuma, Lekh Lekha 5

GOD AND THE NATIONS

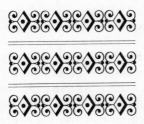

INTRODUCTION

THIS HOMILY, *which, though ascribed to various authors, is undoubt-edly a product of third-century Palestine, has been preserved only in the Babylonian Talmud (where various comments, omitted here, have been added to it). It does not follow any of the conventional formal patterns which we have met so far. Without preliminaries, it begins with a dramatic account of God's dealings with the nations of the world in time to come: a kind of eschatological fantasy, popular and humorous, or satirical, in style. The entire homily is based on Isaiah 43:9: "All the nations are gathered together, and the peoples are as-sembled; who among them can declare this, and announce to us former things? Let them bring their witnesses, that they may be justified; and let them hear, and say, 'It is truth.'" The constituent parts and phrases of this verse are expounded one by one. The entire exposition has been turned into a continuous narrative, uninterrupted by sayings or interpretations quoted in the names of individual au-thors.*

The dramatic effect is increased by dialogue and disputation, in which each clever or impertinent argument of the "nations" is refuted by a crushing reply. The whole is effectively structured: three argu-ments are presented by Rome and a corresponding three by Persia; in each case, God replies to the first two arguments, "All that you have done, you have done only to satisfy your own desires," while to the third His reply is different and unexpected. To Rome: "As to silver and gold—they are Mine"; to Persia: "As to waging war—I am the Lord of battles." There is a close analogy between the arguments proffered by Rome and Persia respectively and between the respective replies; while not identical, they follow the same threefold pattern and create the same rhythm: "We have established many market-places / we have erected many baths / we have accumulated much gold and silver," followed by the threefold reply: "You have established marketplaces—to place courtesans therein / you have erected baths—to revel in them / as to silver and gold—they are Mine"! Of course, the preacher does not hesitate to put biblical verses into the mouths of the contending nations, and the effect is further enhanced by rhetorical questions ("he who has not troubled on the eve of the Sabbath, what shall he eat on the Sabbath?") and recurring phrases ("They will then depart crushed in spirit").

From its conclusion, the sermon appears to have been preached on the Feast of Tabernacles. The idea that the nations might save themselves by observing the commandment of the Tabernacle would seem to be derived from Zechariah 14:16ff.; in its original form the homily probably quoted this passage. Isaiah 43:9, which is quoted throughout, is not connected with Tabernacles in present-day liturgy. However, it may very well have been part of the reading from the Prophets for one of the days of the Festival when the sermon was preached, since it does allude to the Exodus and to Israel's wanderings in the desert (e.g., verse 16: "Thus says the Lord, who makes a way in the sea, and a path in the mighty waters"; verse 19: ". . . I will even make a way in the wilderness, and rivers in the desert"; verse 20: ". . . Because I give waters in the wilderness, and rivers in the desert, to give to drink to My people . . ."); this is the more likely because of the strong associations of Tabernacles with water, rain, and prayers for rain (e.g., Mishnah Rosh Ha-shanah I, 2; Sukkah chapter V).

Moreover the preacher found in the Isaiah passage some "confirmation" for the idea which he develops of the nations being unable to bear living in the tabernacles in the blazing sun, while of Israel it is said: "When you walk through the fire, you shall not be burned, neither shall the flame kindle upon you (Isa. 43:2)."

GOD AND THE NATIONS

R. Hanina bar Papa—some say R. Simlai—preached: In times to come, the Holy One, blessed be He, will take a scroll of the Law in His embrace and proclaim: "Let him who has occupied himself herewith, come and take his reward." Thereupon all the nations will crowd together in confusion, as it is said: *All the nations are gathered together* (Isa. 43:9). The Holy One, blessed be He, will then say to them: "Come not before Me in confusion, but let each nation come in with its scribes"; as it is said: *and let the peoples be gathered together.* Thereupon the kingdom of Edom [a] will enter first before Him. The Holy One, blessed be He, will then say to them: "Wherewith have you occupied yourselves?" They will reply: "O Lord of the universe, we have established many marketplaces, we have erected many baths, we have accumulated much gold and silver, and all this we did only for the sake of Israel, that they might have leisure for occupying themselves with the study of the Torah." The Holy One, blessed be He, will say in reply: "You foolish ones among peoples, all that you have done, you have done only to satisfy your own desires. You have established marketplaces to place courtesans therein. You have erected baths, to revel in them; as to silver and gold, they are Mine, as it is written: *Mine is the silver and Mine is the gold, says the Lord of Hosts* (Haggai 2:8). Who among you who have been declaring this? As it is written: *Who among them can declare this?* And 'this' is nought else than the Torah, as it is said: *And this is the Torah which Moses set before the Children of Israel* (Deut. 4:44)." They will then depart crushed in spirit.

On the departure of the kingdom of Rome, Persia will step forth. The Holy One, blessed be He, will ask of them: "Wherewith have you occupied yourselves?"; and they will reply: "Sovereign of the Universe, we have built many bridges, we have captured many cities, we have waged many wars, and all this for the sake of Israel, that they might

---

[a] *Edom* is the symbol of the Roman empire.

engage in the study of the Torah." Then the Holy One, blessed be He, will say to them: "You foolish ones among peoples, all that you have done, you have done only to satisfy your own desires. You have built bridges in order to extract toll, you have subdued cities to impose forced labor; as to waging war, I am the Lord of battles, as it is said: *The Lord is a man of war* (Ex. 15:3). Are there any among you who have been declaring this? and 'this' means nought else than the Torah, as it is said: *And this is the Torah which Moses set before the Children of Israel.*" They, too, will then depart crushed in spirit.

And so will every nation fare in turn. The nations will then contend: "Lord of the Universe, did we accept the Torah and fail to observe it?" [b] Thereupon, the Holy One, blessed be He, will say to them: "Let us then consider the happenings of old, as it is said: *Let them announce to us former things* (Isa. 43:9). There are seven commandments [c] which you did accept, did you observe them?"

The nations will then say, "Sovereign of the Universe, has Israel, who accepted the Torah, observed it?" The Holy One, blessed be He, will reply, "I can give evidence that they observed the Torah." "O Lord of the Universe," they will argue, "can a father give evidence in favor of his son? For it is written: *Israel is My son, My firstborn* (Ex. 4:22)." Then will the Holy One, blessed be He, say: "Heaven and Earth can bear witness that Israel has fulfilled the entire Torah." But they will

---

[b] *did we accept the Torah and fail to observe it*: According to MS 44830 of the Jewish Theological Seminary of New York. In the Talmud there follows a series of further arguments and their refutation; these, however, are not part of the original sermon (which is obvious from their being presented in Aramaic, not in Hebrew) and have been omitted (together with other additions to, and embellishments of, the original homily).

---

[c] *seven commandments*: According to Rabbinic tradition, seven commandments were given to Noah (Gen. 9:1–7) and accepted by him on behalf of all his descendants.

object, saying: "Lord of the Universe, Heaven and Earth are partial witnesses, for it is said: *If not for My covenant* [d] *with day and with night, I should not have appointed the ordinances of Heaven and Earth* (Jer. 33:25)." Then the Holy One, blessed be He, will say: "Some of you yourselves shall testify that Israel observed the entire Torah. Let Nimrod come and testify that Abraham did not [consent to] worship idols; let Laban come and testify that Jacob could not be suspected of theft; let Potiphar's wife testify that Joseph was above suspicion of immorality; let Nebuchadnezzar come and testify that Hananiah, Mishael, and Azariah, did not bow down to an image; let Darius come and testify that Daniel never neglected the [statutory] prayers; [e] let Bildad the Shuhite, and Zophar the Naamathite, and Eliphaz the Temanite [and Elihu the son of Barachel the Buzite] testify that Israel has observed the whole Torah, as it is said: *Let them* [*the nations*] *bring their* [*own*] *witnesses, that they* [*Israel*] *may be justified* (Isa. 43:9)."

The nations will then plead, "Offer us the Torah anew and we shall obey it." But the Holy One, blessed be He, will say to them, "You foolish ones among peoples, he who took trouble [to prepare] on the eve of the Sabbath can eat on the Sabbath, but he who has not troubled on the eve of the Sabbath, what shall he eat on the Sabbath? Nevertheless, I have an easy command which is called Sukkah, [f] go and carry it out." Straightway will every one of them betake himself and go and make a booth on the top of his roof; but the Holy One,

---

[d] *if not for My covenant:* The verse is taken to mean, that were it not for the Torah and its acceptance by Israel, Heaven and Earth could not exist.

---

[e] *the [statutory] prayers:* Cf., Daniel 6:11.

---

[f] *Sukkah:* Booth, tabernacle.

blessed be He, will cause the sun to blaze forth over them as at the summer solstice,[g] and every one of them will trample down his booth and go away, as it is said: *Let us break their bands asunder and cast away their cords from us* (Psalms 2:3). Thereupon the Holy One, blessed be He, will laugh at them, as it is said: *He that sits in heaven laughs* (ibid.: 4).

Bab. Avodah Zarah 2b–3a

[g] *summer solstice:* The Feast of Tabernacles is celebrated in autumn.

THE POOR MAN'S SACRIFICE

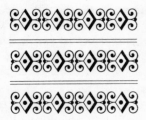

This chapter *from* Leviticus Rabba, *and the following section from* Deuteronomy Rabba, *are examples of the "literary" homily. Such homilies, in fact, were not delivered as live sermons before an audience, but were the creations of authors or editors of literary works. Undoubtedly these editors made use of traditional materials which had first served as sermons or parts of sermons; however, they did not limit themselves to a particular sermon but collated and combined many different parts in composing their own, more extensive, homilies. In order to appreciate the aims and methods of composition, one must look upon each chapter as one unit and analyze its structure as a whole, even though it is made up of a considerable number of smaller parts. The art and skill of the author of the Midrash will emerge fully only when one considers the arrangement of material in, and the inner structure of, each homily as a self-contained entity. The homily is concerned with the opening verse(s) of Leviticus 2 which formed the beginning of one of the weekly pericopes in the "Triennial Cycle." The chapter lays down details of the meal-offering which, as compared with animal sacrifices, is inexpensive and is therefore considered the typical "poor man's sacrifice." The entire homily concentrates on this aspect of the matter.*

The first proem (§1) elucidates Ecclesiastes 4:6 in a variety of ways, interpreting it in its concluding section—the one relevant to the entire homily: "Better a handful of quietness," that is a handful of flour of the meal-offering of a poor man, "than two handfuls of labor and striving after the wind," that is the incense of spices of the congregation, . . . (on the basis of two plays on words: nahat and minhah; ruah and reah, i.e., "a sweet savor").

The second proem (§2) which opens with Psalms 22:24, utilizes effectively the element of surprise—the words "You that fear the Lord, praise Him, . . ." do not provide any link with the meal-offering. Only when, toward the end of the proem, the preacher proceeds to quote the verse following: "For he has not despised or abhorred the affliction of the lowly," does the connection become apparent: "Even as he despises not his prayer, he despises not his offering."

The third proem (§3) emphasizes that God "pardons abundantly" (Isa. 55:7); hence, He provided us with an additional, inexpensive, means of obtaining forgiveness—the tenth of an ephah of flour that makes up the meal-offering.

The body of the sermon (§4–5) begins in this case (though this is by no means the pattern of all "literary" homilies), with the question, "what is written prior to this matter?" It refers the reader to the latter part of Chapter 1 of Leviticus, dealing with the burnt-offering of a fowl which, being comparatively cheap, may also be considered a poor man's sacrifice. This provides a transition to the charming folktale about King Agrippa, followed by two more stories about poor people and their sacrifices, the last about a woman who brings a handful of fine flour and is insulted by the priest.

So far, all the various items elaborate upon one general theme: the poor man's offering is by no means inferior to the sumptuous sacrifices of the rich, but is, on the contrary, even more precious in the eyes of God; for the poor man, no matter how little he can offer, is regarded "as if he had sacrificed his own life." The homilist does not develop the subject of the Biblical chapter—namely, the meal-offering and its detailed regulations—but emphasizes his own particular conception of this offering. The motif of God's regard for the sacrifice of the poor is illustrated by the story of the poor man's turtledoves, offered up in spite of the king's injunction; but because this story concerns an offering of fowls, not of flour, the homilist has to lead up to it by expositions referring to "what is written prior to this matter." However, the last tale—the meal-offering of the *poor woman—completing the section, brings one back to the actual subject of the homily.*

At first sight, §6 would seem to digress from the main theme, being connected with the Bible text only by a slender link—an exposition of Leviticus 2:3: "That which is left of the meal-offering shall be Aaron's and his sons." But this section complements, by way of contrast, the story told at the end of the preceding section. The tale of the grievance of a poor woman insulted by haughty priests has its counterpart in the story of the man who brings his meal-offering from a faraway country: "When he saw that the priest took off a handful and ate the rest, he said, 'woe unto me. All this trouble I have gone to was but for the benefit of this man!'"—an unjustified complaint, for Scripture states explicitly: "He shall take thereout his handful of the fine flour to offer up," and not "all the fine flour." And, indeed, those present pacify the aggrieved pilgrim: if the priest has the right to enjoy the meal-offering in return for the little trouble he has taken in offering up some of it, how much more so will you, who have come such a long way, receive great reward for your trouble! Here we come to a turning point in the homily. The tales which illustrate the contempt felt by the aristocracy and especially by the priests for the meager sacrifices offered by the poor are counterbalanced by a hymn of praise to the ideal priest. The priest who is without a share in the land and takes his portion from the hand of God is truly himself the poorest of the poor and yet he devotes himself wholeheartedly to the service of God; hence he is worthy of the praise bestowed upon him by the prophet Malachi: "For the priest's lips should keep knowledge, and they should seek the law at his mouth; for he is the messenger [or: angel] of the Lord of Hosts."

It is not merely because of its outward connection with Leviticus 2:3, then, that the author introduces the material contained in the concluding section; he successfully integrates it into the structure of the homily as a whole and, indeed, uses it in fashioning its climax.

❧

THE POOR MAN'S SACRIFICE

§1   R. Isaac opened his discourse: *Better a handful of quietness than both the hands full of labor, and it is the desire of the spirit* (Eccles. 4:6).[a] Better he who studies two orders [of the Mishnah] and is conversant with them, than he who learns *halakhot* [b] and is not conversant with them, but *it is the desire of the spirit,* namely, it is his ambition to be acclaimed an adept at *halakhah.* Better is he who studies *halakhot* and is conversant with them than he who studies legal decisions and hermeneutics and is not conversant with them but, *it is the desire of the spirit:* namely, it is his ambition to be acclaimed an adept at hermeneutics. Better is he who studies *halakhot* and hermeneutics, and is conversant with them, than he who studies *halakhot* and hermeneutics and Talmud, and is not conversant with them, but *it is the desire of the spirit:* namely, it is his ambition to be acclaimed adept at the Law. Better is he who has ten gold pieces of his own, and engages in business and earns a livelihood with them, than he who goes and borrows on interest; (as the saying goes: "He who borrows on interest loses that which is his, and also that which is not his"), which is but *the desire of the spirit:* it is his ambition to be acclaimed a businessman. Better is he who goes and works and gives charity of that which is his own, than he who goes and robs or takes by violence and gives charity of what belongs to others (as the saying goes: "She whores for apples, and distributes them among the sick"), which is but *the desire of the spirit*—it is his ambition to be acclaimed a charitable

---

[a] *it is the desire of the spirit:* A possible rendering of the phrase usually translated as "striving after wind."

---

[b] *Mishnah . . . halakhot:* The various clauses refer to progressive degrees of scholarship.

man. Better is he who has one garden and fertilizes it and hoes it and earns his livelihood out of it, than he who takes gardens from others on terms of half-profits. (As the saying goes: "One who rents one garden eats birds; one who rents many gardens, the birds eat him"), which is but *the desire of the spirit*—it is his ambition to be acclaimed a landowner.

R. Berekhiah said: Better one footstep trodden by the Holy One, blessed be He, in Egypt, as it is said, *For I will go through the land of Egypt in that night* (Ex. 12:12), than both the hands full of soot thrown by Moses and Aaron (Ex. 9:8 ff.), for through the former there was redemption, but through the latter there was no redemption.

R. Hiyya bar Abba said: *Better is a handful of quietness* means the Sabbath; *than both the hands full of labor* refers to the six workdays; but there is *the desire of the spirit*; it is one's desire to do his work in these six days. You have proof that this is so, in that Israel is to be redeemed only by the merit of the Sabbath, as it is said, *Through rest and quietness shall you be saved* (Isa. 30:15).ᶜ

R. Jacob b. Kurshai said: *Better is a handful of quietness*; that is the world to come. *Than both hands full of labor*; that is this world. But *it is the desire of the spirit*; it is the desire of the wicked to do their wicked deeds in this world, in retribution for which penalty is exacted from them in the world to come. Even as we have learned: Better is one hour of repentance and good deeds in this world than the whole life of the world to come; and better is one hour of the even-tempered spirit of the world to come than all the life of this world (Mishnah Avot IV, 17).

R. Isaac explained the verse as referring to the tribe of Reuven and to the tribe of Gad. When these entered the land, and saw how much sowing capacity and planting capacity was there, they said,

---

ᶜ *Through rest and quietness etc: Shuvah* ["rest"] in Isaiah is taken as a reference to the Sabbath, the name for which, in Palestinian Aramaic, it resembles in sound.

"Better is a handful of satisfaction in this land, than both hands full of trouble on the other side of the Jordan." In the end they said: "Have we not ourselves chosen it for ourselves?" [d] For so it is written, *Let this land be given unto your servants for a possession* (Num. 32:5). This is meant by *The desire of the spirit;*—it was their own wish.

Another interpretation: *Better is a handful of quietness* [nahat] that is a handful of the flour of the freewill meal-offering [minhah] of a poor man, *than two hands full of labor, and striving after the wind,* that is, the finely ground incense of spices of the congregation, since the latter carries with it expiation,[e] while the former does not carry expiation. And which is this [meal-offering of the poor]? The tenth part of an ephah, as it is said *And when one brings a meal-offering,* etc. (Lev. 2:1).

§2 *You that fear the Lord, praise Him; All you the seed of Jacob, glorify Him; And stand in awe of Him, you seed of Israel (Psalms 22:24). You that fear the Lord* said R. Joshua ben Levi, means those that fear Heaven.[f] R. Samuel bar Nahman said: It means the righteous proselytes.[g]

---

[d] *"Have we not ourselves chosen it for ourselves?":* Having crossed the Jordan, they realized how fertile and desirable the chosen land proved to be.

---

[e] *carries with it expiation:* The incense has atoning faculties (Lev. 16:13). The superiority of the meal-offering is here found in the fact that it is a voluntary offering and not brought about by the need to atone for sins.

---

[f] *those that fear Heaven:* Gentiles who believe in the One God but have not become proselytes.

---

[g] *righteous proselytes:* Those who have become fully converted to Judaism.

R. Hezekiah and R. Abbahu said in the name of R. Eleazar: If righteous proselytes will come in times to come,[h] Antoninus [i] will come at the head of them.[j] And what does Scripture mean by saying, *All you seed of Jacob, glorify Him*. This means the ten tribes.[k] If so, why is it also said, *And stand in awe of Him, all you seed of Israel?* Said R. Benjamin b. Levi: this means the tribe of Benjamin who came [into the world] last.[l]

It is further written, *For He has not despised or abhorred the lowliness of the poor* (Psalms 22:25). The usual experience is: Two men go before a judge, one of them poor and the other rich; toward whom does the judge turn his face? Is it not toward the rich man? But here, *He has not hidden His face from him; but when he cried unto Him, He heard.*

R. Haggai decreed a fast, and rain came down. He said: "It is not because I am worthy, but because it is written *For He has not de-*

---

[h] *If righteous proselytes will come . . . :* If proselytes will be accepted in the messianic era (a controversial question).

[i] *Antoninus:* The friend of R. Judah the Prince, supposed to be one of the Roman emperors.

[j] *At the head of them:* He was exceptionally pious and God-fearing.

[k] *the ten tribes:* The Psalmist, himself of the tribe of Judah, addresses the other tribes, v.:23; "I will declare Thy name unto my brethren."

[l] *the tribe of Benjamin who came . . . last:* He was born after the name "Israel" had already been given to Jacob.

spised or abhorred the supplication of the poor." [m] And even as He despises not his prayer, He, likewise, despises not his offering, as it is said, *And when one brings a meal-offering, etc.*

§3   *Let the wicked forsake his way, and the man of iniquity his thoughts* (Isa. 55:7). R. Bibi ben Abaye said: How should a person confess on the eve of the Day of Atonement? He should say: "I confess all the evil I have done before Thee; I stood in the way of evil; and as for all the evil I have done, I shall no more do the like; may it be Thy will, O Lord my God, that Thou pardon me for all my iniquities, and forgive me for all my transgressions, and grant me atonement for all my sins." This is indicated by what is written, *Let the wicked forsake his way, and the man of iniquity his thoughts, and let him return unto the Lord, and He will have compassion upon him.* R. Isaac and R. Jose ben Hanina each offered a simile. R. Isaac said: It is like a man fitting together two boards, and joining them one to another.[n] R. Jose ben Hanina said: It is like a man fitting together two legs of a bed and joining them one to another.

And let him return unto the Lord, and He will have compassion upon him (Isa. 55:7). The Rabbis and R. Simeon bar Yohai commented on this. The Rabbis said: The Holy One, blessed be He, showed Abraham [o] our father, peace be upon him, all the expiatory

---

[m] *the supplication of the poor:* The Hebrew word *"enut"* may be rendered either as "lowliness" or as "supplication."

---

[n] *joining them one to another:* A play on words on "He will have compassion" [*rahem*] and a similar root [*halhem*], meaning "to join together."

---

[o] *showed Abraham:* In the vision in Genesis 15 allusions to all types of sacrifices are found by the homilists.

offerings, except the tenth of an ephah.[p] R. Simeon bar Yohai said: Also that of the tenth of an ephah did the Holy One, blessed be He, show to Abraham our father. Here [the word] "these" is used [viz., *The meal-offering that is made out of these* (Lev. 2:8)], and there, too, the word "these" is used [viz., *And he took him all these* (Gen. 15:10)]. Just as "these" used here is a reference to the tenth of an ephah, so, too, "these" used there is a reference to the tenth of an ephah.

And to our God, for He will abundantly pardon (Isa. 55:7). R. Judah ben Simon said, in the name of R. Ze'ira: This means that the Holy One, blessed be He, gave us an additional means of obtaining forgiveness, namely the tenth of an ephah—*And when one brings a meal-offering, . . .*

§4 What is written prior to this matter?[q] *And he shall take away its crop with the feathers thereof, and cast it beside the altar, in the place of the ashes* (Lev. 1:16). R. Tanhum bar Hanilai said: This bird flies about and swoops throughout the world, and eats indiscriminately; it eats food obtained by robbery and by violence. Said the Holy One, blessed be He, "Since its crop is filled with the proceeds of robbery and violence, let it not be offered on the altar"; for this reason it is said, *And he shall take away its crop.* On the other hand, the domestic animal is reared at the crib of its master and eats neither indiscriminately nor of what is obtained by robbery or by violence; for this reason the whole of it is offered up. Therefore it is said, *And the priest shall offer the whole and make it smoke on the altar* (Lev. 5:12). Because a living being eats food obtained by robbery and violence, come and see how much trouble and exertion it undergoes before its food issues forth from

---

[p] *the tenth of an ephah:* The meal-offering (which may, on occasion, also have an atoning function).

---

[q] *prior to this matter:* Prior to Leviticus 2 with which the homily is concerned.

it. From the mouth to the gullet,[r] from the gullet to the stomach, from the first stomach to the second stomach, from the second stomach to the maw, from the maw to the intestines, from the small winding intestine to the large winding intestine, from the large winding intestine to the mucal sieve, from the mucal sieve to the rectum, from the rectum to the outside. Come and see how much trouble and exertion it has before its food issues forth from it.

§5   *And he shall rend it by the wings thereof, but shall not divide asunder* (Lev. 1:17). R. Johanan said: An ordinary being, should he smell the odor of burning wings, is nauseated, and you say, *And the priest shall make it smoke upon the altar* (ibid.)! Why then all this? In order that the altar be enhanced by the sacrifice of the poor.

King Agrippa wished to offer up a thousand burnt-offerings in one day. He sent to tell the High Priest: "Let no man other than myself offer sacrifices today!" There came a poor man with two turtledoves in his hand, and he said to the High Priest: "Sacrifice these." Said he: "The King commanded me, saying, 'Let no man other than myself offer sacrifices this day.'" Said he: "My lord the High Priest, I catch four doves every day; two I offer up, and with the other two I sustain myself. If you do not offer them up, you cut off my means of sustenance."[s] The priest took them and offered them up. In a dream it was revealed to Agrippa: The sacrifice of a poor man preceded yours. So he sent to the High Priest, saying: "Did I not command you thus: 'Let no one but me offer sacrifices this day?'"

---

[r] *From the mouth to the gullet*, etc.: This passage, which refers to cattle, is obscure in this context.

---

[s] *you cut off my means of sustenance*: If, contrary to his custom, he will not offer up two of the birds he caught, he fears that in the future he will no longer succeed in catching four of them every day.

Said the High Priest to him: "Your Majesty, a poor man came with two turtledoves in his hand, and said to me: 'I catch four birds every day; I sacrifice two, and from the other two I support myself. If you will not offer them up you will cut off my means of sustenance.' Should I not have offered them up?" Said King Agrippa to him: "You were right in doing as you did."

An ox was once being led to sacrifice, but would not budge. A poor man came along with a bundle of endive in his hand. He held it out to the ox, which ate it, sneezed, expelled a needle,[t] and then allowed itself to be led to sacrifice. In a dream a message was revealed to the owner of the ox: The poor man's sacrifice preceded you.

Once a woman brought a handful of fine flour, and the priest scorned her, saying: "See what she offers! What is there in this to eat? What is there in this to offer up?" It was shown to him in a dream: Do not despise her! It is regarded as if she had sacrificed her own life. And may we not draw [a deduction from] minor to major, since even with reference to one who does not offer up a life the word *nefesh* [soul] is used by Scripture [thus: *And if a nefesh brings a sacrifice* (Lev. 2:1)], surely, then, when one offers a life (nefesh), it is as if one is offering up one's own life.

§6 *And he shall bring it to Aaron's sons* (Lev. 2:2). R. Hiyya taught: Even if they are many.[u] R. Johanan quoted: *In the multitude of people is the king's glory* (Prov. 14:28).

And he shall take thereout his handful of the fine flour thereof, and of the oil thereof (Lev. 2:2). It says *of the fine flour thereof*, and

---

[t] *expelled a needle:* One that had stuck in its throat and might, eventually, have caused it to become unfit for sacrifice.

---

[u] *Even if they are many:* Nevertheless, "the handful of fine flour" is divided among them.

not, "all the fine flour thereof," *of the oil thereof,* and not "all the oil thereof." There was a case of a man who brought his meal-offering from Gallia or from Aspamia. When he saw that the priest took off a handful and ate the rest, he said: "Woe unto me! All this trouble I have gone to was but for the benefit of this man." They all began pacifying him, saying: "Even though this man has gone to no more trouble than to take two steps between the hall and the altar, he has, nevertheless, earned the right to enjoy your meal-offering; how much more so, then, will you, who have taken all this trouble [receive for your merit the good that is treasured up]." Moreover, it is said, *That which is left of the meal-offering, shall be Aaron's and his sons'* (Lev. 2:3).

R. Hanina bar Abba went to a certain place and found this verse at the beginning of the *Seder*,[v] viz., *And that which is left of the meal-offering shall be Aaron's and his sons'* (Lev. 2:3). What text did he employ with which to open his discourse? *From men, by Thy hand, O Lord, from men of the world, whose portion is in this life, and whose belly Thou fillest with all Thy treasure; who have children in plenty, and leave their abundance to their babes* (Psalms 17:14). *Who are men of Thy hand, O Lord,* meaning, who are the mighty men? They who took their portion from beneath Thy hand, O Lord. *Who are the men without a share of the world?* They who took no portion of the land. *They whose portion is in life* refers to the holy things to be eaten only in the Sanctuary. *And they whose belly Thou fillest with all Thy treasure* refers to the holy things that may be eaten in the entire territory. *They whose sons shall be satisfied with food* has reference to *Every male among the children of Aaron may eat of it* (Lev. 6:11). *And leave their abundance to their babes* has reference to *And that which is left of the meal-offering shall be Aaron's and his sons'* (ibid.: 2:3). Aaron passed on the privilege

---

[v] *and found this verse at the beginning of the Seder:* In Amoraic times in Palestine, no uniform lectionary had yet been introduced; but on each Sabbath a "seder" of at least 21 verses from the Pentateuch was read and on the following Sabbath the following passage would be read. Eventually, the so-called triennial cycle (extending, probably, over three years and some months) became customary in Palestine.

to his descendants both fit and unfit,ᵂ as it is said, *My covenant was with him, yea with the living* (Mal. 2:5); *Peace* (ibid.), for the ensured peace in Israel. *And I gave them to him for the fear wherewith he feared me* (ibid.), since he took upon himself the injunctions of the Torah, in awe, in fear, in trembling and quaking.

Why does Scripture say in addition, *And before My name he was dismayed* (ibid.)? At the time when Moses poured the oil of anointing on Aaron's head, he trembled and recoiled, and cried out, "Woe is me! Perchance I have made improper use of the consecrated oil of anointing?" Whereupon the Holy Spirit answered, saying to him: *Behold how good and how pleasant it is for brethren to dwell together in unity! It is like the precious oil upon the head, coming down upon the beard; even Aaron's beard, that comes down upon the collar of his garments; like the dew of Hermon, that comes down upon the mountains of Zion* . . . (Psalms 133:1–3). Even as the law of trespass does not apply to dew, so does that law not apply to the oil. *It is like the precious oil upon the head, coming down upon the beard, the beard of Aaron.* Had Aaron then two beards, that it is said *The beard, the beard,* etc.? No, but when Moses saw the oil coming down on the beard of Aaron he rejoiced as if it had been coming down on his own beard. *The Torah of truth was in his mouth, and unrighteousness was not found on his lips* (Mal. 2:6), in that he neither declared the permitted forbidden, nor declared the forbidden permitted. *He walked with Me in peace and uprightness* (ibid.), since he did not entertain misgivings about the ways of the All-Present, even as Abraham had not entertained misgivings. *And he did turn many away from iniquity* (ibid.), in that he made transgressors turn to the study of Torah. And thus it says, *Sincerely do they love thee* (Song 1:4). What is written in conclusion? *For the priest's lips should keep knowledge, so that they may seek the law at his mouth; for he is the messenger of the Lord of Hosts* (Mal. 2:7).

Leviticus Rabba, chapter III

ᵂ *both fit and unfit*: Even priests who were prevented from taking part in the sacrificial service because of a physical blemish were permitted their share of the meal-offering.

THE LORD YOUR GOD HAS MULTIPLIED YOU

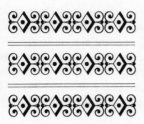

INTRODUCTION

DEUTERONOMY RABBA *belongs to the Tanhuma-Yelammedenu group; in common with other such Midrashim, each of its chapters opens with a question of Halakhah and concludes with the first verse of the weekly portion from Deuteronomy. After this special opening, there follow a number of proems and the body of the sermon, as in the other homiletic Midrashim. The chapter presented here refers to Deuteronomy 1:10–11, which must have marked the beginning of a pericope (not attested elsewhere), even though this would seem to imply that the preceding Seder, starting with the beginning of Deuteronomy, consisted of only nine verses.*

The entire homily is devoted to the subject of the fruitfulness of Israel both as a positive duty and as a blessing long since granted to Abraham. This theme fits perfectly the verses with which the pericope opens; but it disregards the contents of the rest of the biblical chapter, which deals with the appointment of "heads" or judges. Only one section of the homily refers to this subject; but it obviously does not constitute an integral part of the original homily, having probably been transferred by a copyist from a different Midrash; for this reason it has been put in brackets in the passage below.

181

The halakhic question (§1) *introduces the "commandment" to be fruitful and multiply. It proceeds to emphasize that mankind was created for the purpose of procreation. Nevertheless, Adam abstained from intercourse for 130 years after his son Abel was slain and Cain, the killer, put under a curse—until God "added desire to his former desire" and he begat another son. And just as Adam and his descendants multiplied, so did Israel in Egypt, in spite of Pharaoh's cruel decrees, until Pharaoh himself exclaimed in despair: "What can I do to you whom the Holy One saw fit to make more and more numerous?"*

The first proem (§2) offers different expositions of Psalms 119:89 —"For ever, O Lord, Thy word stands fast in heaven"—among them that God always conducts Himself mercifully and fulfills His promises. Thus He acted in the case of Adam and, especially, in the case of Abraham, whom "He raised above the vault of the firmament," and His promise to Abraham—"look now toward heaven and count the stars . . . so shall your seed be"—He fulfilled in the time of Moses.

In the second proem (§3) the interdependence of rebuke and blessing is stressed. Because Israel accepted rebuke from Moses, it received the blessing of the good—"The Lord your God has multiplied you, etc."

In the body of the sermon (§4–5) the preacher returns to the motif of Israel's increase in Egypt, in spite of Pharaoh's decrees. God miraculously saved the children born in the fields from the Egyptians who sought to kill them and provided each child with two angels to cater to its needs; God Himself eventually led them back to their parents' homes. Not only the birth of the children but also their conception came about in a miraculous way: the Egyptians compelled the men to work far from their homes during the day and forced them to stay during the night. A number of highly dramatic and ingenious stories illustrate the miracles of conception and birth in spite of all the efforts made by the oppressor to make "the seed of Abraham diminish."

The following section (§6) emphasizes that the promise of increase was fulfilled at the time of the Exodus, and also that Israel was "as the stars of heaven" in a spiritual sense as well: "As the heavenly bodies encompass Me, with My glory in their midst, so your children will . . . encamp [in the wilderness] . . . with My Presence in their midst." Moreover, the blessing: "The Lord . . .

*make you a thousand times so many more as you are," which ap-
pears to set a limit upon the promised increase, is Moses' own (§7),
while God's blessing will be far greater, without limit. When He
promised "to add to you a thousand times as many . . . ," it is to
be understood that with God—contrary to human custom—the "addition" is liable to be greater than the specified amount. Furthermore,
at the time of the redemption from Egypt there was no "addition,"
but in the world to come God will "make an addition" to the redemption.*

*The thematic integrity of all the parts of this homily is self-evident.
Each consecutive section strengthens and develops the motifs already touched upon. The entire homily uses a variety of literary
devices, as well as striking parables and attractive narratives, rich
in folk motifs. Apart from the main theme—the blessing of increase
and multiplication—which all sections have in common and which
each illuminates from a different angle, every section elaborates upon
one or more of the phrases of the two scriptural verses to which they
specifically refer. The halakhic opening develops, in particular, the
expressions "multiplied" and "multitude": the first proem concentrates on the words "The Lord, the God of your fathers" and on "the
stars of heaven"; the second develops, especially, Moses' words, "and
bless you." In the body of the sermon all these expressions recur in a
variety of interpretations. In §7–8, finally, a threefold climax is
created: the simile, "like the stars of heaven," is taken up again and
given a spiritual interpretation; "a thousand times" is given an unexpected meaning, as it is pointed out that the "addition," will be
greater than the amount specified; and all the signs and wonders
of the redemption from Egypt are now shown to have been but a
"redemption without addition"—hence the Messianic redemption
of the future will be incomparably greater and more miraculous than
anything yet known in the world.*

*Even though the homily also stresses the spiritual dimension of the
blessing granted to Abraham, it is primarily devoted to the multiplication and increase of his seed in the physical sense—clearly a
subject of topical importance. When tens of thousands of Jews were
killed in the revolts against Rome, many must have asked themselves*

whether the blessings given to Abraham and confirmed by Moses had not been somehow forfeited. By implication our homily rejects any such doubts and apprehensions: just as in the past the promise that Israel would grow and increase was fulfilled in spite of all efforts on the part of enemies to limit their numbers or kill them off altogether, so it will happen again; persecutions and tribulations are themselves but the proof of this. In the darkest hours, circles of Jews came to the bitter conclusion that it was no longer worthwhile to beget children who, like Cain and Abel, would be "under a curse" and doomed; our homily takes an unequivocal stand against such a counsel of despair.

The tendency to refrain from leading normal lives, followed by groups calling themselves "mourners of Zion," is described in the Talmud: "Our Rabbis taught: When the Temple was destroyed for the second time, large numbers in Israel refrained from eating meat or drinking wine. R. Joshua said to them: 'My sons why do you not eat meat nor drink wine?' They replied: 'Shall we eat meat which used to be brought as an offering on the altar, now that the altar has been destroyed? Shall we drink wine which used to be poured as a libation on the altar, now that it has been destroyed?' He said to them: 'If so, we should not eat bread either, because the meal-offerings have ceased!' They said: 'We shall be satisfied with eating fruit.' He said: 'We should not eat fruit either, because there is no longer the offering of first fruits.' They said: 'We shall be satisfied with other fruit [than the "seven kinds" of which firstfruit was offered]'. He said: 'We should not drink water, because there is no longer the ceremony of pouring water' (cf., Mishnah Sukkah, chapter IV). To this they could find no answer. He said to them: '. . . not to mourn at all is impossible . . . but to mourn overmuch is also impossible, because one must not impose on the community a hardship which the majority cannot endure . . . .'" And again: "R. Ishmael ben Elisha said: Since the day of the destruction of the Temple we should refrain from eating meat and drinking wine . . . and from the day that the government has issued cruel decrees against us and has forbidden us to observe the Torah and its commandments and to celebrate 'the week of the son' [i.e., apparently, circumcision] we should by rights refrain from taking wives and begetting children, and the seed of Abraham our father would come to an end of itself . . . :" (Bab. Bava Batra 60b). Our homily in its entirety militates against such destructive doctrines by holding up the example of Israel in Egypt, a people who did not despair and did not doubt that the blessing of Abraham, which ensures the future of the nation, would eventually be fulfilled.

⬥⬥⬥

THE LORD YOUR GOD HAS MULTIPLIED YOU

§1 How many children must a man have to consider himself exempt from the command to be fruitful and multiply? [a] Our masters taught: A man is never to consider himself exempt from the command to be fruitful and multiply. Assuming, however, that he must have at least a certain number of children to be exempt from the command, how many must he have? At least two males, according to the school of Shammai. According to the school of Hillel— so said R. Eleazar ben Azariah—at least a male and a female.

What is the reason for the school of Shammai ruling that two males are required for the exemption? Corresponding to Cain and Abel. And what is the reason that the school of Hillel says a male and a female are required? Corresponding to Adam and Eve.

R. Eleazar said: He who neglects propagating the race is deemed to be one who diminishes the image of God, for it is said *In the image of God made He man* (Gen. 9:6). Hence no man is to neglect the propagation of the race.

For 130 years—so said R. Simon—Adam abstained from intercourse with his wife. Why? Because after begetting Cain and Abel and Cain's subsequent slaying of Abel, as though the anguish of Abel's slaughter were not enough, Adam also knew that Cain would end his days under a curse, as it is said: *A fugitive and a wanderer shall you be in the earth* (Gen. 4:12)—so both Abel and Cain were doomed. What did Adam do? He abstained from intercourse with

---

[a] *the command to be fruitful*: Genesis 1:28.

his wife for 130 years, as it is said *Adam lived for a hundred and thirty years* (Gen. 5:3), and only after that *he begot in his own likeness after his image* (ibid.). What did the Holy One do? He added desire to Adam's former desire, and so he once again had intercourse with Eve and begot Seth.

For the Holy One said: I created the world with no purpose other than that the human race be propagated, as it is said *He created the earth not to be empty, but to be inhabited* (Isa. 45:18). And it is said: *Be fruitful and multiply* (Gen. 1:28). Thus from the very beginning the Holy One, in creating Adam and Eve, intended that they be fruitful and multiply—that they keep begetting children and keep on being fruitful and multiplying. Why? Because the propagation of mankind redounds to the glory of the Holy One. Therefore when Israel went out of Egypt, they went forth as sixty myriads, as is said: *The children of Israel journeyed from Rameses . . . about six hundred thousand . . .* (Ex. 12:37). After they came into the wilderness they continued to be fruitful and multiply, and they gathered against them proudly,[b] as Scripture points out about them: *The children of Israel were fruitful, and increased abundantly* (Ex. 1:7). Hence he exclaimed: "What can I do to you whom the Holy One saw fit to make more and more numerous?" Whence do we know this? From what we read in the lesson for the day, *the Lord your God has multiplied you* (Deut. 1:10).

§2 *For ever, O Lord Thy word stands fast in heaven* (Psalms 119: 89).[c] What is intended by the words: *For ever, O Lord?* R. Berekhiah

---

[b] *and they gathered against them proudly:* The text, as it stands, is obscure; it would seem that this part of the homily has been displaced, and that it referred, originally, to Israel in Egypt (cf., Ex. 1:7). "Hence he exclaimed," presumably, was said of Pharaoh.

---

[c] *For ever, O Lord, etc.:* The Tetragrammaton (rendered "Lord") is taken to stand for the quality of divine mercy (as against the appellations *el, elohim* ["God"] which designate stern justice).

said: That for ever He conducts Himself toward us in the measure of mercy [for he is designated "Lord of mercy"]: *the Lord, the Lord, being a merciful God* (Ex. 34:6). Hence, *for ever, O Lord, ...*

R. Eliezer taught: The creation of the world was begun on the twenty-fifth day of Elul, so that Adam was created on the New Year which was the sixth day. In the first hour of the day, according to R. Judah, Adam came into existence as a thought in God's mind; in the second hour, God consulted [the ministering angels as to whether He should create him]; in the third hour, God gathered up the dust from which He was to make him; in the fourth, God made him into a *golem*; in the fifth, God jointed his limbs; in the sixth, God put the breath of life into him; in the seventh, God stood Adam up on his feet; in the eighth, God brought him into the Garden of Eden; in the ninth, God gave him the command; in the tenth, Adam transgressed it; in the eleventh, he was brought to judgment; in the twelfth, he was driven out of Eden. For, as God was about to impose death sentence upon Adam, having said to him previously *In the day you eat thereof you shall surely die* (Gen. 2:17), He realized that it was the New Year day, and so had mercy upon him and pardoned him.

Thereupon the Holy One said: As you live, even as I pardoned you freely, so will I pardon your children on this day, on the New Year day, as it is said, *in the seventh month* (Lev. 23:24).[d] Hence *For ever, O Lord Thy word stands fast in heaven,* that is, God conducts Himself in the measure of mercy. What is implied by *stands fast in heaven?* That Thou art not like a man who makes a promise and is then compelled to disregard it. For whatever Thou sayest endures, as it is said *The words of the Lord are [steadfast] words* (Psalms 12:7). Thus a king of flesh and blood may promise to do something, but may not be able to accomplish it. He may enter a province where the people praise him, so that he says to them: "Tomorrow I shall build you marketplaces and bathhouses, tomorrow I shall build an aqueduct for you." But at night he goes to sleep and rises no more. Then where is he and where are his promises? But the Holy One does not act thus. *The Lord is the God of truth, because He is the living God and the*

---

[d] *in the seventh month:* The text has "on this day"; however, this phrase does not occur in Scripture with reference to New Year's day.

everlasting King (Jer. 10:10). This is the meaning of *For ever, O Lord, Thy word stands fast in heaven.*

However, when Balaam said *God is not a man that He should lie . . . that which He has promised, will He not do it?* (Num. 23:19), he meant the first part of the verse to apply to good things. When God promises to do good, He will do it. Thus He said He would bring Israel into the Land and give it to them, and indeed He gave it to them. But when He promises to bring evil, He repents. What did He say to Moses when Israel did that deed? *e Let Me alone, that I may destroy them* (Deut. 9:14). But He did not do so. He repented of what He intended to do, as it is said *And the Lord repented of the evil* (Ex. 32:14). But when good is promised, His promise is carried out. Hence *For ever, O Lord, Thy word stands fast in heaven.* And so, too, *The word of our God shall stand for ever* (Isa. 40:8).

Another comment: *For ever, O Lord, Thy word stands fast in heaven.* Does the word of God stand fast only in heaven and not upon earth? What is meant, then, by the words, *stands fast in heaven?* It means that the word which God uttered to Abraham [in heaven] was fulfilled [on earth]. What does Scripture say? *He brought [Abraham] forth beyond, and said: Look toward heaven and count the stars* (Gen. 15:5). *Brought him forth beyond* means—so taught R. Judah bar Simon and R. Hanin in the name of R. Johanan—that the Holy One raised Abraham above the vault of the firmament. For "beyond" implies "beyond the heavens," as in the verse *While as yet He had not made the earth nor the areas beyond* (Prov. 8:26). Accordingly, the word "look" in *look now toward heaven* (Gen. 15:5), means, so said R. Samuel bar Isaac, looking downward from above, as in the verse *Look down from heaven, and behold* (Psalms 80:15). And so when Israel went forth out of Egypt and came into the wilderness, Moses saw them in great multitudes. Thereupon Moses said to them: "The words which the Holy One uttered to your father Abraham are now fulfilled: *Look now toward heaven and count the stars . . . so*

---

e *when Israel did that deed:* Made the golden calf and worshiped it.

shall your seed be. The Lord your God has multiplied you, and behold, you are this day as the stars of heaven for multitude (Deut. 1:10)."

§3 *Upon those who give rebuke shall be delight, upon them shall come the blessing of the good* (Prov. 24:25). R. Simeon ben Lakish and R. Johanan commented on this verse. R. Simeon ben Lakish pointed out that the text may be taken to say [that delight will not be only] "upon him who gives rebuke" but also *upon those who accept rebuke.* And R. Johanan went on to point out that the text says *upon them shall come the blessing of the good*—upon him who gives the rebuke as well as upon them who receive it.

What is meant by *the blessing of the good?* R. Judah, R. Nehemiah, and the Rabbis differ on the meaning of the phrase. R. Judah said: It means the blessings of the Holy One who is called "good" as in the verse *The Lord is good to all* (Psalms 145:9). R. Nehemiah said: It means the blessing of the Torah that is called "good," as in the verse *I have given you a doctrine which is good* (Prov. 4:2). And the Rabbis said: It means the blessing of Moses who is called "good" as it is said *And his mother saw the infant [Moses] that he was goodly* (Ex. 2:2). And where in Scripture does Moses bless Israel? At the end of Deuteronomy.[f] After he had rebuked them saying *These are the words,* . . . . (Deut. 1:1), he blessed them because they willingly received his rebukes.[g] Therefore the Holy One said: Since Israel willingly received Moses' rebukes, let them now receive his blessings. And how did Moses bless them? After he said *The Lord your God has*

---

[f] *At the end of Deuteronomy:* Chapter 33. Originally this homily must have been delivered on the occasion of the reading of that chapter; it is here connected, somewhat artificially, to Deuteronomy 1:10–11.

---

[g] *willingly received his [Moses'] rebukes:* Contained in Deuteronomy; e.g., 1:22ff., 4:25ff., 8:11ff., etc.

multiplied you (Deut. 1:10), he went on to say, *The Lord God of your fathers make you a thousand times so many more as you are, and bless you as He has promised you* (Deut. 1:11).

[§4   How is the statement *The Lord your God has multiplied you* (Deut. 1:10) relevant (to the preceding words *I am not able to bear you alone*)? Because the words are to be read "has heightened your worth (over that of your judges)." [h] Thus you find Ben Azzai saying: Even the ear of a Jew's dog is of greater consequence than Israel's judges. How so? It happened that a man came to his friend and said: "Will you trade with me—take this kid and give me your dog?" His friend said: "Yes." While they were standing there, another acquaintance came along and said: "Take two kids in exchange." Still a third came along and said to him: "Take three." And yet a fourth came along and said to him: "Take four." When the four men could not work out the dispute among themselves, they went to court and told the judges what had happened. Thereupon the judges decreed: Let the dog be divided among the four contestants. (According to the Sages, be it noted that the one who made the first offer should be declared in the right. As it was, the judges divided the dog among the four.)

[h] *"has heightened your worth over that of your judges"*: The bracketed section is not an integral part of the homily presented here, the theme of which is the blessing that Israel shall multiply, but of an alternative sermon to this section, which concentrated on verses 9 and 13ff., dealing with the appointment of judges. Originally, this sermon must have made use of Proverbs 26:17: *"He that passes by and meddles with strife not his own, is like one that takes a dog by the ears"*; hence the strange story of a quarrel concerning the ear of a dog. The entire section is satirical and directed against local [lay] judges, who, in spite of their utter ignorance, had themselves appointed to office by using their power and influence. The section of the verse, "and meddles with strife not his own," is applied to them in the sense that they take upon themselves judicial functions for which they are unfit.

[Thus justice was perverted, and one of the four was, in fact, given more [1]—by the ear of a dog—than his fellows. What will befall such judges? Their lives and the lives of their children, and all that is theirs will perish. What is the cause of this? That more was given to one contestant than to the others. Hence a dog's ear (unjustly assigned) can be deemed more important than (some) Jewish judges. And so the verse is to be understood "The Lord your God has heightened your worth over that of your judges."]

§5   *The Lord your God has multiplied you.* When did he multiply you? When you were in Egypt, for so it is said *I have caused you to multiply as a seedling [j] of the field* (Ezek. 16:7). What does this mean? When Pharaoh charged his people *Every son that is born, you shall cast into the river* (Ex. 1:22), what did the Jewish women do? When a Jewish woman felt that her time for giving birth was near, she would go out into the field, and as she was giving birth, she would raise her eyes on high and say, "I have done my duty in keeping with what you said, *Be fruitful and multiply.* Now do what you are to do."

In the meantime what were the Egyptians doing? When the Egyptians saw the daughters of Israel go out into a field to give birth, they would crouch down at some distance from the women. After the women gave birth and went back to the city, the Egyptians would take up stones and set forth to slay the infants. But the infants would be swallowed up in the field, then after a while be seen in the dis-

---

[1] *was, in fact, given more—by the ear of a dog:* Obviously, it is patently impossible to divide an animal bodily into four equal parts.

---

[j] *I have caused you to multiply as a seedling . . . :* The entire allegory in Ezek. 16—signifying the relationship between God and the people of Israel in its "infancy"—is here taken literally as an account of what happened to the infants in Egypt who, at the time of the persecution, were growing "as seedlings in the field."

tance, and again be swallowed only to be seen again after a while, so that eventually the Egyptians would weary and go away. How did the children remain alive in the field? The Holy One, so said R. Levi, assigned two angels to each infant, one to wash him and one to clothe him, and to suckle and to anoint him, as it is said *He made him suck honey out of the rock, and oil out of the flinty rock* (Deut. 32:13); and as it is said *I washed you with water . . . and I anointed you with oil, I clothed you also with broidered work* (Ezek. 16:9–10). According to the elder R. Hiyya, it was not angels who attended the infants, but the Holy One in His own glory, for the text reads *I washed you.* If the text read, "I had you washed," one might have said, "washed at the hands of an angel," but the text reads *I washed you*—hence not at the hands of an angel. May the name of the Holy One be praised! He, in His own glory, thus attended the infants.

And so like seedlings, the infants grew up in the field and when they were grown, they came in bands to their homes. Of these children, Ezekiel said: *I have caused you to multiply as a seedling of the field* (Ezek. 16:7).

But how did these children know where to find their parents? Again it was the Holy One who went with them and showed each and every one of them his father's home, saying to him, "Call out to your father by his name, and to your mother by hers." Then the child would say to his mother, "Do you not recall when five months ago you gave birth to me in such and such a field on such and such a day?" When she asked him, "Who took care of you?" he would reply, "A young man with beautifully curled locks—you never saw one like him! He is outside and he brought me here." The mother would then say, "Come, show him to me." They would go outside and walk around among all the lanes, everywhere, but would not find him. Therefore when they came to the Red Sea and saw Him, they pointed Him out with their fingers to their mothers and said *This is my God who I said was so beautiful* (Ex. 15:2).[k] He is the one that took care of me."

---

[k] *this is my God who I said was so beautiful:* The usual rendering is "And I will prepare him a habitation" or "I will glorify him."

§6 You find, said R. Joshua, that when the Egyptians issued their decrees to prevent Israel's multiplying, they carefully considered all occupations to determine which most diminished a man's potency, and found that it was ploughing. Why ploughing? Because, said R. Simeon ben Yohai, the act of ploughing exhausts a man.[1] In addition, the Egyptians decreed even harder work—they had the Israelites go out and labor at making bricks in the field. Despite these decrees, the children of Israel, upon returning to their homes after their labors, would find rest in sleep and then would lie with their wives and conceive children. Thereupon the Egyptians said: "It is as though we had decreed nothing." So they decreed: "Let us make the Israelites sleep wherever they work." And this the Israelites had to do. But then the daughters of Israel—so taught R. Simeon ben Halafta—would go down to fill their pitchers with water from the river. And whenever they went down to draw water, the Holy One had fish come along and enter the pitchers. Upon returning from the river, each woman would sell the fish, buy wine and oil, and cook food therewith; then, with a mirror in her hand, she would go out to her husband in the field where the two would eat and drink. After they had eaten and drunk, she would say to her husband, "Come and see in this mirror who is the most handsome," and thus slowly she aroused desire in her husband and he would lie with her, and at once the Holy One would remember her. With how many children? With two in her womb at the same time, some say. With six, others say. With ten, others say. With twelve, still others say. And all these opinions derive from the verse *And the children of Israel were fruitful, and increased abundantly*, etc. (Ex. 1:7). According to the opinion that there were six in her womb, the phrase *were fruitful* implies one; *increased abundantly*, one; *multiplied*, one; *waxed*, one; and *exceeding mighty*, two more—hence, six. According to the opinion that there were ten, the verse is expounded as follows: *were fruitful* implies two; *increased abundantly*, two; *multiplied*, two; *waxed*, two; and *exceeding mighty*, two—hence, ten. And according to the opinion that there were twelve, *exceeding* is taken to imply two and *mighty* two—hence, twelve.

---

[1] *the act of ploughing exhausts a man:* In Hebrew, this is based on a play on the two similar roots—*h-r-sh / h-l-sh*.

R. Hanina of Sepphoris commented: By *yishretzu* (increased abundantly), Scripture gives us an idea of just how fertile the Israelites were, for it implies that the Israelites in Egypt were as fertile either as the largest of small animals (*sheretz*), or as the smallest of small animals: if the largest of small animals, the mouse, is meant, it bears no less than six young at a time; if the smallest of small animals, the scorpion, is meant, it bears no fewer than sixty at a time.

To the Egyptians, the Holy One said: The seed of Abraham, to whom I said *so* [like the stars] *shall your seed be* (Gen. 15:5), you sought to diminish? By your lives (Scripture says of you), *But the more they afflicted them, the more they multiplied and grew* (Ex 1:12). What was it you said of them? *Lest they multiply* (Ex. 1:10). Indeed, by your lives [More and] *the more they multiplied,* [more and] *the more they grew* (Ex. 1:12). To what extent? To such an extent, said R. Simeon ben Lakish, that the Egyptians *came to have a sickening abhorrence of the children of Israel* (ibid.). Hence when an Egyptian was about to stop a while with a friend, he would see a thousand Israelites, and [would be so sickened that] unable to go on to see his friend, he would put his hand upon his nose and all but wish he were dead, saying "I can't bear this people—how numerous it is!" With regard to Israel's increase in Egypt, the Holy One said: *I have caused you to multiply as the seedling of the field, and you have increased, and waxed great* (Ezek. 16:7). And upon seeing Israel going forth out of Egypt, marching as innumerable camps under innumerable standards, Moses said: *The Lord your God has multiplied you* (Deut. 1:10). Remember that the Holy One multiplied you in Egypt even as He promised your father Abraham.

§7 *And, behold, you are* [hinkhem] *this day as the stars of heaven* (Deut. 1:10)—R. Hanina said in the name of R. Jose bar Hanina: What is meant by *You are this day?* That your encampment [haniyyatkhem] this day is like the stars of heaven—your camps are set up the same way as are the stars of heaven, which the Holy One showed Abraham when He showed him all heavenly bodies encompassing the Divine Presence. The Holy One said to Abraham: As the heavenly bodies encompass Me, with My glory in their midst, so your children will become numerous and encamp under many standards with My presence in their midst, as it is said *Then the Tabernacle of the congregation shall set forward with the camp of the Levites in the midst of the camp: as they encamp so shall they set forward, every man in his place by their standards* (Num. 2:17). So as Israel set forward, they encompassed the Ark in their midst. When Israel came up from the Red Sea, the Holy One said to Moses: "Array them in many standards so that they set forward in the order of royal armies." Upon being drawn up according to their standards they went forward in the orderly fashion of royal armies, with the Levites encompassing the Ark. And so Moses said to them: *The Lord your God has multiplied you, and, behold, you are this day as the stars of heaven are for multitude* (Deut. 1:10), your encampment is like the stars of heaven which God showed to Abraham when He said to him *Thus shall your seed be* (Gen. 15:5).

§8   *The Lord God of your fathers make you a thousand times so many more as you are* (Deut. 1:11). Israel said to Moses: Moses, you appear to set a limit upon our blessings,ᵐ for you said to us: *The Lord . . . make you a thousand times so many more.* This may be likened to a king who had an administrator to whom he said: Go and distribute gifts among the legions. The administrator went and distributed among them a thousand gold coins. The legions said, "Is this all you give us? The king said that he would give us much and you give us only a thousand gold coins?" The administrator replied, "All that I have given you is my own. But the king, when he said he would give you much, will indeed give you gifts without limit." Moses also said to Israel: "The Holy One declared: *Your seed shall be as the dust of the earth* (Gen. 28:14), and also *look now toward heaven, and count the stars* (Gen. 15:5). When I blessed you a thousandfold, I bestowed blessing of my own, but when the Holy One said to you *and bless you* (Deut. 1:11), He meant that He will add to the blessings *so many times more.*" R. Simeon ben Lakish said: The amount the Holy One adds is greater than the amount He specifies.

ᵐ *set a limit upon our blessings*: By requesting that we multiply only a thousandfold.

Among mortals, the amount specified is greater than the amount added.[n] But with the Holy One it is different: the amount He adds is greater than the amount He specifies.

The Holy One said: When I redeemed you from Egypt, there was no addition to the redemption. But when I come to bestow upon you the redemption of the world to come I will make an addition to your redemption,[o] as it is said . . . *Twofold with His hand the Lord will add when He recovers the remnant of His people, that shall remain from Assyria, and from Egypt, and from Pathros, and from Cush, and from Elam, and from Shinar, and from Hamath, and from the islands of the sea* (Isa. 11:11).

Deuteronomy Rabba, Lieberman, editor, pp. 9–17

[n] *the amount specified is greater than the amount added:* Of goods sold by a merchant, e.g.

[o] *I will make an addition to your redemption:* Another exposition of Deuteronomy 1:11, which says (rendered literally), "The Lord, God of your Fathers, shall add to you a thousand times so many . . . ."

NOTES

INTRODUCTION

1. See Saul Lieberman, *Greek in Jewish Palestine* (New York: Jewish Theological Seminary, 1942), pp. 161–62.
2. See H. L. Strack, *Introduction to the Talmud and Midrash* (Philadelphia: Jewish Publication Society, 1945), pp. 210–16.
3. See Joseph Heinemann, "The Proem in the Aggadic Midrashim: A Form-Critical Study," in *Studies in Aggadah and Folk-Literature: Scripta Hierosolymitana* XXII (Jerusalem: The Hebrew University, Magnes Press, 1971), pp. 100–22.
4. ———, s.v. "Preaching [In the Talmudic Period]," in *Encyclopaedia Judaica* (Jerusalem: 1971), vol. 13, pp. 994–98.

THE SIN OF MOSES AND THE SIN OF DAVID

1. Cf., Heinemann, "The Proem," pp. 112ff.

ABRAHAM AND SARAH IN EGYPT

1. N. Avigad and Y. Yadin, *A Genesis Apocryphon: A Scroll from the Wilderness of Judaea* (Jerusalem: The Hebrew University, Magnes Press and Heikhal Ha-Sefer, 1956). Cf., G. Vermes, *Scripture and Tradition in Judaism* (Leiden: E. J. Brill, 1961), pp. 96–126.

SUGGESTIONS FOR FURTHER READING (*in English*)

Ginzberg, Louis. *The Legends of the Jews* I (Philadelphia: Jewish Publication Society, 1954), "Preface," pp. vii–xv.

———. "Jewish Folklore: East and West," in *On Jewish Law and Lore* (Philadelphia: Jewish Publication Society, 1955), pp. 61–73.

Heinemann, Joseph. "Leviticus Rabbah," in *Encyclopaedia Judaica*. Vol. 11, pp. 147–50.

———. "Preaching [in the Talmudic Period]," in *Encyclopaedia Judaica*. Vol. 13, pp. 994–98.

———. "The Proem in the Aggadic Midrashim: A Form-Critical Study," in *Studies in Aggadah and Folk-Literature: Scripta Hierosolymitana* XXII (Jerusalem: The Hebrew University, Magnes Press, 1971), pp. 100–22.

———. "Profile of a Midrash: The Art of Composition in Leviticus Rabbah," in *Journal of the American Academy of Religion* XXXIX (1971), pp. 141–50.

———. "The Triennial Lectionary Cycle," in *Journal of Jewish Studies* XIX (1968), pp. 41–48.

Mann, Jacob. *The Bible as Read and Preached in the Old Synagogue*, vol. I. revised edition (New York: Ktav Publishing House, 1970), "Prologomenon," by B. Z. Wacholder, pp. xl–l; "Prolegomena" by Jacob Mann, pp. 3–19; vol. II (Cincinnati: Hebrew Union College, 1966), "Preface" by Isaiah Sonne, pp. xxi–xxxviii.

Spiegel, Shalom. "Introduction," in *Legends of the Bible* by Louis Ginzberg (New York: Random House, 1956) in *The Jewish Expression*. Edited by Judah Goldin (New York: Bantam Books, Inc., 1970), pp. 134–62.

Strack, Hermann L. *Introduction to the Talmud and Midrash* (Philadelphia: Jewish Publication Society, 1945).

PART THREE

THE POETRY OF THE SYNAGOGUE

JAKOB J. PETUCHOWSKI

PREFACE

EVERY TRANSLATOR from one language into another is painfully aware of the difficulty—occasionally, the sheer impossibility—of his task. In translating poetry, the difficulty is infinitely compounded. It can probably be said that no translator of poetry is ever completely satisfied with his accomplishments. That is why, for his German translation of Judah Halevi's poems, Franz Rosenzweig used as his motto the words of Friedrich Leopold von Stolberg, the German translator of Homer's *Iliad*: "O dear reader, learn Greek, and throw my translation into the fire."

Happily, the English reader has long had at his disposal some felicitous translations of medieval synagogal poetry, the work of such skilled translators as Nina Salaman, Alice Lucas, and Israel Zangwill. And yet, all three of them, as well as others, have seen fit to substitute English schemes of rhyme and meter for the original Hebrew schemes, and in the process they have also frequently been forced to give a paraphrase of the original, rather than a translation.

Those paraphrases are frequently encountered in the commonly used Hebrew-English editions of the Festival liturgy. They have a certain charm of their own, and they undoubtedly still manage to contribute something to the worshipful mood. However, after carefully considering all the relevant aspects of the problem, I have decided, for the purposes of this volume, to sacrifice literary grace for greater literalness. The present collection is not intended for worship and edification but to give the reader an insight into the actual thinking of the various poets, and a knowledge of their skill in utilizing traditional source materials. It is precisely this which all too often gets lost in English re-creations of traditional piyyutim.

Therefore, no attempt has been made in my own translations, either to provide English poetic equivalents or to preserve the Hebrew schemes of rhythm and rhyme (although in a few instances I have carried over something of the beat of the original and in others I have rendered early payyetanic rhyme by the use of English jingles). Nevertheless, I did find it desirable, out of the fifteen pieces, to use the work of other translators in the following five selections: "In the Middle of the Night," "Dew, Precious Dew," "The Royal Crown," "O God, Thy Name," and "When the Portals of Grace Will Open." The last of these was especially translated for this volume by Elizabeth R. Petuchowski.

I have, in the case of each of the piyyutim, given one of the more readily accessible Hebrew sources. In addition, I have, where available, given the reference to the appropriate listing in Davidson's thesaurus. By using the latter, the reader may obtain additional information about the piyyutim and about their utilization in the various traditional rites. All the printed sources of each selection are indicated in the end notes.

Jakob J. Petuchowski
Cincinnati, Ohio

INTRODUCTION

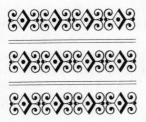

THE TRADITIONAL Jewish liturgy, as it has come down to us, not only consists of the standard prayers ordained in the Talmud and the ritual codes, but also contains poetic embellishments of all kinds. Such poetic embellishments take the form of hymns to be sung prior to, and after, the standard prayers—such as the *Adon Olam* and the *Yigdal*[1] and of poetic inserts in the standard prayers themselves. Thus, for example, there are occasions when each of the first three benedictions of the Sabbath or Festival Amidah is interrupted by one or more poems. The same can happen to the first two benedictions before the Shema, and to the one benediction after the Shema in the morning service, or to the two benedictions after the Shema in the evening service.

Technically, such poetic embellishments and inserts are known as *piyyutim* (singular: *piyyut*), a word which comes from the same Greek root that gives us the English words "poet" and "poem." Scholars differ in their use of the term, *piyyut*. Some would apply it to all poetic compositions for the synagogue, from the first such written until the eighteenth-century Enlightenment;[2] others would regard the "age of the piyyut" as having come to an end in the tenth century,[3] and call synagogal poetry composed after that date *shirei kodesh*, religious poetry.

But this difference in nomenclature (to which we shall pay no attention in the following pages) is not nearly as significant as are

205

some other problems. First of all there is the question of content. Some synagogal poems are mere elaborations on the themes of the standard prayers. If, for example, a prayer mentions the celestial choirs praising the Lord, a poem inserted into that prayer may go into detailed descriptions of how the angels were organized, how they took turns in singing, etc. But very often a piyyut will bring in extraneous matter; thus, into the standard benedictions of the Amidah it may introduce a poetic treatment of the Torah and Haftarah readings of that particular day, elaborating on the legal (halakhic) and homiletical (aggadic) interpretations of the biblical texts.

This brings us to the origins of the piyyut, an issue on which, as yet, there is no unanimous opinion. For a long time, scholars have been particularly intrigued by two twelfth-century reports. One is by Judah ben Barzillai al-Bargeloni, who makes the point that in the past piyyutim were introduced during times of persecution:

> The enemies decreed that Israel must not occupy themselves with the Torah. Therefore the Sages among them ordained for them, in the midst of the prayers, to mention, and to warn the ignorant about, the rules of Tabernacles on Tabernacles, and the rules of the [other] festivals and the rules of the Sabbath and the minutiae of the commandments by way of praises and thanksgivings and rhymes and *piyyutim*.[4]

Modern scholars have interpreted this passage as referring to the law of the Byzantine Emperor Justinian, who, in 553 c.e., ruled in favor of reading the Greek translation of the Scriptures in the synagogues, while at the same time prohibiting *deuterosis*, a word which is generally taken to mean the aggadic exegesis of the Midrashim.[5] On this basis they have dated the origin of the piyyut in the late sixth century, and have located it in the Byzantine realm.

Yet another twelfth-century report specifically locates the origin of the piyyut in the Persian realm. That report comes from Samau'al b. Yahya al-Magribi, a Jewish convert to Islam, whose father was himself a synagogal poet of note. Samau'al writes:

> The Persians forbade them [i.e., the Jews] the practice of circumcision and likewise prayer, because they knew that most of the prayers of that community were invocations of God against the nations—that He destroy them and make the world desolate, except their own fatherland which is the Land of Canaan. But when the Jews saw that the Persians were serious about the prohibition of the worship

service, they composed [new] prayers in which they inserted passages of the customary prayer. They called those [new] prayers *al-hizana*. They composed for them many tunes. At times of prayer they would congregate in order to sing and to read. The difference between the *hizana* and the obligatory prayer [*salat*] is that the obligatory prayer is recited without a tune. It is recited by the precentor alone, and nobody accompanies it with shouting. But, in the case of *al-hizana*, many accompany the precentor with shouts and singing, and assist him with the tunes. . . . The remarkable thing about this is that, when Islam permitted the *Ahl al-dimma* ["tolerated people," i.e., the Jews under Muslim rule] the practice of religion, and when the obligatory prayer was permitted to them again, the *hizanat* had become for the Jews a meritorious religious exercise on festivals and holy days. They made them a substitute for the obligatory prayer, and were satisfied with it without being forced to do so.[6]

While Samau'al does not give any specific date for the introduction of al-hizana (which is what piyyutim are called in the Arabic-speaking world), we do know that the period between 450 and 589 C.E., the end of the Sassanian reign in Persia, was a period of persecution for the Jews. There may well be some substance to Samau'al's report, and the Jews of Persia may well have substituted the singing of poetry for other (prohibited) religious exercises. However, it is now beyond any doubt that the geographical origin of the piyyut lies in Palestine. If, therefore, Samau'al's report is true, all it means is that the Persian Jews adopted a Palestinian practice.

For that reason Al-Bargeloni's account, read in the light of Justinian's law, tends to gain authority, since Palestine in the sixth century was part of the Byzantine world. Nevertheless, Al-Bargeloni's report does not compel us to date the beginning of the piyyut in the sixth century, for as one scholar has cogently argued, "what is meant is that the Sages, at that time, included in the service piyyutim that were already in existence." [7]

The earliest known payyetanim (authors of piyyutim) are Yose ben Yose, Yannai, and Eleazar Ha-Kaliri, in that order. (There are a number of anonymous piyyutim of even earlier date.) It is now generally conceded that all three were Palestinians; a) because their poetry is based on a Palestinian, not Babylonian, lectionary of the Pentateuch; b) because the fragments of the standard prayers contained in their poetry point to the Palestinian, and not to the Babylonian, rite; and c) because, in Babylonia, the introduction of the piyyut was opposed by many rabbis as a Palestinian import.

But if we know where these three poets lived, we do not know when. All dates remain tentative and approximate. Thus one scholar dates Yose ben Yose in the sixth century; [8] a second puts him as early as the second to the third centuries; [9] while a third points again to the sixth century "or even earlier." [10] Yannai, who is known to have lived before Ha-Kaliri, is said by one writer to have lived about the fourth century,[11] by another "between the end of the fourth and the beginning of the sixth centuries." [12] And as for Ha-Kaliri, the view of recent scholarship may be summed up by saying that he must have lived before the Arab conquest of Palestine in 635.[13]

Yose, Yannai, and Ha-Kaliri are the first three poets whose names are known to us. They are not, however, the first to have embellished the standard prayers with poetic elaborations. As Aaron Mirsky has argued, we must look for the origins of the piyyut in the Talmudic age; [14] indeed, Mirsky has devoted a whole volume to demonstrating that the early piyyutim reflect both the thought patterns and the speech patterns of Talmudic halakhah and agadah.[15] The literary historian, Jefim Schirmann, goes further, holding that piyyutim must have already existed in the second century. He insists that in the oldest standard prayers there may be found an embryo of the kind of rhyme which later on was to become a characteristic feature of the piyyut.[16] Similarly, Salo W. Baron points out that "for a long time, there was little to distinguish the new creations [i.e., the piyyutim] from other prayers . . . ." [17]

As against this, a later dating of the piyyutim has been argued by Ezra Fleischer, who maintains that the payyetanim did not begin their work until after the majority of the standard prayers had already crystallized; [18] and that, according to Fleischer, would get us— at the earliest—to the fifth century.[19] Fleischer sees in the piyyutim not an embellishment of the standard prayers but a substitute for them,[20] even a kind of rebellion against them.[21] (Only later editions of the liturgy, including both the standard prayers and the piyyutim, make the latter look like inserts into the former.) Consequently, we have to assume the existence of fixed standardized prayers before we can account for the existence of the piyyutim.

What we have to remember here is, that until the ninth century, there was no such thing as a Jewish prayerbook. The content of certain prayers was fixed, and so was the sequence of prayers as well as the concluding eulogies of the major benedictions. But when it came to the actual wording of the prayers, a great deal of leeway was given—and more in Palestine than in Babylonia. Not only did the precise wording of the prayers differ from congregation to congregation—so that, even in later centuries, no two manuscripts of the Palestinian rite are exactly alike—but also the same prayer-leader in the same congregation may have chosen different words on different occasions for the same prayer. A prayer-leader who also happened to be poetically gifted may well have elaborated a prayer poetically here and there—thereby laying the foundations of the later, more formalized, piyyut. In that sense, the piyyut would indeed represent a rebellion against the *idea* of standardized fixed prayers, although we need not assume (as Fleischer does) the existence of an actual body of such prayers against which the poet rebelled.

One thing is quite clear: it was the prayer-leader, in public worship, and not the congregation itself, who introduced and recited the piyyutim.[22] This point seems reasonable because written prayer manuals were non-existent. It is also evidenced by one of the names given to one particular form of the early piyyut. That name is *kerovah*: and it denotes the poetic embellishment of the Amidah. Now, the name, *kerovah* is derived from the name by which, in Talmudic times, the prayer-leader in public worship was known, and it may be argued on the basis of this nomenclature that the institution of the *kerovah* must necessarily go back to those early times when, in public worship, the prayer-leader began his function with the recitation of the Amidah.[23]

All this suggests, therefore, that at a time when prayer texts were not yet fixed, several versions of the same prayer vied for popular acceptance—some more simple, others more elaborate (or more poetic). As prayer-texts then became more fixed and more "traditional," particularly in the Babylonian rite, the earlier freedom to create liturgically presented itself—and was often fought—as an *alternative* to fixed prayer, until a compromise solution was arrived at. Not that the early stirrings of liturgical poetry were in any way elaborate structures of rhyme and meter; on the contrary. But the later kind of "technical" piyyut, which may well have come to full flower as late as the sixth century, would nevertheless have been unthinkable without that earlier and much simpler foundation.

In the eighth, ninth, and tenth centuries, we find Babylonian

Geonim taking various positions on the question of the permissibility of piyyut. A few of them, under Palestinian influence, championed the piyyut's cause, but there were many who vehemently argued against its introduction in Babylonia, and some went so far as to declare it wrong for the Palestinians themselves.[24] What was at stake here was not only an issue of halakhah, but also the question of hegemony over Jewish life, for which both the Palestinian and the Babylonian authorities were struggling at that time.[25] The piyyut had come to Babylonia from Palestine, and this fact alone made the Babylonians reluctant to give up their own tradition in favor of Palestinian practice.

Ultimately, however, a compromise was achieved. Once certain halakhic specifications were met, the piyyutim could be tolerated. This becomes evident from a responsum of the ninth-century Gaon Natronai:

> As for those who say *piyyutim* in the first two benedictions of the *Amidah*, and in all the prayers, and include in them the subject matter of the festival on every single festival, as well as inserts on the Ninth of Ab and on Purim—if, in every single benediction, they also deal with the subject matter of that benediction, and then, on Rosh Ha-shanah and Yom Kippur, they add words of appeasement and prayers for forgiveness, they are permitted to do so. But the main thing is, that in every single benediction, they bring in the theme of its beginning and of its end. And if, in between, they recite words of *Aggadah* and praises of God, that is all right. . . .[26]

The initial halakhic argument against the piyyut had been that it interrupts the flow of ideas in the traditional prayers and benedictions. This "halakhic compromise," as we may call it, is willing to set that argument aside as long as the piyyut, at its conclusion, provides a bridge to the theme of the concluding eulogy of the traditional benediction. It was on this basis that the piyyut won legitimacy in Jewish liturgy in those communities—they were to become the majority—which accepted the authority of the Babylonian scholars. But two points ought to be borne in mind. First, the halakhic compromise was not universally accepted; at all times and in all places there have been great scholars who continued to oppose the piyyut.[27] And second, it should be noted that the halakhic compromise declared the piyyut to be "permitted," *not* to be mandatory.

Thus, Rav Amram Gaon, in the ninth century, declares that

if the prayer-leader wants to insert a *kerovah*, he may do so. But Amram goes on to say: "This is not something fixed nor is it an obligation. Rather is it whatever the congregation desires—be it to add or to decrease." [28] And Rav Saadya Gaon, in the tenth century, seeing that "now the majority have accepted the custom of saying Atonement piyyutim also in the morning service," feels encouraged to set down three of his own.[29]

Two centuries later, however, Maimonides finds in the recitation of the piyyutim "the major cause for the lack of devotion and for the lightheartedness of the masses which impels them to talk during the prayer . . . . In addition to this, the piyyutim are occasionally the words of poets who are not scholars." [30] This last point Maimonides elaborates in his *Guide of the Perplexed*, where he castigates the "truly ignorant" poets and preachers, "or such as think that what they speak is poetry," for composing prayers and sermons in which attributes are predicated of God that run counter to true belief, and which constitute "vituperative utterances against what is above." [31] A century later, the author of the *Sepher Hasidim* complains about a man who left the synagogue after the special poetic penitential prayers in the morning service, without waiting for the recitation of the regular liturgy. This man was giving primary importance to secondary matters.[32]

But such objections notwithstanding, the piyyut, having once gained entry into the synagogue, continued to flourish. The mere listing of the names of payyetanim takes up twelve pages in the new *Encyclopaedia Judaica*.[33] Yet many of the old Palestinian piyyutim got lost, and some were only recently rediscovered in the Genizah. They were lost a) because newer piyyutim crowded out the older ones; b) because festivals observed for two days in the Diaspora made necessary the creation of new piyyutim for the second day, and they, in turn, stimulated the writing of new piyyutim for the first day as well; and c) because of the change from the Palestinian Scripture lectionary (on which the old piyyutim were based) to the Babylonian cycle of readings.[34]

In Europe, we find the piyyut first developing in southern Italy, in the second half of the ninth century. From there, it spread, in the tenth century, to central and northern Italy. French-German Jewry, at first under Italian-Jewish influence, produced its own great school of payyetanim in the tenth and eleventh centuries—many of them composing in the style of Ha-Kaliri, with his manifold allusions to biblical and rabbinic literature and his grammatical peculiarities.

The Spanish piyyut began to flourish in the tenth century. It is quite different in style and content from the French-German variety; it is couched largely in biblical vocabulary, adheres to classical Hebrew grammar, and adopts, often from Arab sources, sophisticated schemes of meter and rhyme.

While the piyyut continued to enjoy popularity, and while the number of piyyutim recited by congregations increased with the invention of printing and the availability of the printed prayerbook, few, if any, great *piyyutim* were composed after the thirteenth century.

Only in the nineteenth century did the preponderance of piyyut in the synagogue service (particularly on festivals) begin to wane. Reform Judaism, in its endeavor to shorten the services, removed most of the piyyutim from its prayerbooks. But since then the number of piyyutim has also been severely curtailed in several Orthodox and Conservative rituals. In part, this is due to the fact that, without a learned commentary, many of the piyyutim—especially those of the Ha-Kaliri type which predominated in the German-Polish rite—have become completely unintelligible to the modern worshiper.

The major types of payyetanic creations in the traditional liturgy are these:

1. *Yotzerot:* Poetic embellishments of the two benedictions before, and the one benediction after, the Shema in the morning service.

2. *Kerovot:* Poetic embellishments of the Amidah.

3. *Ma'aravot:* Poetic embellishments of the two benedictions before, and the two benedictions after, the Shema in the evening service.

4. *Avodah:* Poetic treatment of the Atonement service of the ancient high priest, included in the additional service of the Day of Atonement.

5. *Azharot:* Enumeration and poetic treatment of the 613 commandments, included in the additional service of Pentecost (Shavuot).

6. *Hosha'not:* Poetic compositions recited during the processions with the *lulav* on Tabernacles (Sukkot).

7. *Selihot:* Various penitential poems, recited on fast days, during the week before Rosh Ha-shanah, and during the Ten Days of Repentance.

8. *Kinot:* Elegies and dirges on the destruction of the Temple and Jewish suffering in general, recited on the Ninth of Ab.

9. *Akedah:* A *selihah* type of piyyut, dealing with the Binding of Isaac.

10. *Reshut:* Literally: "permission" i.e., the asking of permission (from God and from the congregation) for the inclusion of piyyutim in the service. Usually this is the first piyyut recited by a prayer-leader when he takes over a given part of the service. Thus, there are *reshut* prayers introducing the Kaddish, the *Nishmat* (cf., Birnbaum, p. 331, and "The Kaddish"), and the first *kerovah* in a series of *kerovot.*

EL BARUKH
A PRE-PAYYETANIC *PIYYUT*

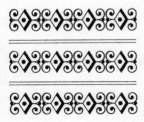

INTRODUCTION

THE DAILY YOTZER *benediction, thanking God for the light of a new day (see "The Shema and Its Benedictions") leads into a passage of angelology and the recitation of a Kedushah. One of the links joining the angelology to the benediction, in all traditional prayer-books, is, on weekdays, a sentence beginning with the words, El barukh. Presumably it was already included in Rav Amram's prayer-book;[1] and Saadya Gaon provides this text as well as an alternative,[2] thereby indicating, that in his time, it was not yet a permanent part of the standard liturgy but that several such passages were used alternatively.[3] One scholar goes so far as to attribute this sentence to "the early payyetanim who lived in the Talmudic age," but is unable to adduce any evidence from the Talmud itself.[4]*

Although the sentence has no rhyme or meter, it does represent an artistic creation—if only because the author opens with the letter aleph *and begins subsequent words with a subsequent letter until he exhausts the alphabet.*

215

EL BARUKH

A literal translation would read as follows:

> The blessed God, great in knowledge, prepared and made the bright rays of the sun. The Beneficent One created glory for His Name. He placed luminaries 'round about His might. His chief hosts are holy beings that extol the Almighty. They continually recount the glory of God and His holiness.

The literal translation fails to convey the artistry and flavor of the Hebrew composition. An English paraphrase, using all the letters of the English alphabet, comes closer:

> A Blessed Creator Does Ever Fashion Glorious Heavenly Illuminations—Jubilating Knowingly, Lauding, Ministering, Nurturing Orbs, Praising Quotidiously, Rehearsing Sanctifications, Telling Unquestionable Verities With eXultation—Yea—Zeal.

The heavenly luminaries are here identified with the angelic hosts. The physical light, therefore, which man enjoys, also contributes to the glory of God. Moreover, these luminaries are the angels who sanctify God by singing Isaiah 6:3 and Ezekiel 3:12, as the rest of this insert in the Yotzer benediction spells out in some detail.

A VINE FROM EGYPT
A PALESTINIAN *AHAVAH* BENEDICTION

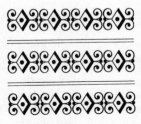

INTRODUCTION

IN A GENIZAH FRAGMENT *of a Palestinian order of service, the following text takes the place of the second benediction before the
morning Shema, i.e., it comes between the Yotzer benediction and
the Shema itself ("The Shema and Its Benedictions"). It is note-
worthy that this text, which is written in the style of a simple piyyut,
is* not *inserted into the standard* Ahavah *benediction, but actually
displaces that benediction. This would tend to show that the Palestinian rite was less standardized and more flexible than the Babylonian rite. It would also lend support to that view of the piyyutim
which sees in them not so much an embellishment of the standard
prayers but rather an attempt to displace them.*

A VINE FROM EGYPT

A vine from Egypt our God has brought up.
He drove out nations and planted it.
From Sinai He gave it water to drink,

217

Yea, running waters from Horeb.
5   Praised are You, O Lord, who loves Israel.

1–2. *A vine from Egypt . . . He drove out nations and planted it:* See Psalm 80:9 for the thought and for the image of Israel as "vine."

3–4. *Sinai . . . Horeb:* Rabbinic tradition understands "Horeb" to be one of the names of Mt. Sinai. Cf., Exodus Rabbah 2:4; 51:8.

3. *He gave it water:* The Hebrew text says "them," but the reference is clearly to Israel.

3–4. *water . . . running waters:* (Hebrew: *mayim . . . nozelim.*) This forms a pair of synonyms in the parallelism of biblical poetry. Cf., Psalm 78:16; Proverbs 5:15.

Water is frequently understood as a metaphor for Torah in Rabbinic literature. Cf., for example, Canticles Rabbah, chapter I.

This prayer says: God has redeemed Israel from Egyptian bondage, and has settled Israel in its own land. He has also given the Torah to Israel. All of this shows that God loves Israel.

Simple though the prayer is—and brief—the fact that Israel, the Land of Israel, and the Torah are all referred to by circumlocution shows that it has been composed in the payyetanic mode. It is, however, far less complicated in language and structure than the piyyutim of Yannai and Ha-Kaliri.

HOW BLESSED IS THE FOUNTAIN OF ISRAEL!
from a KEDUSHTA by YANNAI

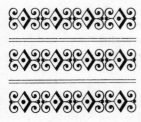

INTRODUCTION

THE FOLLOWING *is the fourth section of a Kedushta (i.e., a kerovah for the Sabbath morning service) by Yannai. It is meant for recitation on the Sabbath when, according to Yannai's Scripture lectionary, the Pentateuchal lesson begins with Deuteronomy 6:4 (i.e., the Shema). The first two lines end with the word, "Israel." The remaining lines end in "-im," which achieves the rhyme in this poem. Obviously, this cannot be reproduced in English, but I have tried to preserve something of the flavor in this rendition.*

HOW BLESSED IS THE FOUNTAIN OF ISRAEL!

How blessed is the fountain of Israel!
They say the blessings and recite the "Hear, O Israel."
They sit in Your presence, thinking of Your Name,
Audible to one another, as together they proclaim.

5 How beautiful they who proclaim it morn and night,
Pleasant their looks, their voices a delight!
Pledged one to another in Unity's affirmation,
They meddle not with those who seek its alteration.

Loving with their heart and soul and might,
10 They bow their heads in holy fright.
Worshiping, they bend the knee.
Twice every day, perpetually,
They bless and sanctify Your Name, O Holy One.

1. *fountain of Israel*: Refers to those of Jewish origin. See Psalm 68:27, where those "from the fountain of Israel" are called upon to bless God in their assemblies.

2. *They say the blessings and recite*: In both the evening service and the morning service, the recitation of the Shema is preceded by two blessings—the first praising God in nature, the second praising God as giver of the Torah. See Mishnah Berakhot 1:4.

3. *They sit in Your presence*: The schools of Hillel and Shammai argued whether the Shema should be recited in a sitting or in a standing position. The decision was in accordance with Hillel, who contended that if one were standing prior to the Shema one should remain standing; but, if seated, remain seated. (Mishnah Berakhot 1:3.) In Leviticus Rabbah 27:6, God is made to say to Israel: "I did not put you to any trouble, and I did not ask you to recite the *Shema* either standing upon your feet or with your heads uncovered." It is interesting to note, however, that the poet here bases himself on classical sources rather than on the custom

of his own Palestinian environment, which, contrary to the Babylonian custom, was, in fact, to stand up for the Shema.[1]

---

4. *Audible to one another:* The Shema must be recited au-
dibly. Cf. Mishnah Berakhot 2:3 and the *Gemara* ad loc.

---

7. *Pledged one to another:* Cf., "All Israel are pledged one
to another." (Bab. Shevuot 39a)

---

8. *They meddle not . . . :* Cf., Proverbs 24:21. "And meddle not with them that are given to change." This verse is explained,
in Deuteronomy Rabbah 2:33, in terms of Ecclesiastes 4:8, "There
is one that is alone, and he hath not a second; yea, he hath neither
son nor brother." The play on words—*shonim* ("they that are given
to change") and *en sheni* ("not a second")—is meant to underline
the uncompromising nature of Jewish monotheism and its difference
from the religion of the dominant culture.

---

9. *Loving with their heart and soul and might:* A reference to
the Shema itself. Cf., Deuteronomy 6:5.

---

12. *Twice every day:* The commandment to recite the Shema
applies to evening and morning. Cf., Deuteronomy 6:7.

IN THE MIDDLE OF THE NIGHT
from a KEROVAH by YANNAI

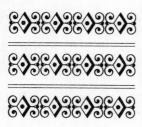

INTRODUCTION

THE FOLLOWING POEM *is a section of a* kerovah *composed by Yannai for the Sabbath preceding Passover. It is based on the Rabbinic view that "all the miracles which were wrought for Israel, and the punishment of the wicked on their behalf, took place in the night." (Numbers Rabbah 20:12.) This particular section of Yannai's kerovah has become so popular that it was incorporated in the Ashkenazi version of the Passover Haggadah for recitation on the first seder night. The first letters of each line form a complete alphabetical acrostic; and each line ends with the word* layelah (night) *or with a form thereof.*

IN THE MIDDLE OF THE NIGHT

Translation by Jacob Sloan

And so it came to pass in the middle of the night.
It was then You worked many miracles at night.

223

At the beginning of the watches on   this night,
You gave victory to the convert when
        divided was   the night.
5 And so it came to pass in the middle of   the night.

You sentenced the king of Gerar in a dream   of the night
You terrorized the Aramean in the yester   night.
And Israel with an angel fought and
        overcame him   at night.
And so it came to pass in the middle of the   night.

10 You crushed the firstborn seed of Pathros in
        the middle of   the night.
They found their strength gone when they rose   at night.
The lord of Harosheth's host were levelled
        by the stars   of night.
And so it came to pass in the middle of   the night.

The blasphemer thought to ravage Your chosen;
        You rotted his corpses   at night.

15 Bel and his pedestal fell in the middle of   the night.
To the greatly beloved man was bared
        the secret vision   of night.
And so it came to pass in the middle of   the night.

He who grew drunk from the sacred vessels
        was slain on that   very night.
He who was saved from the lions' den
        interpreted dread dreams   of night.

20 The Agagite nurtured hate, and wrote scrolls   at night.

And so it came to pass in the middle of   the night.
You began to overpower him when sleep fled   at night.
You will trample down the winepress
    for him who asks, "Watchman, what   of the night?"
He will sing out like a watchman, saying,
        "The morning cometh and also   the night."

25 And so it came to pass in the middle of   the night.

O bring near the day that is neither day nor   night.
O, Most High, announce, yours the day is, yours   the night.
Set watchmen to watch your city all the day
                        and all   the night.
Brighten, like the light of day, the dark   of night.
30 And so it came to pass in the middle of   the night.

This commentary, based on the commentaries of E. D. Goldschmidt, is by Nahum N. Glatzer, and appears in his edition of *The Passover Haggadah* (New York: Schocken Books, 1953).

1. *it came to pass:* Cf., Exodus 12:29.

3. *At the beginning:* The night is divided into three watches— the first is called *rosh ashmurot* (Lam. 2:19).

4. *convert:* Abraham.

    divided: During the battle against the four kings (Gen. 14:15).

6. *king of Gerar:* Abimelech, who "sent and took" Sarah, after "Abraham said of Sarah, his wife: 'She is my sister' " (Gen. 20:2–3).

7. *the Aramean:* Laban, whom God told "yesternight" not to harm Jacob (Gen. 31:29).

8. *Israel:* Jacob, whose name was changed to Israel (Gen. 32:29; Hos. 12:5).

10. *Pathros:* Egypt (Gen. 10:14; Jer. 44:1).

12. *Lord of Harosheth:* Sisera, the Canaanite general who "dwelt in Harosheth-goiim," and was defeated by Deborah and Barak (Judges 4:13).

the stars: "The stars in their courses fought against Sisera" (Judges 5:20).

14. *The blasphemer:* Sennacherib, King of Assyria, who sent a messenger "to taunt the living God" (II Kings 19:4, 22).

chosen: Zion, the chosen city (Psalm 132:13).

rotted his corpses: "The angel of the Lord went forth, and smote in the camp of the Assyrians . . ." (II Kings 19:35).

15. *Bel: The idol* (Dan. 3:1; cf., Isa. 46:1).

16. *beloved man:* Daniel (Dan. 10:11), to whom the interpretation of Nebuchadnezzar's dream was revealed (Dan. 2:19).

18. *grew drunk:* Belshazzar, the Babylonian king, who "made a great feast to a thousand of his lords" (Dan. 5), at which he drank from the vessels of the Temple in Jerusalem.

was slain: Daniel 5:30.

THE POETRY OF THE SYNAGOGUE 227

19. *saved from the lions' den:* Daniel (Dan. 6:20).

20. *The Agagite:* Haman who sent letters to the King's provinces to have all the Jews destroyed (Esther 3:13).

22. *when sleep fled:* From Ahasuerus (Esther 6:1).

23. *trample down the winepress:* i.e., destroy (cf., Isa. 63:3).
for him: For the sake of Israel who asks . . . (Isa. 63:3).

24. *"The morning cometh . . .":* Isaiah 21:12. The question is taken to mean: "When will the deliverance from the oppressor come?" The answer given is "The morning cometh" for you, "and also the night—" for your oppressors.

26. *neither day nor night:* The day of Messianic deliverance (Zech. 14:7).

27. *yours the day is, yours the night:* Psalm 74:16.

28. *Set watchmen:* Isa. 62:6.

REMEMBER THE PATRIARCH
from the PRAYER FOR RAIN by ELEAZAR HA-KALIRI

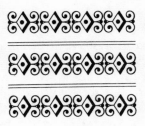

INTRODUCTION

WINTER *is the rainy season in the Land of Israel. As an adequate supply of rain is crucial for the economy of an agricultural society, prayers for rain were an important aspect of the ancient liturgy. One of those prayers, describing God as "causing the wind to blow and the rain to fall," is known as gevurot geshamim, "God's mighty acts manifested in the rain." It is inserted in the standard liturgy from Shemini Atzeret through Passover (Cf., Mishnah Ta'anit 1:1). It is included in the second benediction of the Amidah, i.e., the benediction which deals with the resurrection of the dead (Mishnah Berakhot 5:2; cf., Birnbaum, p. 83, and the chapter, "The Weekday Amidah"). God's mighty acts, which, one day, will be seen in the resurrection of the dead, are no less manifest in the life-giving qualities of rain. Indeed, what the rain does to the "lifeless" grain of seed is prototypical of the ultimate eschatological expectations—in terms both of individual resurrection and the national restoration from Exile.*

The occasion when gevurot geshamim is recited for the first time in the year, during the recitation of the Amidah of the additional service on Shemini Atzeret, has been embellished by various synagogal poets—in such a way that the "rain-resurrection-restoration" theme is introduced as early as in the first benediction of the Amidah, al-

though it does not reach its climax until the second benediction with the proclamation that "Thou art the Lord our God, causing the wind to blow and the rain to fall."

The poem translated here is the concluding section of a series of lengthy piyyutim by Eleazar Ha-Kaliri. As far as this particular section is concerned, however, doubts have been raised about Ha-Kaliri's authorship on the grounds of diction.[1] Yet the fact remains that this poem displays several of the artistic touches which are associated with the poems of Ha-Kaliri: the use of Midrashic circumlocutions to describe various biblical characters, the complete alphabetical acrostic, and the rhyme scheme with each line ending in the word mayim (water). *If, therefore, this poem was not composed by Ha-Kaliri himself, it is certainly to be attributed to his school.*

REMEMBER THE PATRIARCH

Our God and God of our fathers!

I

Remember the Patriarch who followed Thee   like water.
Thou didst bless him like a tree planted
                              by streams   of water.
Thou didst protect him and save him from fire   and from water.
Thou didst seek him out as he sowed by   every water.
5   For his sake, withhold not   the water.

II

Remember him who was born after the proc-
          lamation of "let there be taken a little   water."
Thou didst tell his father to slaughter him,
                    to spill his blood like   water.
He, too, took care to pour out his heart like   water.

He dug, and he found wells of   water.
10   For his righteousness' sake, favor us
                with an abundance of   water.

III

Remember him who took his staff and crossed
                the Jordan's   water.
With dedicated heart, he rolled away the
                stone from the mouth of a well of   water.
He once wrestled with an angel, composed
                of fire and of   water.
Thou, therefore, didst promise to be with him
                through fire and through   water.
15   For his sake, withhold not the   water.

IV

Remember him, who, in an ark of reeds, was
                drawn out of the   water.
They said: From the well he drew, and let
                the sheep drink   water.
At a time when Thy chosen ones were
                thirsting for   water.
He smote the rock, and there came forth   water.
20   For his righteousness' sake, favor us
                with an abundance of   water.

V

Remember him, the Temple priest, who went
                through five immersions in   water.
He cleansed himself and washed his hands
                with sanctifying   water.
He recited Scripture, and he sprinkled
                the purifying   water.
He was set apart from a people as unstable as   water.
25   For his sake, withhold not the   water.

VI

Remember the twelve tribes whom Thou
      didst bring across the divided   water.
For them didst Thou sweeten the bitterness of   water.
For Thy sake was their offspring's blood
                spilled like   water.
O turn to us, for troubles encompass
          our life like   water.
30   For their righteousness' sake, favor us
        with an abundance of   water.

For Thou art the Lord our God,
    causing the wind to blow and the rain to fall
For a blessing, and not for a curse.   Amen.
For life, and not for death   Amen.
For plenty, and not for famine.   Amen.

I Abraham

---

2. *tree planted by streams of water:* Biblical description of the righteous man. Cf., Psalm 1:3.

---

3. *Thou didst . . . save him from fire and from water:* The Midrash relates that Nimrod had the young Abraham cast into a fiery furnace, from which God delivered him.[2] The Midrash also relates, that as Abraham was on his way to sacrifice his son, Isaac, on Mount Moriah, Satan turned himself into a mighty river in which Abraham all but drowned. At Abraham's plea, God rebuked Satan, and Abraham was saved. Cf., Yalkut Shim'oni, Va-yera, 99.

---

4. *sowed by every water:* Cf., Isaiah 32:20, "Happy are ye that sow beside all waters." The Rabbinic interpretation of this verse, in Bab. Baba Kamma 17a, understands "sowing" as "doing charitable deeds," and "water" as Torah.

II   Isaac

6. *"let there be taken a little water"*: According to Genesis 18:4, Abraham addressed these words to the three angels who visited him. One of those angels later announced to Abraham the forthcoming birth of a son. See Genesis 18:10.

7. *Thou didst tell his father to slaughter him:* The reference is to the story of the "Binding of Isaac" in Genesis, 22.

8. *He, too, took care to pour out his heart:* Genesis 24:63 relates that "Isaac went out to meditate in the field at eventide." According to Rabbi Yosé ben Haninah, in Bab. Berakhot 26b, Isaac's "meditation" was the Minhah prayer, of which Isaac is to be regarded as the originator.

9. *He dug, and he found wells of water:* Cf., Genesis 26:17–22.

III   Jacob

11. *him who took his staff:* In Genesis 32:11, Jacob, contrasting his erstwhile poverty with his present wealth, says: ". . . with my staff I passed over this Jordan; and now I am become two camps."

12. *he rolled away the stone:* Cf., Genesis 29:1–10.

13. *he once wrestled with an angel:* Cf., Genesis 32:25–32.

composed of fire and of water: The word for "heaven" in Hebrew is *shamayim*, which some of the rabbis, in Bab. Hagigah 12a, understand as a compound of *esh* (fire) and *mayim* (water), i.e., a reconciliation of opposites. The angels, as heavenly beings, would be composed of the same elements.

---

14. *Thou, therefore, didst promise*: Cf., Isaiah 43:1–2. The Prophet, of course, was addressing the *nation* of Israel, and used the name of Jacob only metaphorically. But the poet, in this context, takes "Jacob" literally.

IV *Moses*

---

16. *who, in an ark of reeds, was drawn out of the water*: Cf., Exodus 2:3–10.

---

17. *They said*: i.e., the daughters of Jethro said. Cf., Exodus 2:16–19.

---

18. *when Thy chosen ones were thirsting*: Cf., Exodus 17:1–6.

V *Aaron*

This stanza is not so much concerned with the historical Aaron, the brother of Moses, as with Aaron the prototype of the high priest, whose ministrations on the Day of Atonement are described in some detail in the Mishnah tractate of Yoma.

---

24. *He was set apart*: Yoma 1:1 begins with the report that "seven days before the Day of Atonement, the high priest was removed from his own house unto the Chamber of the Counselors."

a people as unstable as water: In Genesis 49:4, Reuben is described as "unstable as water." Reuben, being Jacob's firstborn son, seems, in the poet's view, to exemplify a quality of instability shared by all of the children of Israel.

VI   *The Twelve Tribes*

26. *Thou didst bring across the divided water:* Cf., Exodus 14.

27. *For them didst Thou sweeten:* Cf., Exodus 15:22–25.

29. *troubles encompass our life like water:* Cf., Jonah 2:6, "The waters compassed me about, even to the soul; the deep was round about me."

DEW, PRECIOUS DEW
A PRAYER FOR DEW by ELEAZAR HA-KALIRI

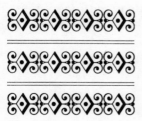

INTRODUCTION

ALL THE TRADITIONAL *Jewish rites include the phrase, "Thou causest the wind to blow and the rain to fall," in the second benediction of the Amidah from Shemini Atzeret through Passover; but the corresponding practice of saying "Thou causest the dew to descend," between Passover and Shemini Atzeret, did not gain universal acceptance. It was a part of the Palestinian rite, and from there it spread to the Italian and Spanish rites. But the Ashkenazim do not have it.*

Nevertheless, on the first occasion of the year when other rites insert the phrase, the Ashkenazi rite does, too—but only on that one occasion: the reader's repetition of the Amidah of the additional service on the first day of Passover. Possibly this is due to the fact that the Ashkenazi rite took over so many of Ha-Kaliri's piyyutim.

In form, the "Prayer for Dew" is the exact counterpart to the "Prayer for Rain." Ha-Kaliri's authorship of the concluding poem in the prayer has here again been questioned on grounds of diction, in this case with perhaps greater justice.

The poem consists of six stanzas. Each stanza begins with the word tal *(dew), and ends with the word* betal *(in, with, by, dew). There is also an acrostic of the Hebrew alphabet from the end to the beginning, i.e., backward. Each stanza consists of four lines. The first two lines deal with hoped-for agricultural bounties, and take "dew" in a literal sense. The last two lines construe the word in a metaphorical sense, as a symbol of national restoration and resurrection. This usage is already found in the Bible. Cf., Isaiah 26:19.*

DEW, PRECIOUS DEW

Translation by Israel Zangwill

Our God and God of our fathers!

Dew, precious dew, unto Thy land forlorn!
Pour out our blessing in Thy exultation,
To strengthen us with ample wine and corn
And give Thy chosen city safe foundation

5   In dew.

Dew, precious dew, the good year's crown, we wait,
That earth in pride and glory may be fruited,
And the city now so desolate
Into a gleaming crown may be transmuted

10   By dew.

Dew, precious dew, let fall upon the land,
From heaven's treasury be this accorded,
So shall the darkness by a beam be spanned,
The faithful of Thy vineyard be rewarded

15   With dew.

Dew, precious dew, to make the mountains sweet,
The savor of Thy excellence recalling!
Deliver us from exile, we entreat,
So we may sing Thy praises, softly falling

20   As dew!

Dew, precious dew, our granaries to fill
And us with youthful freshness to enharden!

Belovèd God, uplift us at Thy will
And make us as a richly watered garden
25   With dew.

Dew, precious dew, that we our harvest reap,
And guard our fatted flocks and herds from leanness!
Behold our people follows Thee like sheep,
And looks to Thee to give the earth her greenness
30   With dew.

For Thou art the Lord our God,
        causing the wind to blow and the dew to descend
For a blessing, and not for a curse.   Amen.
For life, and not for death.   Amen.
For plenty, and not for famine.   Amen.

---

4. *And give . . . safe foundation:* Literally: "Raise up again Thy chosen city."

---

8. *the city now so desolate:* Literally: "The city left as a booth." Cf., Isaiah 1:8.

13–14. Literally, these lines say: "To give light out of the darkness to the stock which is drawn after Thee." "The stock" refers to Israel, as in Psalm 80:16, ". . . the stock which Thy right hand hath planted."

---

23. *Beloved God, uplift us at Thy will:* Literally: "Beloved, establish our name corresponding to Thine own worth." "Beloved" (Hebrew: *dod*) is a favorite payyetanic name for God, based on the Rabbinic interpretation of the Song of Songs. The sense of this line seems to be, that just as God is eternal, so Israel, at the time of the eschatological fulfillment, will be eternal.

28–29. Literally, these two lines say: "The nation Thou hast led forth like sheep, O let it obtain favor." For this description of Israel, see Psalm 78:52. The phrase, "let it obtain favor" is based on Proverbs 8:35. By referring to the earth's greenness, in line 29, Zangwill does violence to the structure of this poem, in which the first two lines of each stanza deal with agricultural boons, while the last two lines invariably sound the messianic theme. The "favor" of the original of line 29 has messianic, not agricultural, implications.

THE MEN OF FAITHFULNESS ARE LOST
AN ANCIENT *SELIHAH*

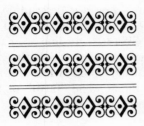

INTRODUCTION

SAADYA GAON (882–942) *includes this penitential prayer in the liturgy for fast days.*[1] *He himself may possibly have been its author. In the Spanish and Portuguese rite, it is recited every Monday, and repeatedly on the Day of Atonement.*

It is an alphabetical acrostic, from aleph *through* tav, *with two additional lines. Each line has three—occasionally, four—words. There is no attempt at a rhyme.*

The selihah is an elaboration on the theme that Israel's exile is due to Israel's sins. The great men of piety lived in the past; we suffer because we are unable to rise to their heights; nevertheless, let us in contrition return to God.

THE MEN OF FAITHFULNESS ARE LOST

The men of faithfulness are lost,
They who came by the strength of their deeds.

Mighty to stand in the breach,
They averted the evil decrees.

5 A wall they were to us,
A refuge on the day of wrath.
They extinguished anger by their whisper.
They restrained rage by their cry.
Before they called You, You answered them.

10 They knew how to pray and appease.
Like a father, You showed mercy for their sake;
You did not dismiss them empty-handed.
Because of our many iniquities, we have lost them;
They were taken away from us because of our sins.

15 They have gone on to their eternal rest,
Leaving us to our sighs.
The repairers of the wall have vanished;
Cut off are they who turned away wrath.
Of such as could stand in the breach we have none;

20 Those worthy to appease You have come to an end.
We have wandered about in the earth's four corners,
But healing we have not found.

We now turn to You with shameful faces,
To seek You, God, at the time of our distress.

---

4. *They averted the evil decrees:* Cf., Bab. Shabbat 63a: "Even if the Holy One, praised be He, makes a decree, He annuls it [for those who keep the commandments]."

---

9. *Before they called You, You answered them:* Cf., Isaiah 65:24.

I SAID, BE GRACIOUS UNTO ME
A *SHIV'ATA* by SAADYA GAON or HIS SCHOOL

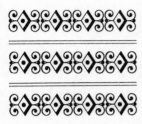

INTRODUCTION

A SHIV'ATA *is a poetic treatment of the seven benedictions of Sabbath and festival Amidot other than those of the morning service. The shiv'ata presented here has been attributed to Saadya Gaon or to his "school."* [1]

The poem is composed according to an acrostic of the complete alphabet (substituting, however, the letter sin for the letter samekh— a frequent device in acrostic poems). The last line of each stanza, before its concluding eulogy, is a biblical quotation adumbrating the theme of the eulogy. With few exceptions, there are four Hebrew words to the line, and each stanza has its own rhyme scheme (not reproduced in the English).

It is somewhat strange to see a shiv'ata, which, according to the concluding eulogy of the fourth stanza, is definitely meant for the Sabbath, so completely devoted to the themes of exile and oppression. Perhaps it was composed for one of the three sabbaths preceding the Ninth of Ab.

244 LITERATURE OF THE SYNAGOGUE

I SAID, BE GRACIOUS UNTO ME

I said: Be gracious unto me, my God,
Look upon my affliction and see my travail.
Deliver me from my oppressors and from the hand of him
who loathes me.
O Lord, be my helper!
5   Praised are You, O Lord, Shield of Abraham.

You have thrust me out of Your Temple.
Now I am driven about by the hand of Your enemies.
How long will You remain silent about Your chosen sons?
Revive me with dew, O Lord, as You have promised.
10   Praised are You, O Lord, reviver of the dead.

Remember me in Your mercy, to draw me out of the mire.
Hasten, O Comforter, restorer of my soul.
Establish my turret, and forgive my foolish transgression.
O Lord, my God, my Holy One.
15   Praised are You, O Lord, the Holy God.

I have grown weary in captivity and faint for lack
of restoration.
My eyes fail from waiting, and my joy has ceased.
For Your sake grant me joy, and guard me like the apple
of the eye.
"The Lord has given you the Sabbath."
20   Praised are You, O Lord, who hallows the Sabbath.

Reign over us forever.
Bear us and exalt us by means of the rebuilt shrine.
Make us happy, and let us spend our days in pleasant places.
The Lord is great in Zion, and exalted over the peoples.
25   Praised are You, O Lord, who restores His Presence to Zion.

To the prayer of Your beloved people
Turn, and accept it as You did incense in your meeting-place.
The sheep of Your hand are they, Your witnesses, too.
O Lord, my God, I will give thanks unto You forever.
30   Praised are You, O Lord, whose Name is the Good One.

We have hoped for Your salvation; requite us with Your goodness.
Lead us by it, to make us full of sap and green.
Dwell in our borders as of old.
O Lord, grant us peace.
35   Praised are You, O Lord, who blesses His people
                              with peace.

Lines 5, 10, 15, 20, 25, 30, and 35 are the concluding eulogies of the seven benedictions of the Sabbath Amidah.

1. A direct quotation of Psalm 41:5a.

4. Psalm 30:11b.

9. Psalm 119:25b: Dew is mentioned here because, during the summer months, the (Palestinian) standard form of this benediction describes God as "causing the dew to descend." Dew as a metaphor for the resurrection is already found in Isaiah 26:19.

13. *Establish my turret:* (Hebrew: tirati.) The reference is to the Jerusalem Temple. Cf., Ezekiel 46:23.

14. Habakkuk 1:12.

19. Exodus 16:29.

24. Psalm 99:2.

29. Psalm 30:13.

34. Isaiah 26:12

ABUNDANT SHOWERS
A PRAYER FOR RAIN by SOLOMON IBN GABIROL

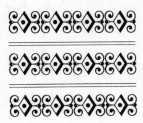

INTRODUCTION

WHILE THE POEMS of Ha-Kaliri and his school dominated the liturgy
of the Ashkenazi Jews, the Sephardi Jews relied upon their own poets.
One of the most popular among them was Solomon ibn Gabirol (ca.
1020–1057). Gabirol, writing both religious and secular poetry, also
composed a prayer for rain, from which the following selection is
taken. It is meant for recitation on Shemini Atzeret, when, for the
first time in the year, the phrase, "You cause the wind to blow and
the rain to fall," is inserted in the second benediction of the Amidah
(cf., "The Weekday Amidah" and "Litanies for Tabernacle").

Unlike the synagogal poetry of the Ashkenazi Jews, which was
mainly composed in the Ha-Kaliri style, the Sephardi poets strove for
greater faithfulness to biblical syntax and vocabulary. At the same
time, they combined the use of biblical Hebrew with more sophisticated schemes of rhyme and meter. In the poem which follows, the
poet uses his first name, Solomon, and the wish, hazak (Be strong!), as
his acrostic.

While Gabirol's syntax and vocabulary are biblical, in several
stanzas (consisting primarily of biblical quotations) a certain knowledge of Rabbinic exegesis of Scripture is assumed on the part of the
worshiper—not as much, admittedly, as in the case of Ha-Kaliri or of

247

Ashkenazi poetry, but enough to make the poem otherwise unintelligible. In this particular instance, it is taken for granted that the worshiper will be familiar with the Rabbinic interpretation of the Song of Songs, in which God figures as the lover, Israel as the beloved. It is, incidentally, somewhat remarkable that Gabirol bases most of this poem on the Song of Songs, the biblical book assigned to the festival of Passover, rather than on a text more in keeping with the rainy season, which the beginning of this poem celebrates.

ABUNDANT SHOWERS

   Abundant showers
   May He bring down from above,
   To give life to the seed,
   To give yield to the fruit.

5 Early rain and latter rain
   May He bring down with heavy drops,
   That all the fruit trees and the leaves
   Be full of strength and sap.

   O hasten and send the fawn
10 Before the shadows flee.
   For my sake, remember him
   Who planted the tamarisk tree.

   Restore the closed-in garden,
   The orchard and its shoots of pomegranates,
15 The city where David dwelt,
   The strong tower of his hosts.

   Return to the neck of ivory,
   With perfect beauty filled,
   To which all nations shall flow.
20 Built it was with turrets;
   A thousand shields
   Are hanging thereon.

9. *O hasten and send the fawn:* Cf., Song of Songs 4:5, "Thy two breasts are like two fawns." The Targum renders this as "Your two redeemers, Messiah ben David and Messiah ben Joseph." Gabirol is here interested only in the more generally expected Messiah ben David; but he uses the word, "fawn," in the singular, in the sense indicated by the Targum.

10. *Before the shadows flee:* Cf., Song of Songs 4:6.

11–12. The reference is to Abraham. Cf., Genesis 21:33. Since this poem is inserted in the Avoth section of the Amidah, some reference to the patriarchs is to be expected. In fact, this whole section of the poem can be seen as a poetic elaboration of the Avoth phrase, "Thou rememberest the pious deeds of the patriarchs, and, in love, wilt bring a redeemer to their children's children." The Hebrew for "tamarisk tree," in Genesis 21:33, is *eshel.* According to one view in the Talmud, Bab. Sotah 10a, eshel, in this Genesis verse, does not mean "tamarisk tree," but "an inn for wayfarers"—which would exemplify one of the" pious deeds" in which Abraham engaged.

13. *closed-in garden:* Cf., Song of Songs 4:12. According to Canticles Rabbah IV, 12, 1, this is a reference to Israel.

14. *orchard:* This continues the metaphor of the previously quoted verse from Song of Songs. Cf., Canticles Rabbah, loc. cit.

15. *The city where David dwelt:* Jerusalem. Cf., Isaiah 29:1.

17. *neck of ivory:* Cf., Song of Songs 7:5, "Thy neck is as a tower of Ivory." According to the Targum, ad loc., this refers to the Hall of Hewn Stones at the Jerusalem Temple, where the Sanhedrin held its sessions. Gabirol seems to understand it as a reference to the Temple as a whole.

19. *To which all nations shall flow:* Cf., Isaiah 2:2.

20–22. *Built it was with turrets;* etc.: Another description of the beloved's neck, this one from Song of Songs 4:4. According to Canticles Rabbah IV, 4, 9, this, too, is a reference to the Jerusalem Temple. The word here translated as "turrets," *talpiyot,* is understood by the Midrash (loc. cit.) as *tel piyot,* "the hill of mouths," i.e., the hill for which, or toward which, all mouths pray.

THE ROYAL CROWN
from A POEM by SOLOMON IBN GABIROL

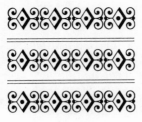

INTRODUCTION

IN ADDITION TO WRITING *religious and secular poetry, Solomon ibn Gabirol also wrote philosophical works. His philosophical position, a form of Neoplatonism, is described in Julius Guttmann,* Philosophies of Judaism *(New York: Holt, Rinehart & Winston, 1964), pp. 89–103.*

The poem, Keter Malkhut *("The Royal Crown"), from which two selected stanzas are presented here, is a unique combination of prayerful contrition and the lofty exposition of a philosophical system. After a liturgical introduction, Gabirol begins with an enumeration of God's attributes. But the poet stresses that these attributes are distinct only in human thinking, whereas in God Himself they mysteriously form a complete unity. The poet then proceeds to a description of God's wonderful revelation in the universe, in a world created out of nothing. The universe is described according to the Ptolemaic scheme, but the Divine Will is emphasized as the instrument of creation. Above it all, is God Himself. Heaven and Hell are described next, and then the poet speaks about man's body and man's soul. This leads into a confession of sins and a prayer for forgiveness. The poet manages to do all this with a largely biblical vocabulary. Of particular note is his use of biblical quotations, taken out of context and imbued with philosophical meaning.*

251

In the Spanish and Portuguese and related rites, "The Royal Crown" is recited at the conclusion of the Kol Nidre service. Some Ashkenazi festival prayerbooks have included it as well—for private meditation after the service.

It has been said of this poem:

Everything the poet knew—what his own thinking had taught him, what his brethren in faith had bequeathed to him by tradition, what he had learned from the science and the wisdom of his own age—all of that he wove together into a diadem of glory for his God.[1]

From the forty stanzas we present here stanza II and stanza VIII.

THE ROYAL CROWN

Translation by Israel Zangwill

II

Thou art One, the first of every number, and the foundation of every structure.

Thou art One, and at the mystery of Thy Oneness the wise of heart are struck dumb,

For they know not what it is.

Thou art One, and Thy Oneness can neither be increased nor lessened,

5   It lacketh naught, nor doth aught remain over.

Thou art One, but not like a unit to be grasped or counted,

For number and change cannot reach Thee.

Thou art not to be visioned, nor to be figured thus or thus.

Thou art One, but to put to Thee bound or circumference my imagination would fail me.

10   Therefore I have said I will guard my ways lest I sin with the tongue.

Thou art One, Thou art high and exalted beyond abasement or falling,

"For how should the One fall?"

VIII

Thou art the God of Gods, and the Lord of Lords,
Ruler of beings celestial and terrestrial,
For all creatures are Thy witnesses
15   And by the glory of this Thy name, every creature
is bound to Thy service.
Thou art God, and all things formed are Thy
servants and worshipers.
Yet is not Thy glory diminished by reason of
Those that worship aught beside Thee,
For the yearning of them all is to draw nigh Thee,
But they are like the blind,
20   Setting their faces forward on the King's highway,
Yet still wandering from the path.
One sinketh into the well of a pit
And another falleth into a snare,
But all imagine they have reached their desire,
25   Albeit they have suffered in vain.
But Thy servants are as those walking clear-eyed
in the straight path,
Turning neither to the right nor the left
Till they come to the court of the King's palace.
Thou art God, by Thy Godhead sustaining all that hath
been formed,
30   And upholding in Thy Unity all creatures.
Thou art God, and there is no distinction 'twixt Thy
Godhead and Thy Unity, Thy pre-existence and Thy existence,
For 'tis all one mystery.
And although the name of each be different,
"Yet they are all proceeding to one place."

II

Both his Jewish heritage and his Neoplatonic philosophical system
compel the poet-philosopher to wrestle with the problem of "the
One" which is the origin of "the many," and yet in no way identical
with them. Cf., the statement of Plotinus, in *Ennead* VI, 9: "For
the nature of *the one* being generation of all things, is not any one of

them. Neither, therefore, is it a certain thing, nor a quality, nor a quantity, nor intellect, nor soul, nor that which is moved nor again that which stands still. Nor is it in place, or in time; but is by itself uniform, or rather without form, being prior to all form, to motion and to permanency." [2]

5. Psalm 39:2.

6. Ecclesiastes 4:10.

VIII

It was a remarkable feat for an eleventh-century poet to recognize, that in spite of all their differences, all religions were really tending toward the same One God. The early Stoics did indeed seem to have such a notion, and they used the universality of the belief in God as a proof of the existence of God (*de consensu gentium*). And, of course, the prophet Malachi (1:11) seems to have had this concept as well. But in the Middle Ages this proof of the existence of God was rarely used by Jewish authors—for the simple reason that what would seem to be proved by it would not be Jewish monotheism but rather the validity of polytheism.[3] Gabirol is an exception to the rule. But contrary to the modern notion that all religions are equally true (or false), Gabirol does not stop with the assertion (line 18) that "the yearning of them all is to draw nigh Thee" (although some recent quotations of this stanza do); in fact he goes on to say, that to the extent to which they do not approach Jewish monotheism, other religions have failed to reach their true destiny. For Gabirol, Judaism is the yardstick by which the truth of religion is to be measured.

26. Cf., Pesikta Rabbati, chapter 8, Friedmann, ed., p. 30a: "The wicked are like the man who walks in darkness . . . , but the righteous are like the man with a light in front of him."

34. Ecclesiastes 3:20.

O GOD, THY NAME
AN INTRODUCTION to THE *KADDISH*
by JUDAH HALEVI

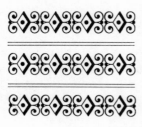

INTRODUCTION

JUDAH HALEVI (1075?–1141) was a poet, philosopher, and physician. He lived in Spain, but toward the end of his life decided to emigrate to the land of Israel. He seems to have died in Egypt, on the way toward his desired goal. Halevi wrote a great number of poems, both secular and religious. Many of his religious poems are incorporated into the liturgy of the Spanish and Portuguese Jews and of related rites. Some, particularly poems which voice Halevi's intense longings for Zion, are also incorporated into the Ashkenazi liturgy.

The poem presented here was written as an introduction to the Kaddish (cf., "The Kaddish"). It is used to introduce the Kaddish before the Call to Worship on the morning of the New Year in the Spanish and Portuguese rite. The four opening words of the second paragraph of the Kaddish form the refrain of this poem, and they also determine the rhythm and meter of the whole composition. The name Judah is spelled out in an acrostic.

O GOD, THY NAME

Translation by Nina Salaman

O God, Thy name! I will exalt Thee, and
    Thy righteousness I will not conceal.
I have given ear, and I have trusted; I will
    not question, I will not prove:
For how should a vessel of clay say unto its
    molder, What doest Thou?
I have sought Him, I have met Him—a tower
    of strength, a rock of trust—
5   The radiant one, like shining light, unveiled,
    uncovered!
Praised be He and glorified, exalted and extolled!

The beauty of Thy glory and the strength
    of Thy hand the heavens declare,
When they dawn and when they wane and
    when they bow their faces;
And angels walk amid the stones of fire and
    water.
10 They testify to Thee, they thank Thee, Who
    createst the fruit of the lips,
For Thou upholdest, and failest not—without
    arms, without hands—
The depths and the heights, the Beings and
    the Throne.
Praised be He and glorified, exalted and extolled!

And who can utter the glory of Him who
    formed the clouds by His word?
15 He liveth eternally, albeit hidden; in the
    highest heights is His abode.
And in His love for the son of His house,
    within his tent He set His presence,

And granted vision to prophecy, to look
    toward His likeness.
And there is no form and no measurement,
    and no end to the knowledge of Him;
Only the vision of Him in the sight of
    His prophets is like a King high and exalted.
20 *Praised be He and glorified, exalted and extolled!*

The tale of mighty acts is beyond telling, and
    who can declare His praises?
Happy is the man who is quick to perceive
    the strength of His great deeds,
And stayeth himself upon God who upholdeth
    the universe in His arms,
And proclaimeth His awe whate'er betide,
    and holdeth right His acts,
25 And giveth thanks for all he doeth, since for
    His own sake are His doings,
And since a terrible day of God cometh when
    there shall be judgment for all work.
Praised be He and glorified, exalted and extolled!

Consider deeply and prepare thyself and reflect
    on thine own secret,
And examine what thou art and whence thine
    origin,
30 Who set thee up, who gave thee understanding,
    whose power moveth thee;
And look unto the mighty acts of God and
    waken the glory in thee.
Search out His works, only upon Himself
    put not forth thine hand
When thou seekest the end and the beginning,
    the too wonderful, the deeply hid.
Praised be He and glorified, exalted and extolled!

The progression of ideas in this poem has been described in the following way by Franz Rosenzweig:

The individual streams of the five stanzas which flow into the common ocean of "Praised be He . . ." come from different directions. The first stanza proceeds from the condition of the creature— of that creature whose desire for the Creator's salvation is immediately paralleled by his receiving of that salvation. Heaven opens for him who is thus certain of salvation; and, blinded, he falls to the ground.

The second stanza dares to open the eyes again. Heaven has been closed. Nature lies stretched out. But the poem climbs from sphere to sphere, up to Nature's Prime Mover, at rest within Himself. Arrived at this point, it beholds the wonders of God's Throne, in Ezekiel's vision, and, again, falls to the ground.

Shaken by the tension between height and depth, which he now measures, the poet begins to comprehend the riddle of Revelation: the Tent of Meeting contains the Eternal One, Him for whom the whole world does not provide sufficient space! The thinker knows that all of our cognition, even prophetic cognition, can only behold a reflection. But he also knows that this "only" is not a mere "only," but the form through which man has a share in the vision of "His likeness." Yet the thought of the "only" throws him to the ground again.

And now he looks around in man's world, which surrounds him, and he recognizes the fate of man in his dependence, and the salvation of man in the free and joyous acceptance of that dependence, in the recognition of Providence, and in waiting for the Judgment. This time, the words of the prayer are but the calm and necessary consequence of that which wisdom has perceived.

But the calm of recognition does not last. Man reaches deeper into himself. He is not wise. He is—nothing. And out of this final and most inward experience of nothingness, he looks up again to the greatness of his Lord. Trembling, he now expresses the last thought unto which his thinking has attained: he recognizes and senses only God's *deeds*. Toward God Himself he may not "put forth his hand" —as he says in the identical words with which God deprives the Tempter of the power over Job's life. And, shuddering at this feeling of the mystery above him, man stammers the words of the prayer which, whispered by the lonely one, now carry further as, from the beginning, they are accompanied by the choir of Creation and the created spirits.[1]

6. Also lines 13, 20, 27, and 34. This is the refrain, consisting of the four opening words of the second paragraph of the Kaddish. Cf., *Birnbaum*, p. 70.

10. *Who createst the fruit of the lips:* Cf., Isaiah 57:19.

16. *the son of His house:* Moses. Cf., Numbers 12:7.

24. *whate'er betide:* Literally: "ran and returned." Ezekiel 1:14.

32. *only upon Himself put not forth thine hand:* Cf., Job 1:12.

33. *the too wonderful, the deeply hid:* The words are from Bab. Hagigah 13a, "Seek not things that are too hard for thee, and search not out things that are hidden from thee." The Talmud is quoting Ecclesiasticus 3:21.

MOSES WENT UP ON HIGH
A POEM ABOUT THE SINAITIC REVELATION
by JOSEPH BAR SAMUEL TOV ELEM (BONFILS)

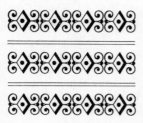

INTRODUCTION

JOSEPH BAR SAMUEL TOV ELEM (*Bonfils*), *born in Narbonne in the eleventh century, served as a rabbi in Limoges. He is noted both for his contributions to Jewish legal literature and for his synagogal poetry—the latter drawing heavily upon the biblical exegesis in the Midrash.*

The selection offered here is one section of Joseph bar Samuel's Ma'aravot (poetic embellishments of the two benedictions before and after the evening Shema) for Shavuot eve (cf., "The Shema and Its Benedictions"). For the overall composition, the poet has chosen a very intricate scheme in which he links his treatment of the Sinaitic Revelation with the main contents of the standard benedictions of the evening service. The opening words of each verse in Exodus 19:19– 20:15, including the opening words of each of the Ten Commandments, form the openings of the poet's sentences. This scheme is integrated with another whereby a complete acrostic of the Hebrew alphabet is produced as well as an acrostic of the poet's name.

In the selection presented on the following pages, however, which is the first poetic insert in the first benediction after the Shema, the poet merely completes the alphabetical acrostic from tet *to* tav, *and* adopts a meter and a rhyme different from the rest of the composition. It is a meditation on the roles of both God and man in the Sinaitic Revelation. Each stanza consists of three stichs. There are three Hebrew words in each of the first two stichs, and two in the last stich, which invariably ends in "-ot."

The effect may be gathered from the following transliteration of the first three stanzas of the poem:

> toviyah lamarom alah / vehorid dat kelulah /
> > behag hashavu'ot.
> yarad tzur be'atzmo / venatan oz le'ammo /
> > bir'amim uzeva'ot.
> kol atzei haya'ar / ahazum hil vasa'ar /
> > veharim ugeva'ot.

MOSES WENT UP ON HIGH

> Moses went up on high, and brought down the perfect Law
> > on the Feast of Shavuot.
> The Rock Himself descended, and gave strength unto
> > His people with thunders and earthquakes.
> All the trees of the forest were seized by fear and trembling,
> > and also the hills and the mountains.
> He taught the holy people the order of solstices and months
> > and the reckoning of the hours.
> 5 He loved them more than all other nations, and brought
> > them to Mount Sinai,
> > > the God of salvation.
>
> He carried them on eagles' wings, He that dwelleth in lofty
> > heights; and underneath the [everlasting] arms.
> They, the comely and beautiful people, rebelled
> > at the very moment they heard [God speaking];
> > > the very heavens shook.
> The shamed ones covered their heads,
> > and the Rock devoted them to the slaughter
> > > when the time for punishment came.

The majestic expanse of the sky and a lofty stretch of earth,
          they were touching each other.
10   The Righteous One turned the mountain over the
     fair and comely people
          like a barrel and like curtains.

The chosen people hearkened to upright statutes and ordinances
          with an attentive ear.
The Lofty One, in His mercy, protected them from the hand
     of all their enemies
          and also from evil decrees.
He sent signs and wonders, and bequeathed to them engraved
     laws
          in wisdom and in knowledge.
He greatly magnified their glory, making them famous and
     praised,
          with the blessing of the cup of salvation.

---

1. *Moses:* The text has "Tobiah"—on the basis of Bab. Sotah
12a, where, in a playful interpretation of Exodus 2:2 (*vateire oto ki
tov hu*), Moses is said to have also been called Tobiah. The poet's
scheme required this stanza to begin with the letter *tet*.

2–3. The "earthshaking" aspects of the Sinaitic Revelation,
indicated in such passages as Exodus 19:16–18, played a significant
role in the Rabbinic typology of Revelation.[1]

    strength, as in Psalm 29:11, is identified by the rabbis with
Torah. See Sifre to Deuteronomy, Finkelstein, ed., p. 398n.

---

4. *The order of solstices and months:* According to the Rabbinic interpretation of Exodus 12:2, God revealed to Moses and
Aaron, by way of setting the stage for the first Passover, the entire
system of the Jewish calendar (as it was later presupposed in the
Rabbinic period). Cf., *Mekhilta*, Lauterbach, ed., Vol. I, pp. 15–22.
This "commandment of the calendar" was the very first commandment which God addressed to Israel as a people. See Rashi on

Genesis 1:1. Since, moreover, the rabbis considered the whole Torah to have been revealed at Sinai, and not just the Ten Commandments, the poet, here addressing himself to the *content* of the Sinaitic Revelation, dwells on this "first commandment" given to Israel.

---

6. *He carried them on eagles' wings:* Cf., Exodus 19:4. *And underneath the [everlasting] arms:* Cf., Deuteronomy 33:27. The transcendent God ("He that dwelleth in lofty heights") is, in the Jewish view, concerned with man, supporting him in his lowly situation.

7–8. The reference is to the narrative of the Golden Calf, in Exodus 32, which describes both the people's idolatry at the very moment when Moses was receiving the Law, and the terrible punishment meted out upon his return. The poet's use of the word "rebelled" (*sorerim*) echoes the identical word in Psalm 68:19, the Shavuot psalm par excellence, which, in Exodus Rabbah 33:2, is understood by the rabbis to refer to the people's idolatrous conduct at the time of the Sinaitic Revelation. Similarly, his use of "the shamed ones" (*aluvim*) recalls Ulla's exclamation, in Bab. Gittin 36b, "Shameful (*aluvah*) is the bride who commits fornication while still under her bridal canopy!"—a statement the Talmud applies to Israel's idolatrous conduct while still encamped at Mount Sinai. Wolf Heidenheim, in his commentary on the festival liturgy, holds that stanzas 7 and 8 refer to the pagan nations, doomed to perdition because of their refusal to accept the Torah. But it seems, on the contrary, that *Israel's* rebellious behavior is an essential element in the poet's treatment of the paradox of Revelation: man ascends and God descends, heaven and earth meet—and man, in his contrariness, shows himself incapable of absorbing the immediate impact of God's word.

the very heavens shook: Literally: "The curtains do tremble" (Habakkuk 3:7). But Psalm 104:2 speaks of God's stretching out the heavens "like a curtain," a simile on which the translation is based.

8. *when the time for punishment came:* Hebrew: *biphro'a pera'ot.* The phrase comes from Judges 5:2, where its meaning is unclear. Suggested translations include "when men let their hair grow wild," "when the leaders took the lead," and "the avenging." Whatever the meaning of this phrase may be in Judges 5:2, it is clear that our poet has in mind a use of *para* which in Rabbinic Hebrew means "to collect payment, to exact punishment."

10. *The Righteous One turned the mountain . . . like a barrel:* Rabbinic literature describes two different states of mind in which Israel accepted the Torah at Sinai. According to one account (Sifré to Deuteronomy, paragraph 343, Finkelstein, ed., pp. 395 ff.), Israel accepted the Torah voluntarily after other nations had rejected it. According to another account, in Bab. Shabbat 88a, which is presupposed here, God held Mount Sinai "like a barrel" over Israel, saying to them: "If you accept the Torah, well and good. If not, this will be your grave."

fair and comely: These are the attributes of the beloved—according to the Rabbinic interpretation, Israel—in the Song of Songs.

13. *engraved laws:* According to Exodus 32:16, the laws were "engraved upon the tables." The word, "engraved" (*harut*), led to the Rabbinic pun, in Bab. Eruvin 54a: "Do not read *harut* ("engraved"), but *herut* ("freedom")." That is to say, in the observance of the Sinaitic Law you will achieve true freedom.

WHEN THE PORTALS OF GRACE WILL OPEN
AN AKEDAH by JUDAH BEN SAMUEL IBN ABBAS

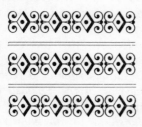

INTRODUCTION

A SPECIAL GENRE *of the piyyut is the akedah. The word means "binding," and, apart from its use as a name for a type of piyyut, it is generally taken to refer to the narration of the events described in the twenty-second chapter of Genesis, the "Binding of Isaac" (cf., "God Tries Those that fear Him"). The akedah as piyyut deals with the events of that biblical chapter. Often the akedah occurs as a part of the penitential prayers (selihot).*

Abraham's willingness to sacrifice his beloved son has always been considered a supreme act of piety—constituting, indeed, the merit on which later, less meritorious, generations could draw in their appeals to God. But in some strands of the (post-biblical) tradition, Isaac, too, figures as the hero of that biblical story. For it was believed that Isaac knew exactly what was in store for him, and submitted willingly and eagerly to his fate. This view of the story was of particular appeal in the centuries when Jews were frequently called upon to give up their lives "for the sanctification of God's Name." The best treatment of this aspect, and of its liturgical utilization, may be found in Shalom Spiegel, The Last Trial (New York: Pantheon Books, 1967).

267

Poetic treatments of the akedah do not confine themselves to the biblical narrative, but draw heavily on the literature of the Midrash, particularly for such items as conversations (not recorded in the Bible) between Abraham and Sarah, and between Isaac and Abraham.

Judah ben Samuel ibn Abbas, who died in 1167, was born in Fez, North Africa, and lived in Aleppo. His akedah, "When the Portals of Grace Will Open," is used in various rites as a selihah. It is featured in a particularly prominent way in the Spanish and Portuguese rite, and in some related rites—it is sung during the solemn moments before the blowing of the shofar on the New Year.

In the alphabetical acrostic of this poem, the author spells his name. The refrain, here translated as "Remember Abraham who bound, Remember Isaac who was bound, And also the altar," consists, in the Hebrew original, of only three words: "The binder, the bound, and the altar."

WHEN THE PORTALS OF GRACE WILL OPEN

Translation by Elizabeth R. Petuchowski

At the time when the portals of grace will open,
On the day when I spread forth my hands to God,
On the day of judgment, remember me, too.
> Remember Abraham who bound,
> Remember Isaac who was bound,
> And also the altar.

5 As the last of ten trials to Abraham God said:
"Bring him up—your dear son whom Sarah bred,
"To whom your soul is so firmly tied—
"As an offering, pure to that mountainside
"Where My glory will shine for you."
> Remember . . .

And he said to Sarah: "Son Isaac, your pleasure,
"Has grown without learning God's service to treasure.
"I will go now to teach him the law of God."
"But not too far!," with an assenting nod.
15 "In God should your dear heart trust."
            Remember Abraham who bound,
            Remember Isaac who was bound,
            And also the altar.

In the morn he rose early to start in time.
Two heathen servants did with him climb.
On the third day they found the place which they sought,
20 Refulgent with glory. He stood and thought
Of the mission that do he must.
            Remember . . .

When he asked them, the servants knew what to say:
"Did you see Moriah's crest shining, I pray?"
25 "Only caverns we saw." "Then stay below,
"You dullards. My son and I will go
"To worship Him and bow."
            Remember . . .

And the two of them went to their holy task.
30 And young Isaac turned to his father to ask:
"Father, I see both the wood and the fire;
"But, O where is the lamb for the sacred pyre?
"Your law you forgot just now?"
            Remember . . .

35 But the father made answer: "On God rely
"For He will provide the lamb for on high.
"And what God desires, that He will do.
"Before Him, today, build a throne I and you,
"To exalt both off'ring and giver."
40   Remember . . .

And they knocked on the gates of mercy to part,
One to be slain, one to render his heart.
They hoped in God, in His mercy's length.
Those who hope in God shall increase in strength.
45 They would join the possession of God.
        Remember Abraham who bound,
        Remember Isaac who was bound,
        And also the altar.

For the offering he readied the wood with power,
And bound Isaac as he bound a lamb any hour.
In their eyes light of day turned to dark of night.
50 Down their cheeks poured the tears with bitter might.
Eyes wept, while rejoiced the heart.
        Remember . . .

"Tell my mother her joy has now utterly turned,
"For the child of her dotage as offering was burned.
55 "Where can I seek him, my mother's consoler?
"How I grieve for my mother, her weeping, her dolor!
"I am part of the slaughtering knife."
        Remember . . .

"Ah, the knife has affected my speech with groan!
"At the time of my binding, the dull blade hone!
"At the time of my burning, show yourself strong!
"The remains of my ashes to Sarah belong.
" 'Isaac's savor!'—thus face your wife."
        Remember . . .

65 All hosts start moan, and for Isaac entreat,
For their chief, and ask mercy for one of their suite.
"A redemption and ransom accept, but not him,"
So plead the angels, ofanim and seraphim:
"Deprive not the world of light!"
70   Remember . . .

God said to Abraham from heaven: "Give ear!
"One of the three who shed light your hand spare!
"All ye hosts of My stronghold, to peace return,
"For Jerusalem's sons this day merit earn.
75 "I forgive Jacob's offspring all slight."
        Remember . . .

Remember, O God who dwellest on high,
Your covenant with those who are storm tossed and sigh.
Do Thou list as they sound shofar's every sound.
80 Do Thou speak unto Zion: "Salvation's come round,
"I send you Yinnon and Elijah."
            Remember Abraham who bound,
            Remember Isaac who was bound,
            And also the altar.

---

5. *As the last of ten trials:* Cf., Mishnah Avot 5:3, "With ten
trials Abraham our father was tried, and he bore them all, to make
known how great was the love of Abraham our father."

11–13. This conversation is based on a Midrash, the Hebrew
fragment of one version of which was published by Jacob Mann,
The Bible as Read and Preached in the Old Synagogue Vol. I (Cincinnati: 1940), Hebrew section: p. 65:

When God said to him [Abraham], "bring him [Isaac] up as an
offering before Me," Abraham went to his house and said to Sarah:
"How long will your son, Isaac, still rest at your bosom? Is he not
already thirty-seven years old? He does not go to the House of Study,
and I have not let him go to school. Arise, and give us provision for
the way, and I and he will go to the Great House of Study."

---

60. *At the time of my binding, the dull blade hone!:* Presupposed here is the idea that the (later) full priestly ritual would be
observed in connection with the intended sacrifice of Isaac. Cf.,
Pesikta Rabbati, Friedmann, ed., pp. 170b, 171a. The knife used
would, therefore, have to be sharp enough for a proper kosher
slaughtering.

---

72. *One of the three who shed light:* A reference to the three
Patriarchs (Abraham, Isaac, and Jacob), of whom Isaac was one.

81. *I send you Yinnon and Elijah:* Cf., Malachi 3:23. ("Behold, I will send you Elijah the prophet before the coming of the great and terrible day of the Lord.") Yinnon, according to Rabbi Yannai (Bab. Sanhedrin 98b), will be the name of the Messiah. This is based on a playful interpretation of Psalm 72:17, "May his name endure for ever; may his name be continued as long as the sun." The Hebrew, here translated as "may . . . be continued," is *yinnon*. Since Psalm 72 speaks about the ideal king, this unusual Hebrew word, which occurs only once in the Bible, lent itself to such an interpretation.

NOW, WHEN WE INVOKE YOU
A PENITENTIAL LITANY
by DAVID BEN ELEAZAR IBN PAKUDA

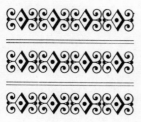

INTRODUCTION

DAVID BEN ELEAZAR IBN PAKUDA *lived in Spain, in the first half of the twelfth century. The poem here presented is a selihah, and is used as such in the Spanish and Portuguese rite. Beginning with the third line, the opening letters of each second line spell out the author's first name as well as the wish,* hazak, *"Be strong!"*

NOW, WHEN WE INVOKE YOU

Now, when we invoke You, to our supplications
                            listen, O Lord.
And our greedy sinning, in Your tender mercies,
                            pardon, O Lord.

To the words I have chosen   Listen, O Lord.
The sin of my conception   Pardon, O Lord.

273

5	From Your lofty dwelling	Listen, O Lord.
	The sin of Your people	Pardon, O Lord.
	When I sing Your praises,	Listen, O Lord.
	But my constant sinning	Pardon, O Lord.
	To the poor and needy	Listen, O Lord.
10	The sins red as scarlet	Pardon, O Lord.
	To the pious in Your presence	Listen, O Lord.
	And me, Your humble servant,	Pardon, O Lord.
	To the praises which I utter	Listen, O Lord.
	But my wicked actions	Pardon, O Lord.
15	To the voice of Jacob's remnant	Listen, O Lord.
	The crooked heart's transgression	Pardon, O Lord.

Now, when we invoke You, to our supplications
                              listen,   O Lord.
And our greedy sinning, in Your tender mercies,
                              pardon, O Lord.

---

4. *The sin of my conception:* Literally: "the sin in which I was conceived." As a rule, Judaism did not share Christianity's emphasis on the doctrine of Original Sin.[1] But, in a moment of extreme contrition, the Psalmist (Psalm 51:7) did say: "Behold, I was brought forth in iniquity, and in sin did my mother conceive me." Ibn Pakuda uses the terminology of this psalm—without necessarily subscribing to any particular *doctrine* of Original Sin.

The phrases, "Listen, O Lord," and "Pardon, O Lord," in lines 1, 2, 17, and 18, are taken from Daniel 9:19. Though the English translation remains the same, the Hebrew of the responses in the other lines is slightly different. Here, the phrase, "Listen, O Lord," is a quotation from Psalm 30:11.

OF ALL THE EARTH THE JUDGE
A *PIZMON* by SOLOMON BAR ABUN

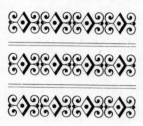

INTRODUCTION

SOLOMON BAR ABUN *lived in France, in the twelfth century. The poem presented here is the most popular of his compositions. Because it begins by invoking God as Judge, and by describing Him as arraigning the world for judgment, it must originally have been designed for the New Year service, where the Yemenite rite and some versions of the Spanish rite still feature it.*[1] *The Ashkenazi rite has it in the Yom Kippur morning service, but also, appropriately enough, as part of the selihot on the day before Rosh Hashanah.*

The poem is, technically, a pizmon: the last line of the first stanza serves as a refrain for all of the other stanzas. The acrostic spells out the poet's first name as well as the wish, hazak, "Be strong!"

OF ALL THE EARTH THE JUDGE

Of all the earth the Judge, You,
    Arraigning it in law,
Grant life and also kindness
    To very needy folk.

5 This prayer of the morning
    In off'ring's place receive,
        Like the off'ring of the morning, the daily sacrifice.

With justice as Your garment,
    Supremacy is Yours.
10 If good works we are lacking,
    Of Hebron's sleepers think.
Let them rise in remembrance
    Before the Lord always,
        Like the off'ring of the morning, the daily sacrifice.

15 Inclining toward kindness,
    Life to Your folk You give.
Be kind unto Your people,
    Be kind, that they may live.
And write the sign of living
20   Upon their brow always,
        Like the off'ring of the morning, the daily sacrifice.

To Zion, my holy city,
    Do good, and favor show.
In Your house, a memorial
25   My holy people grant.
And let the son of Jesse
    Shine in his rule always.
        Like the off'ring of the morning, the daily sacrifice.

Have courage now, my people,
30   Faith in Almighty God.
If you but keep His statutes,
    He, too, will recompense,
Will pardon your transgressions,
    In anger, mercy guard.
35 Search for the Lord, His power;
    His presence seek always,
        Like the off'ring of the morning, the daily sacrifice.

---

1. *Of all the earth the Judge:* Literally: "Judge of all the earth."

That is how Abraham addressed God, in Genesis 18:25, when he pleaded for the innocent of Sodom and Gomorrah.

5–7. The poet here invokes the idea that, since the destruction of the Jerusalem Temple, prayer has taken the place of sacrifice.[2]

---

11. *Of Hebron's sleepers think:* The Patriarchs are buried in Hebron. The idea here is, that even though we may not be able to ask for anything on our own merits (which may be non-existent), God should nevertheless deal kindly with us for the sake of the merits of the Patriarchs. This is the Rabbinic Doctrine of Merits.[3]

---

19. *And write the sign of living:* Cf., Ezekiel 9:4. The rabbis, in Bab. Shabbat 55a, commenting on the verse, explain that there were two signs marked on the people's brows: one marking the wicked for destruction, and one marking the righteous for life. The poet obviously refers here to the latter.

---

26. *the son of Jesse:* A reference to the Messiah.

---

34. *In anger, mercy guard:* Cf., Habakkuk 3:2 ("In wrath remember compassion.").

NOTES AND SOURCES

The following abbreviations have been used for the sources. *Adler-Davis:* Herbert Adler and Arthur Davis, eds., *Service of the Synagogue*, 17th edition (London: Routledge and Kegan Paul, 1949), 6 vols. *Amram Gaon:* E. D. Goldschmidt, ed., *Siddur Rav Amram Gaon* (Jerusalem: Mossad Harav Kook, 1971). *Baer: Seder Abhodath Yisrael*, Seligman Baer, ed. (Berlin: Schocken Books, 1937). *Birnbaum:* Philip Birnbaum, ed., *Daily Prayer Book* (New York: Hebrew Publishing Co., 1949). *Davidson:* Israel Davidson, *Thesaurus of Mediaeval Hebrew Poetry*, 2nd edition (New York: Ktav Publishing House, 1970), 4 vols. *Gaster:* Moses Gaster, ed., *The Book of Prayer and Order of Service According to the Custom of the Spanish and Portuguese Jews* (London: Oxford University Press, 1904–1906), 5 vols. *HUCA: Hebrew Union College Annual* (Cincinnati, 1924ff.). *Saadya Gaon:* Assaf, Joel, and Davidson, eds., *Siddur Rav Saadya Gaon* (Jerusalem: Mekize Nirdamim, 1941). *Zulay:* Menahem Zulay, ed., *Piyyuté Yannai* (Jerusalem: Schocken Books, 1938).

INTRODUCTION

1. *Daily Prayer Book*, Philip Birnbaum (New York: Hebrew Publishing Company, 1949), pp. 11–13.
2. Ezra Fleischer, s.v. "Piyyut," in *Encyclopaedia Judaica*, vol. 13, col. 573.
3. Aaron Mirsky, *The Origins of the Piyyut* [Hebrew] (Jerusalem: Jewish Agency, 1965), p. 69.
4. Judah b. Barzillai Al-Bargeloni, *Sepher Ha'ittim*, R. J. Schorr, ed. (Cracow: 1902), p. 252.
5. Michael Avi-Yonah, *In the Days of Rome and Byzantium* [Hebrew] 3rd edition (Jerusalem: Mossad Bialik, 1962), p. 215.
6. Martin Schreiner, "Samau'al b. Jaḥjâ al-Magrabi und seine Schrift 'Ifḥâm al-Jahûd'," in *Monatsschrift für Geschichte und Wissenschaft des Judentums*, vol. 42 (1898), p. 220; and cf., Moshe Perlmann in *Proceedings of the American Academy for Jewish Research*, vol. XXXII (1964), p. 57.
7. Mirsky, op. cit., p. 47.
8. Ibid., pp. 61ff.
9. A. M. Habermann, *A History of Hebrew Liturgical and Secular Poetry* [Hebrew] (Ramat Gan: Massada, 1970), p. 33.

10. Ezra Fleischer, op. cit., col. 574.
11. A. M. Habermann, op. cit., p. 36.
12. Hayyim (Jefim) Schirmann, "Appendix on the Age of Yannai's Life" [Hebrew] in *Keshet*, vol. VI, no. 3 (1964), pp. 64–66.
13. Mirsky, op. cit., pp. 86ff.
14. Ibid., pp. 11ff.
15. Aaron Mirsky, *Origins of the Piyyut Forms* [Hebrew] (Jerusalem and Tel Aviv: Schocken Books, 1968).
16. Jefim Schirmann, "Hebrew Liturgical Poetry and Christian Hymnology," in *Jewish Quarterly Review*, n.s. vol. 44 (1953/54), p. 134.
17. Salo W. Baron, *A Social and Religious History of the Jews*, 2nd edition, vol. VII (Philadelphia: Jewish Publication Society, 1958), p. 89.
18. Ezra Fleischer, "*The Liturgical Function of Ancient Piyyut*" [Hebrew] in *Tarbiz*, vol. XL (1970), p. 52.
19. Ibid., p. 60.
20. Ibid., pp. 55ff.
21. Ibid., p. 53.
22. Ibid., pp. 44ff.
23. Menahem Zulay, *Zur Liturgie der babylonischen Juden* (Stuttgart: 1933), pp. 83ff.
24. Cf., Pirkoi ben Baboi in *Ginzei Schechter*, vol. II, Louis Ginzberg, ed. (New York: Jewish Theological Seminary, 1929), pp. 504–73.
25. Salo W. Baron,, op. cit., p. 100.
26. *Otzar Hageonim*, Benjamin M. Lewin, ed., vol. I (1928), p. 70.
27. Cf., A. A. Wolff, *Die Stimmen der ältesten glaubwürdigsten Rabbinen über die Pijutim* (Leipzig: 1857).
28. *Seder Rav Amram Gaon*, E. D. Goldschmidt, ed. (Jerusalem: Mossad Harav Kook, 1971), pp. 167ff., no. 127.
29. *Siddur Rav Saadya Gaon*, Assaf, Joel, and Davidson, eds. (Jerusalem: Mekize Nirdamim, 1941), p. 264.
30. Moses Maimonides, *Responsa*, J. Blau, ed., vol. II (Jerusalem: Mekize Nirdamim, 1960), pp. 467ff.
31. Moses Maimonides, *The Guide of the Perplexed*, Shlomo Pines, tr. (Chicago: University of Chicago Press, 1963), pp. 137–43.
32. *Sefer Hasidim*, R. Margaliot, ed. (Jerusalem: Mossad Harav Kook, 1957), p. 221.
33. *Encyclopaedia Judaica* (Jerusalem: 1971), vol. 13, cols. 575ff.
34. A. M. Habermann, op. cit., p. 77.

EL BARUKH

Birnbaum: *p. 71*
Davidson: *I, p. 146, no. 3514*

1. *Amram Gaon*, op. cit., p. 13.
2. *Saadya Gaon*, op. cit. pp. 36ff.

3. See Ismar Elbogen, *Der jüdische Gottesdienst in seiner geschichtlichen Entwicklung*, 4th edition (Hildesheim: Georg Olms, 1962), p. 18.
4. W. Jawitz, *Meqor Haberakhoth* (Berlin: 1920), p. 53.

A VINE FROM EGYPT

Jacob Mann in HUCA, vol. II (1925), p. 323
Davidson: II, p. 97, no. 189

HOW BLESSED IS THE FOUNTAIN OF ISRAEL!

Zulay: p. 240

1. Cf.,*Hilluph Minhagim*, Joel Mueller, ed. (Vienna: 1878), p. 10.

IN THE MIDDLE OF THE NIGHT

Baer: pp. 707–09
Davidson: I, p. 102, no. 2175

REMEMBER THE PATRIARCH

Adler-Davis: Tabernacles, p. 138
Davidson: II, p. 209, no. 91

1. Ismar Elbogen in *HUCA*, vol. III (1926), p. 218.
2. Cf., Louis Ginzberg, *The Legends of the Jews*, vol. I (Philadelphia: Jewish Publication Society, 1947), pp. 198–203.

DEW, PRECIOUS DEW

Adler-Davis: Passover, p. 148
Davidson: I, p. 222, no. 4823

THE MEN OF FAITHFULNESS ARE LOST

Gaster: vol. I, pp. 39–40
Davidson: I, p. 311, no. 6850

1. *Saadya Gaon*, op. cit., pp. 338ff.

I SAID, BE GRACIOUS UNTO ME

Saadya Gaon: p. 380

1. Menahem Zulay, *The Poetical School of Rav Saadya Gaon* [Hebrew] (Jerusalem: Schocken Books, 1964), p. 45.

ABUNDANT SHOWERS

Gaster: vol. IV, p. 176
Davidson: III, p. 507, no. 2107

THE ROYAL CROWN

Gaster: vol. III, pp. 47–63
Davidson: II, p. 490, no. 581

1. Michael Sachs, *Die religiöse Poesie der Juden in Spanien*, 2nd edition (Berlin: 1901), pp. 224ff.
2. Quoted in *Philosophers Speak for Themselves: From Aristotle to Plotinus*, T. V. Smith, ed. (Chicago: Chicago University Press, 1956), p. 283.
3. Cf., Jakob J. Petuchowski, *The Theology of Haham David Nieto*, 2nd edition (New York: Ktav Publishing House, 1970), p. 156, *n.*17.

O GOD, THY NAME

Gaster: vol. II, pp. 79–80
Davidson: II, p. 309, no. 1143

1. Franz Rosenzweig, *Jehuda Halevi*, 2nd edition (Berlin: Lambert Schneider, 1927), pp. 171ff.

MOSES WENT UP ON HIGH

Adler-Davis: Pentecost, pp. 144–45
Davidson: II, p. 189, no. 257

1. Cf., Jakob J. Petuchowski, "*Qol Adonai*—A Study in Rabbinic Theology," in *Zeitschrift für Religions-und Geistesgeschichte*, vol. XXIV (1972), pp. 13–21.

WHEN THE PORTALS OF GRACE WILL OPEN

> *Gaster: vol. II, pp. 106–09*
> *Davidson: III, p. 296, no. 1053*

NOW, WHEN WE INVOKE YOU

> *Gaster: vol. III, p. 27*
> *Davidson: I, p. 285, no. 6245*

1. Cf., Samuel S. Cohon, "Original Sin," in *HUCA*, vol. XXI (1948), pp. 275–330.

OF ALL THE EARTH THE JUDGE

> *Adler-Davis: Atonement, p. 86*
> *Davidson: III, pp. 436ff., no. 712*

1. Israel Abrahams, *By-Paths in Hebraic Bookland* (Philadelphia: Jewish Publication Society, 1920), p. 98.
2. Cf., Jakob J. Petuchowski, *Understanding Jewish Prayer* (New York: Ktav Publishing House, 1972), pp. 31ff.
3. Cf., A. Marmorstein, *The Doctrine of Merits in Old Rabbinical Literature* (London: Jews' College Publications, 1920).

SUGGESTIONS FOR FURTHER READING (*in English*)

Most of the literature on synagogal poetry was written in German in the last generation, and now is written in Hebrew. For the reader who is restricted to works in English, only the following can be recommended:

Fleischer, Ezra. "Piyyut," in *Encyclopaedia Judaica*. Vol. 13, cols. 573–602.

Spiegel, Shalom. "On Medieval Hebrew Poetry," in Louis Finkelstein, ed., *The Jews: Their History, Culture and Religion* II (Philadelphia: Jewish Publication Society, 1949), pp. 528–66.

Translations of piyyutim may be found in the Adler-Davis edition of *Service of the Synagogue*, 17th edition (London: Routledge and Kegan Paul, 1949), 6 vols., as well as in various other editions of Orthodox and Conservative prayerbooks.

In addition, the following are recommended:

Goldstein, David. *The Jewish Poets of Spain, 900–1250* (Baltimore: Penguin Books, 1971).

Selected Poems of Moses ibn Ezra, tr. Solomon Solis-Cohen (Philadelphia: Jewish Publication Society, 1934).

Selected Religious Poems of Solomon ibn Gabirol, tr. Israel Zangwill (Philadelphia: Jewish Publication Society, 1923).

Selected Poems of Jehudah Halevi, tr. Nina Salaman (Philadelphia: Jewish Publication Society, 1924).

GLOSSARY

Aggadah, Aggadot (pl.): The homiletic traditions contained in the Talmud and Midrashim, consisting of legends, parables, expositions of Scripture, etc.

Amora, Amoraim (pl.): The sages of the third to fifth centuries, who created the Jerusalem and the Babylonian Talmud.

Ashkenazi: In the narrow sense: the rites and liturgy of German Jews; in the wider sense: of the Jews of western and eastern Europe and, now, of American and Israeli Jews of European origin.

Amidah, Amidot (pl.): Lit., "standing"; the name (current mainly among Sephardim) of the main obligatory prayer, recited in each of the daily services; its weekday version is also known as "Eighteen Benedictions."

Berakhah, Berakhot (pl.): Lit., "blessing," benediction; in the specific liturgical sense: a) the formula "Blessed art thou, etc.," occurring invariably at the beginning and/or conclusion of each unit of the prescribed prayer; b) the name applying to each such unit.

Gaon, Geonim (pl.): Title of the heads of the great rabbinic academies in Babylonia (and Palestine) from the sixth to the eleventh centuries.

Halakhah, Halakhot (pl.): Law, legal ruling.

Mahzor: Order of prayers; used to denote the prayerbook for Festivals.

Midrash, Midrashim (pl.): a) A method of homiletical exegesis; b) literary works in which expositions in the Midrashic manner (and other, mainly Aggadic, material) are collected.

Mishnah: The compendium of Jewish law, compiled by R. Judah the Prince (end of second, beginning of third centuries).

Payyetan, Payyetanim (pl.): Composer of liturgical poetry.

Piyyut, Piyyutim (pl.): Poetical composition of liturgical character.

Seder, Sedarim (pl.): The portion of the Pentateuch read on any given Sabbath according to the so-called Triennial Cycle, in vogue in Palestine and some neighboring countries till about the twelfth century (as against the Annual Cycle, of Babylonian origin, current in all rites today).

Sephardi: In the narrow sense—the rites and liturgy of the Jews of Spain and Portugal (and of Jews of Spanish-Portuguese origin elsewhere); in the wider—the rites of oriental communities.

Shofar: The ram's horn, sounded on the New Year, Rosh Ha-shanah.

Talmud, Talmudim (pl.): The Jerusalem and the Babylonian Talmud. In form the Talmud is a detailed commentary and analysis of the Mishnah; in effect, it is the record of the creative activity in the field of Halakhah (and, to a lesser extent, of Aggadah) of the Amoraim in the three centuries following the redaction of the Mishnah.

Tanna, Tannaim (pl.): The sages of the first and second centuries C.E., whose teaching is incorporated mainly in the Mishnah.

Torah: Lit. "teaching." In the narrow sense—the Pentateuch; in the wider—the entire Bible as well as all Rabbinic law and teaching ("the Oral Torah"), contained in the Talmudim, etc.

Yavneh: A town in the southern coastal plain of Palestine, where the Sanhedrin was reestablished by Rabban Yohanan ben Zakkai after the destruction of the Second Temple.

INDEX